UNION

This book is due

- 7 SEP

0333613880.

Also by Linda Hantrais

Le vocabulaire de Georges Brassens: vol. 1 Une étude statistique et stylistique; vol. 2 Concordance et index des rimes
*Contemporary French Society
The Undergraduate's Guide to Studying Languages
Managing Professional and Family Life: A Comparative Study of British and French Women

Published by Macmillan

Social Policy in the European Union

Linda Hantrais

Consultant Editor: Jo Campling

First published 1995 by
MACMILLAN PRESS LTD
Houndmills, Basingstoke, Hampshire RG21 2XS
and London
Companies and representatives
throughout the world

ISBN 0–333–61388–0 hardcover
ISBN 0–333–61389–9 paperback

A catalogue record for this book is available from the British Library.

10   9   8   7   6   5   4   3
04   03   02   01   00   99   98   97   96

Copy-edited and typeset by Povey–Edmondson
Okehampton and Rochdale, England

Printed in Malaysia

Contents

List of Figures and Boxes   vii

Preface   viii

① **The Social Dimension of the European Union**   1
    The development of the social dimension   2
    Conceptualising European social policy   15

② **Harmonisation of Social Policies**   19
    Progress towards harmonisation of national social
      policies   20
    Recognising national diversity   27
    Welfare states in the European Union   30
    Converging or diverging welfare regimes   34

3 **Education and Training**   38
    'Educational space' in the European Union   38
    Union initiatives on education and training   46
    Trends in education and training in member states   51
    The impact of European policy on national education and
      vocational training systems   56

4 **The Improvement of Living and Working Conditions**   59
    Community policy on living and working conditions   60
    Working conditions in member states   68
    Living conditions in member states   73
    Towards convergence of working conditions and living
      standards   75

5 **Family Policies**   79
    European family policy in embryo   80
    Conceptualising families and family policies   82
    Defining and making family policy   91
    The family impact of public policy   97

6 Women, Welfare and Citizenship   **102**
European legislation for the welfare of women   104
Women's access to rights as workers and mothers   112
The gendering of welfare   118

7 Policy for Older and Disabled People   **124**
The development of European social policy for older and
    disabled people   125
The impact on social policy of the ageing of the Union's
    population   129
Formal and informal provisions for older and disabled
    people   133
The impact of policy on the living standards of older and
    disabled people   141

8 Social Exclusion   **146**
The development of European policy on poverty and
    social exclusion   147
Defining and measuring poverty and social exclusion   155
National responses to social exclusion   160
Concerted action against poverty   165

9 Social Policy and Mobility   **168**
European legislation on freedom of movement   169
The impact of Union policy on mobility   172
Overcoming obstacles to intra-European migration   176
Union policy and non-European immigration   181
Freedom of movement in a multi-speed Europe   186

10 Assessing European Social Policy   **191**
The parameters of a European social policy   193
The Union as a social policy actor   205
The future of European social policy   211

Appendices
    1. *The European Social Policy-Making Process*   214
    2. *The Structure of Welfare in Member States*   220

Bibliography   227

Index   235

List of Figures and Boxes

FIGURES

2.1 Trends in social protection spending in member states (as
    % of GDP, 1981–91)   30
2.2 Social protection receipts in member states in 1991 (in %) 31
5.1 Total period fertility rates in member states (1965–91)   84
5.2 One-person households in member states (as % of
    households, 1981/82–91)   84
5.3 Extramarital births in member states (per 1000 live births,
    1965–91)   85
5.4 Marriage rates in members states (per 1000 population,
    1965–91)   86
5.5 Divorce rates in member states (per 1000 population,
    1965–91)   86

BOXES

1 Official documents relating to the social dimension of the
  European Union   17
2 Union documents relating to the harmonisation of social
  policies   37
3 Union documents relating to education and training   58
4 Union documents relating to living and working
  conditions   77
5 Union documents relating to family policies   100
6 Union documents relating to women, welfare and
  citizenship   122
7 Union documents relating to policy for older and
  disabled people   144
8 Union documents relating to social exclusion   166
9 Union documents relating to social policy and mobility   188

Preface

In preparing for the twenty-first century, the European Union is facing a number of challenges which have confirmed the importance of social affairs for the policy agenda. Demographic trends in combination with technological and structural change, the prospects for enlargement of the Union and the extension of its sphere of influence have created new pressures on welfare systems and raised questions about the feasibility and desirability of achieving a common social policy. The ambivalence of member states over the Union's responsibility for social affairs, together with these other concerns, explains the enduring interest shown in the social dimension of the Union by policy analysts and justifies a wide-ranging review of developments in European social policy since the 1950s.

The primary aim in this book is to examine the interconnections between social policy making at European level and national policy formulation and implementation. By comparing the policy-making styles and objectives of national governments and by analysing the possible impact of social policies formulated by the Union on measures adopted by member states, an attempt is made to unravel this complex interactive process. Rather than describing national welfare systems one by one and subsequently comparing them across member states, the book is organised thematically. The main areas of social policy that the Union has addressed are examined using international comparisons to exemplify the measures introduced in different member states in response to similar social problems. Cross-national comparisons afford an opportunity to gain a better understanding of conceptual variations in the frameworks created by national systems of welfare while also illustrating the specificity of each country and the effect of cultural embedding.

This approach is based on the assumption that students and analysts of comparative social policy are concerned with identifying the social determinants of policy and are looking for 'culturally specific causes, variables, institutional arrangements and outcomes' (Higgins, 1981, p. 14). They will also want to be aware of the range of policy options available (Room, 1994, p. 23). The underlying hypothesis in the book is that national governments differ in their policy responses to common social problems. All member states have had to tackle broadly similar issues over the period since the European Economic Community (EEC) was created in 1957: for example how to prepare their workforce for rapidly changing labour markets in a context of widespread unemployment and marginalisation; or how to cope with the growing demand for ever higher standards of health care, particularly amongst older people during retirement, in the face of the rising cost of providing services. The solutions adopted to common problems reflect varying socio-economic conditions as well as differing political ideologies and conceptions of the legitimacy of state intervention.

The first chapter provides an insight into the factors shaping European social policy by charting the Union's social remit over time. A major obstacle to effective social policy making at European level has been the lack of a common understanding of central concepts and the societal contexts within which social policy is formulated and implemented. In both the first and second chapters a number of questions are therefore raised about the status of social policy in the Union and the problems associated with harmonisation and convergence of national systems: Why has the Union developed a social policy? What are its aims and objectives? How does it operate? Should it be aimed at achieving a minimum or maximum level of protection? These questions lead on to the debate about citizenship versus workers' rights, equalisation, competition, economic and social cohesion, including discussion of the notions of social dumping, welfare tourism and social devaluation.

The social protection systems of the six original EEC member states can be considered as variants of what has come to be known as the continental model of welfare. The new members which joined the Community in the 1970s and 1980s did not share the same welfare models. While the goal of harmonising social protection would seem to have become more pressing with the move towards the Single European Market (SEM), economic and monetary union, doubts were increasingly expressed about the feasibility and desirability of harmonising very different welfare systems. In the second chapter the main obstacles to harmonisation are examined, and the shift away from the original policy aims is charted through co-ordination, co-operation, cohesion, mutual recognition and convergence, leading to an analysis of national welfare systems in the context of the three waves of membership of the Community in the 1950s, 1970s and 1980s.

Education and training provide a good example of the shift towards a more pragmatic approach to harmonisation. After many years work comparing the content and level of qualifications across the Community in an attempt to reach agreement over transferability from one member state to another, general directives were issued on the mutual recognition of the equivalence of diplomas. Measures of output suggest, however, that recognition does not mean vocational and educational training have been standardised. In the third chapter, after a review of the lengthy process leading to the mutual recognition directive and a survey of initiatives at European level to encourage mobility amongst students and young workers, comparisons are made of developments in the educational and training systems of individual member states.

Several articles in the EEC Treaty were devoted to the improvement of living and working conditions as a means of equalising opportunities and promoting mobility. Despite the early interest shown by the Community, comparisons of working conditions and health and safety at work, as governed by national labour law, demonstrate that member states are far from sharing common standards. In the fourth chapter attention is given to the relationship between European regulations and national policies for health and safety at work, work-time arrangements and public health.

Family policy is only indirectly affected by employment rights. It is therefore an area where member states have been reluctant to seek agreement on a common policy and where the Commission, like many national governments, has preferred to monitor the situation rather than prescribing family policy measures. Although some convergence in family patterns may be occurring spontaneously due to common demographic trends, member states have continued to hold differing views on what constitutes the 'benefit' family and on the aims and objectives of family policy. In the fifth chapter family policies are situated in relation to demographic trends in an attempt to assess the extent of convergence, whether automatically or as a result of intervention at European level.

The employment model of social protection that has become increasingly dominant in the Union puts women at a disadvantage in access to welfare. It also raises the issue of eligibility for social citizenship rights. Directives on equal opportunities in respect of equal pay for work of equal value, equal treatment and employment-related social insurance rights have sought to redress the balance for women who are economically active for the greater part of their working lives. Not all women, however, remain in paid employment, and European law has not properly responded to the needs of women as mothers. In the sixth chapter the relationship between European and national policies is analysed with regard to the situation of women as recipients of social welfare.

In a context where greater life expectancy has been accompanied by heavy demands on health and care services, member states have become increasingly concerned, individually and collectively, about the effects of the ageing of the population on social protection systems. In the seventh chapter the focus is on different forms of provision for older and disabled people, including maintenance and caring, arrangements for transferring rights for mobile workers and pensioners and the overall impact of policy on living standards.

The effects of the emphasis placed on employment rights by most member states in a context of economic recession, rising unemployment and demographic ageing may have been offset to some extent by the Structural Funds. In the 1970s the core-periphery debate intensified, as the problem of poverty moved onto the policy agenda. Much of the discussion focused on the question of whether social insurance should provide a minimum or maximum level of benefits. The prospect of greater freedom of movement heightened concern about welfare tourism and the exporting of poverty from one member state to another. In the eighth chapter these issues are examined with reference to the process of marginalisation, attempts to define and measure poverty and policies designed to combat social exclusion.

Co-ordination of social protection systems, mutual recognition of qualifications, the general improvement of living and working conditions, monitoring of family policy, directives on equality of access to social benefits and measures to reduce poverty at European level were all intended, at least in part, to break down barriers to the free movement of workers within the Union. Information about intra-European mobility suggests that, despite changes in the pattern of labour flows, net mobility has remained relatively low. Even if the Union's policies on the recognition of qualifications or the co-ordination of social protection systems may have some impact on the formal obstacles to mobility, other difficulties associated with linguistic and cultural traditions may be more resistant to European social policy initiatives. In the ninth chapter these issues are considered with regard to both intra-European and non-European mobility.

In the final chapter the progress of the social dimension of the Union is tracked across the topics which are identified in the introductory chapters and recur throughout the book in discussion of different areas of social policy: the unequal weight given in policy measures to the social dimension in relation to economic aspects of the internal market;

the centrality of workers' as compared to citizenship rights in the provision of welfare and income maintenance; the shift away from the objective of harmonisation towards a convergence strategy; disparities between national social protection systems as an obstacle to convergence and the development of different models of welfare from one policy area to another; the interconnections between European and national policies; the coherence and autonomy of European social policy and the Union's competence as a social actor. In retracing these themes an attempt is made to show how European social policy has been shaped and constrained by strong national policies while, nonetheless, developing a focus of its own. In conclusion the prospects are examined for a more broadly based European social policy by the end of the twentieth century.

Although the chapters in the book are linked by common themes and approaches so as to provide a cumulative and wide-ranging overview of social policy in the Union and its member states, each of Chapters 3 to 9 can be studied independently by readers wishing to explore any one policy area in isolation. To supplement the Bibliography which covers works cited throughout the book, separate lists have been compiled of the key policy documents and legislation referred to in each chapter. Throughout the text, references in square brackets indicate the Union documents cited in the boxes at the end of chapters. The appendices briefly describe the Union's policy-making framework and the main organisational features of the welfare systems in the member states that were signatories to the Maastricht Treaty in 1992.

My thanks are due to all those who generously gave of their time to comment on the manuscript for this book and to the staff in the European Documentation Centre in the Pilkington Library at Loughborough University for their assistance in checking information and accessing relevant data sources.

LINDA HANTRAIS

1 The Social Dimension of the European Union

When the Treaty establishing the European Economic Community (EEC) was signed in Rome in 1957 [1.2], the dominant political philosophy was market driven. The six original EEC member states – Belgium, France, the Federal Republic of Germany, Italy, Luxembourg and the Netherlands – believed that, if enterprises were allowed to compete on equal terms, the distribution of resources would be optimised, enabling untrammelled economic growth which would automatically result in social development. Social harmonisation was seen as an end product of economic integration rather than a prerequisite. For these reasons, no specific social provisions were written into the Treaty, and EEC responsibility was limited to promoting co-operation rather than defining precise social policy objectives (Collins, 1975; Shanks, 1977). Member states did recognise the need to establish a social fund to help declining areas of the economy, but it was to operate on a very small scale.

As the optimistic assumptions of the founder members proved to be ill conceived, and as Denmark, Ireland and the United Kingdom joined the European Community (EC) in 1973, a more active approach to social reform was advocated on the grounds that the unevenness which had been created by giving free rein to market forces was unacceptable and not in the long-term interests of member states. The next twenty years therefore saw a growing commitment, at least in principle, to the social dimension as a necessary complement to economic policy.

This chapter provides a brief overview of the historical development of the Union's social dimension within the context of the Community's and Union's Treaties, Charter and social action programmes. Some of the central concepts underlying European social policy are introduced: social space, social dialogue, social plinth, subsidiarity, proportionality and social dumping. As well as identifying the changing aims, objectives and nature of European social policy, the chapter explores why and how the social dimension became a concern of the Union.

1

THE DEVELOPMENT OF THE SOCIAL DIMENSION

In several respects the Treaty of Paris, which set up the European Coal and Steel Community (ECSC) in 1951 [1.1], and the Treaty establishing the European Atomic Energy Community (EAEC) in 1957 [1.3] were more interested in social policy than the EEC Treaty. The ECSC had to deal with the social impact of structural change in two major industries and was endowed with funds to cover the resettlement of displaced workers. It also conferred responsibility for looking into the living and working conditions of miners and steel workers. The EAEC laid down basic standards for the health and protection of workers and the general public as well as procedures for monitoring and checking their implementation. Although the EEC Treaty had a limited, albeit specific, social remit, for example through its commitment to raising standards of living (Article 2) and the provision of a social fund (Article 3), it did not set the framework for a fully developed European social policy. This was done by the Council of Europe in 1961 with the signing of its Social Charter, which was later to serve as a source of inspiration for the Community Charter of the Fundamental Social Rights of Workers in 1989 [1.7]. In this section the development of social policy since the 1950s is examined with reference to the Union's legislative framework (see also Appendix 1).

The social dimension of the EEC Treaty

Twelve of the 248 articles of the EEC Treaty were devoted explicitly to social policy (Articles 117–28). Since the aim of the Treaty was to create an economic union, the relatively low priority given to social affairs was understandable. Justification for the inclusion of any reference to the social dimension can be found in the overriding principle that distortion of the rules of competition was to be avoided at all costs. In the negotiations leading up to the signing of the Treaty, the French had argued that the high social charges which the state imposed on employers and workers in France in the best interests of the workforce, in conjunction with the principle of equal rights for men and women, which was written into the French constitution, would put France at a competitive disadvantage. They therefore advocated harmonisation of provision in these areas. The Germans countered the French case by arguing that social charges were a result of the operation of market forces and should not therefore be regulated by EEC law.

A compromise solution was eventually reached whereby the Treaty included a section on social policy but did not stipulate how most of the provisions should be implemented. Article 118, for example, gave the Commission the task of promoting close co-operation between member states in the social field, particularly in matters relating to training, employment, working conditions, social security and collective bargaining, but without specifying the form such co-operation should take (see Chapters 3 and 4). Article 119, which defined the equal pay principle in response to the demands of the French (see Chapter 6), and Article 121, which was concerned with implementing common social security measures for migrant workers (see Chapter 9), were more explicit. Similarly Articles 123–8 set out specific arrangements for operating the European Social Fund. The ESF was intended to make the employment and re-employment of workers easier and to encourage geographical and occupational mobility within the EEC by providing assistance with the cost of vocational retraining and resettlement allowances (see Chapters 3 and 9).

When discrepancies between the laws and practices of member states were considered to be distorting competition, Article 101 of the Treaty allowed for directives to eliminate any differences. The EEC was, however, premised on the principle that rules avoiding distortion of competition would make it unnecessary to interfere with redistributive benefits, which should remain a matter for individual states (Collins, 1975, p. 9). Provision was made for equal pay, the improvement of standards of living and social harmonisation only in so far as they supported the goal of economic integration (see Chapter 2).

A second justification for the 'social' concerns of the original member states was free movement of labour, which had been a fundamental aim of the EEC Treaty. In addition to the establishment of the ESF, provision was made in the two chapters of the Treaty on the free movement of persons, services and capital for issuing directives or adopting other measures to facilitate the mobility of workers (Articles 48–51) and the right of establishment (Articles 52–8), covering information on job availability in other countries, arrangements for mobile workers to retain social security entitlements and the recognition of professional qualifications (see Chapters 3 and 9).

Although the signatories to the Treaty had flagged their interest in the social dimension of the EEC, the compromise which resulted from their failure to agree about objectives and to set up mechanisms for achieving them led to what could be described as a modest, cautious and narrowly focused social policy. The Treaty which merged the

ECSC, EEC and EAEC in 1965 [1.4] to constitute a single Council and a single Commission of the European Communities (referred to here as the Community) did not bring any formal changes in the social policy field, although the clear social protection remit of the two other Treaties may have had some impact on the subsequent development of European social policy, particularly in the area of health and safety at work (see Chapter 4).

The Council of Europe's Social Charter

While the EEC's approach to social policy was cautious, the Council of Europe was much more explicit and affirmative in the Social Charter it adopted in 1961. With twenty-six members in the early 1990s and a still larger number of countries, including the former Soviet bloc, taking part in its programmes, the Council had become the widest intergovernmental and interparliamentary forum in Europe. Its aims are to work for greater European unity, to uphold the principles of parliamentary democracy and human rights, to improve living conditions and promote human values. Its Social Charter has been described as the economic and social counterpart of the Convention on Human Rights, which future member states pledged themselves to respect when the Council was created in 1949 (Council of Europe, 1988, p. 5).

Like the Convention, the Council's Social Charter guaranteed a number of fundamental rights for workers and citizens, making explicit reference to the rights of the family, mothers and children to social, legal and economic protection. Building on these precedents, the Protocol adopted in 1988 by the members of the Council of Europe further emphasised and extended the terms of the Social Charter, guaranteeing four fundamental social principles: the right to equal opportunities and treatment without discrimination on grounds of sex; the rights of workers to information and consultation and to participation in the determination and improvement of working conditions and the working environment; and the right of older people to social protection (Council of Europe, 1988, p. 7).

Although it did not have the same legally binding status as the Convention, the Council of Europe's Social Charter established a comprehensive and coherent set of policy objectives, which would later serve as a blueprint for the Community Charter.

The 1974 Community social action programme

Signs of a growing political commitment to social legislation and to a more positive and interventionist social policy within the Community can be found more than a decade after the Council of Europe's Social Charter in the Commission's social action programme. In 1974 a Resolution from the Community's Council of Ministers (subsequently referred to as the Council) 'concerning a social action programme' noted that economic expansion was not to be seen as an end in itself but should result in an improvement of the quality of life [1.8]. The programme provided for action in three areas primarily concerned with the working environment, aimed at achieving a number of broad objectives: the attainment of full and better employment; the improvement of living and working conditions; the increased involvement of management and labour in economic and social decisions, and of workers in the life of undertakings. The Council's view of Community competence in the area of social policy at that time was presented in cautious terms, foreshadowing the concept of subsidiarity, discussed below:

> [The Council] Considers that the Community social policy has an individual role to play and should make an essential contribution to achieving the aforementioned objectives by means of Community measures or the definition by the Community of objectives for national social policies, without however seeking a standard solution to all social problems or attempting to transfer to Community level any responsibilities which are assumed more effectively at other levels. [1.8, p. 2]

Since the EEC Treaty did not require a social programme, and the Community did not have direct powers of intervention, its responsibility being confined to promoting co-operation between member states, action had to be justified on political rather than legal grounds. The Resolution expressed the 'political will' to adopt the measures required. In keeping with the priorities of the Treaty, the principles of free movement of labour and equalisation of competitive conditions between enterprises were stressed, and the importance of the ESF was reiterated as a means of palliating the uneven effects of economic growth on weaker sectors of the population.

— The social action programme set the scene for the development of the Community's social policy over the next decade. The 1970s saw a spate of action in the areas of education and training, health and safety at work, workers' and women's rights and poverty, leading to the establishment of a number of European networks and observatories to stimulate action and monitor progress in the social field (described in subsequent chapters).

The social dimension and the Single European Act

By the mid-1980s pressure was building up for a more regulatory social policy. The idea of creating a social space (*espace social*), put forward by the French President, François Mitterrand, in 1981, was taken up by Jacques Delors when he became President of the Commission in 1985. The social space was first mooted during the French presidency of the Community at a time when the revitalisation of social policy was still very much associated with economic performance (Beretta, 1989, p. 5). In line with the policy-making stance adopted by France's own left-wing government, employment was placed at the heart of proposals for European social policy, the dialogue between management and labour was intensified, and co-operation and consultation on social protection were strongly advocated. Social policy was promoted as the means of strengthening economic cohesion and was therefore to be developed on the same basis as economic, monetary and industrial policy. According to this neo-functionalist logic, social policy was a 'functional prerequisite of economic integration' (Room, 1994, p. 21).

Delors made clear his own commitment to the social dimension of the Community, stating that: 'The European social dimension is what allows competition to flourish between undertakings and individuals on a reasonable and fair basis. . . . Any attempt to give new depth to the Common Market which neglected this social dimension would be doomed to failure' (Delors, 1985, p. xviii). For Delors the social space was a natural complement to the completion of the internal market and a means of resolving the stalemate which had arisen over endeavours to establish the social dimension of the Community through legislation. Some member states opposed the legislative route on the grounds that it would go against national provision, but without legislation European social policy was not binding. By referring to a social space, Delors appeared to be seeking to introduce an equivalence of standards, which would be agreed and accepted by both sides of industry through social dialogue, a concept central to his thinking. The social dialogue was intended to make trade unions and employers act as the initiators of social policy, on the understanding that, in return, the Commission would refrain from developing new initiatives itself. The social partners would thus be concerned with principles and objectives, leaving member states to implement them within existing industrial relations frameworks, thereby achieving 'convergence in the employment and labour policy goals of the member states, rather than the standardisation of industrial relations institutions and processes' (Teague, 1989, pp. 69–70).

In order to secure the involvement of the social partners, a series of discussions on socio-economic issues were organised at Val Duchesse (a castle in Belgium) in 1985. Major participants were the European Trade Union Confederation (ETUC), the Union of Industries of the European Communities (UNICE) and the European Centre of Public Enterprises (CEEP). Although the talks fulfilled the objective of encouraging social dialogue between management and workers' representatives, the employers refused to sign the final texts unless Delors gave an undertaking that the Commission would not use the joint opinions as a basis for legislation, thereby preventing the outcome which he had been seeking to engineer. A more positive result of the discussions was the renewed emphasis on social cohesion, involving closer co-ordination of the activities of the ESF in order to focus aid on the poorer member states.

When the Single European Act (SEA) was signed in 1986 [1.5] by the then twelve member states, relatively little progress had been made towards building social policy into the legislative framework of the Community, although significant changes were introduced to speed up and facilitate the social policy-making process (see Appendix 1). The new Article 118a, a supplement to Article 118 of the EEC Treaty, stressed the importance of the working environment and the health and safety of workers and provided for decisions to be taken in this area by qualified majority voting (see Chapter 4). By extending the use of qualified majority voting to health and safety at work and by introducing a new co-operation procedure, which imposed time limits for the passage of legislation and strengthened the role of the European Parliament, the SEA gave the Council an opportunity to tackle more controversial issues in some of the areas of social policy where agreement had previously been difficult to reach.

The other new 118 Article (118b) placed emphasis on the idea of a social dialogue at European level, as initiated in the Val Duchesse talks in 1985. Article 100, on the rights and interests of employed persons, was modified by 100a to enable decisions on approximation of provisions aimed at the establishment and functioning of the internal market to be taken by qualified majority voting. Fiscal provisions, free movement of people and workers' rights were still governed by the unanimity rule.

Under Subsection IV a new Title V was added on economic and social cohesion (Articles 130a-e). Article 130b was intended to strengthen economic and social cohesion, particularly through closer co-ordination of the Structural Funds, namely the European Social Fund (ESF), the European Regional Development Fund (ERDF) and the European Agricultural Guidance and Guarantee Fund (EAGGF) (see Chapter 8).

Despite these changes, the SEA still left the issue of the social space largely unresolved. Interest in the proposal was, however, revived by the Belgian Government during their presidency in the second half of 1987, when the idea was developed of a social policy based on a 'plinth' (*socle social*) of social rights which would not undermine established statutory guarantees for workers (Teague, 1989, p. 76). The Belgian Minister for Labour spoke of the need 'to establish a platform [*socle* in the French version] of basic rights which would give the two sides of industry a stable, common basis from which they could negotiate to guarantee that the internal market has a real social dimension' (Soisson, 1990, p. 10). The proposed social rights to be contained in such a plinth closely resembled the list presented in the Council of Europe's Social Charter, as outlined above. In 1988 before the ETUC, Jacques Delors had stressed the need for a 'revival of social policy', advocating a 'minimum platform [*socle* in the French version] of guaranteed social rights with a view to the implementation of the single European market of 1992'. Echoing the words of the Belgian Minister for Labour, he went on to explain his conception of minimum employment rights: 'This mandatory platform could be negotiated between the two sides of industry and then incorporated into Community legislation. It would serve as a basis for the social dialogue and for strengthening European cohesion' (Soisson, 1990, p. 10).

The Community Charter of the Fundamental Social Rights of Workers

While the SEA did not provide a blueprint for European social policy, the preamble offered a statement of principle in which the signatories agreed to work together to promote fundamental rights as laid down in the Convention for the Protection of Human Rights and Fundamental Freedoms and the European Social Charter. Meeting in Strasbourg on 8–9 December 1989, the heads of all member states, with the exception of the United Kingdom, adopted the Community Charter of the Fundamental Social Rights of Workers [1.7], heralded as the social dimension of the SEA. The preamble to the Charter stated resolutely that 'the same importance must be attached to the social aspects as to the economic aspects and . . ., therefore, they must be developed in a balanced manner'. Although preliminary drafts of the Charter had referred to 'citizens' rather than 'workers', the final version did not define rights in terms of citizenship. Most clauses in the Community Charter implicitly or explicitly referred to workers, a focus which was clearly identified in the title and in the section devoted to employment and remuneration, whereas the Council of Europe's Social Charter had included the right to social and medical assistance and social services without linking them to employment.

— Like the Council of Europe's Social Charter, the Community Charter did not have force of law and was not therefore binding on its signatories. It took the form of a solemn declaration, leaving decisions on implementation procedures to individual member states. The social plinth had been an attempt to ensure that the areas to be covered by social protection would be accepted throughout the Community. Much of the debate about the Charter focused on the related issue of knowing whether the Community and individual member states were aiming for a maximum or minimum level of social provision. Should equalisation be based on an average, the highest or lowest level in the Community? A particular fear in some states intent on defending what they considered as a higher level of social protection was that the internal market would result in a downward alignment of social security allowances and benefits towards the lowest common denominator.

The nebulous terms 'adequate', 'sufficient', 'appropriate' and 'satisfactory', used in the Charter to refer to the levels to be achieved, are indicative of the problems in reaching agreement on how to define targets; they point to the Council's reluctance to impose standards by regulation, the most binding form of legislation (see Appendix 1). This lack of precision left open the possibility that some states would seek competitive advantage by not offering the same level of social protection to their workers, resulting in what has come to be known as 'social dumping', whereby companies may decide to move to countries, such as Greece and Portugal, with low labour and social costs. The term 'dumping' was used in Article 91 of the EEC Treaty in the economic context to describe the practice of differential pricing of goods with no economic justification. An example of what is meant by social dumping is the case of the firm Hoover, which decided in January 1993 to move from Dijon to Glasgow where labour costs were lower. Since the United Kingdom had not accepted the stipulations of the Community Charter, it was accused by the French of unfair competition, and the term 'social dumping' was used (and disputed) to describe the advantage that the United Kingdom was gaining from not having to observe the same standards and conditions of employment as countries which had signed the Charter. The reverse of the coin is that disparities in social protection between member states may also serve as an obstacle to mobility of labour and capital. It has been argued that firms will not invest in low social wage countries unless other factors, for example infrastructure and productivity, justify such investments, and that economic integration may lead rather 'to a more gradual and indirect process of social policy erosion) (Leibfried and Pierson, 1992, p. 350).

Another metaphor frequently used in this context is the 'level playing field' of competition, implying that everybody should be playing by the same rules and with equal chances of success in the market place. Accordingly, a higher level of social spending should be sought uniformly across member states to avoid putting national governments which do want to introduce more generous provisions at a competitive disadvantage.

These concepts were not invented with the SEA and the Community Charter. Fears of social dumping and the creation of an unlevel playing field were, however, exacerbated when Greece joined the Community in 1981 and Portugal and Spain in 1986, since they were all countries with less developed social protection systems than in both the original EEC member states and those which became members in the 1970s (see Chapter 2). Although the Charter may not have produced any innovations in the area of social protection, the surrounding debate did serve the purpose of focusing attention on a number of important issues concerning the social dimension of the Single European Market (SEM), or internal market, which came into operation on 1 January 1993. The different bodies of opinion which emerged over the interventionist role of the Community in social policy and the basis on which it should be founded were symptomatic of the diverging principles underlying systems of social protection in the twelve member states. They also signalled the concern felt in some countries about the possibility of losing national sovereignty and being forced to take action in areas where national governments have at times been reluctant to intervene.

The action programme applying the Community Charter

In the absence of any direct legal means of enforcement, provision was made in the Community Charter for an action programme. Under point 28 of the Charter, the Council invited the Commission to prepare initiatives with a view to the adoption of legal instruments for the effective implementation of the rights which fall within the Community's area of competence. The Commission responded with an action programme containing forty-seven initiatives for developing the social dimension of the SEM [1.9].

The Commission's description of its goals in the first annual report [1.14] is indicative of the status of the social dimension and the constraints within which policy makers were operating. The aim was 'to establish a sound base of minimum provisions, having regard on the one hand to the need to avoid any distortion of competition, and on the other to support moves to strengthen economic and social cohesion and contribute to the creation of jobs, which is the prime concern of completion of the internal market' [1.14 p. 15]. The measures proposed by the Commission were, however, wide ranging. They covered all the topics dealt with in the Community Charter and also added a chapter on the labour market. The methods to be used for implementing the action programme relied heavily on the consultation process, with explicit reference to advisory committees and the social dialogue.

The first annual report on the application of the Community Charter reiterated the point raised at the Luxembourg Council meeting in June 1991 that the achievements made in implementing the SEM programme had not been accompanied by comparable progress in the field of social policy [1.14, p. 26]. This and subsequent reports [1.15; 1.11] stressed the importance of maintaining a balance between the three fundamental principles underlying the Commission's initiatives: subsidiarity (see below), diversity of national systems, cultures and practices, and the preservation of the competitiveness of undertakings, thereby confirming the secondary status of the social dimension. It has been argued that the SEA had added nothing new in the field of social welfare, which remained no more than an area of indirect and limited competence for the Community (Berghman, 1990, p. 9). Some co-ordination of national systems of social security was needed to ensure free movement of workers, but these contingencies had already been covered in the early 1970s by relatively uncontroversial legislation on the application and implementation of social security schemes to employed persons and to members of their families moving within the

Community (see Chapter 9). In all the policy areas encompassed by the Charter, action had been initiated before 1989. The action programme can, however, be credited with providing an impetus for a more concerted and coherent approach to social affairs.

The 'social chapter' in the Maastricht Treaty

The principles set out in the Community Charter were taken up in the Agreement on Social Policy annexed to the Treaty on European Union (EU) signed in Maastricht on 7 February 1992 [1.6]. The Maastricht summit again illustrated the difficulty in reaching agreement over the 'social chapter', which, on the insistence of the United Kingdom, was removed from the Treaty. By including a separate Protocol on Social Policy the other eleven member states could proceed with the Community Charter and make decisions without taking account of the views of the United Kingdom.

The Agreement on Social Policy laid down the basis for management and labour to enter into collective agreements at European level. Decisions could be taken on the basis of qualified majority voting in the areas of health and safety at work, working conditions, information and consultation of workers, equality between men and women and integration of persons excluded from the labour market (Article 2). Issues still requiring unanimous voting by the eleven signatories to the Protocol were social security and social protection of workers, protection of workers made redundant, representation, collective defence of workers and employers, conditions of employment for third-country nationals and financial contributions for job promotion. The distinction between the areas subject to qualified majority and unanimous voting was important since it tended subsequently to dictate the social agenda, limiting it to topics where some degree of consensus already existed.

Article 2 of the Agreement empowered the Council to act in the area of social affairs to adopt 'by means of directives, minimum require-ments for gradual implementation, having regard to the conditions and technical rules obtaining in each of the Member States'. Action was constrained by the principle of subsidiarity (Article 3b of the Treaty), one of the three principles regarded as 'cardinal' by the Commission.

The principle of subsidiarity was set out in a Communication of 27 October 1992 [1.10]. The Commission emphasised the importance of three related issues: greater democratic control, more transparency in

European legislation, and respect of the principle of subsidiarity. While the Treaty stipulated which competencies are attributed to the Union, the principle of subsidiarity was to remain important in determining how those competencies should be exercised. By virtue of the principle, the Union is empowered to act when its aims can be more effectively achieved at European rather than national level, for example in order to establish minimum standards which member states should introduce, or to allow them to maintain higher standards if this is not incompatible with the Treaty. The burden of proof is on the Union's institutions to show that there is a need to legislate at European level and at the intensity proposed, with recourse to the most binding instruments as a last resort. Accordingly, wherever possible, preference should be given to support measures and framework directives rather than to detailed rules and regulations. The Union should only intervene if, and in so far as, the objectives of the proposed action cannot be satisfactorily achieved by member states themselves, as judged by an evaluation of comparative efficiency and value added.

Applied in the area of social protection, subsidiarity could be taken to mean that, if the most appropriate level of provision is found to be the family or smaller local agencies, European, or even national, provision is justified only if it can be seen to provide benefits which could not be obtained by other means. The role of the Union would, in this case, most probably be minor. Where the benefits being sought are to be universally applied, European-level intervention may be justified (Spicker, 1991, pp. 3–8).

The choice of the most appropriate policy instrument is made on the basis of the principle of both subsidiarity and proportionality. According to the principle of proportionality, the means employed should be commensurate with the objectives pursued. Decisions should therefore be taken as closely as possible to the citizens themselves, without endangering the advantages which are to be gained from common action at the level of the whole of the Union and without changing the institutional balance.

These constraints on action at Union level were to some extent offset by the new powers which the Agreement on Social Policy gave to management and labour. Article 3 required that the Commission should 'consult management and labour on the possible direction of Community action' (paragraph 2) and the content of proposals (paragraph 3), as well as enabling them to forward an opinion or recommendation to the Commission and to initiate agreements with the Community (paragraph 4).

The Green and White Papers on European social policy

While the Community Charter of 1989, the action programmes and the Agreement on Social Policy in the Maastricht Treaty together provided a clearer statement of thinking on social policy at European level than was present in the Treaties of the European Communities drawn up in the 1950s, they did not signal that the Union had become strongly committed to social affairs as an objective in its own right nor that the necessary administrative structures had been put in place for producing a common European social policy. By incorporating the principle of subsidiarity in the Maastricht Treaty, member states seemed to be confirming their continued reluctance to develop an overarching social policy which might impinge on national sovereignty. In 1993, however, the Commission published a consultative document which demonstrated that the issue of a European social policy remained firmly on its agenda. The Green Paper of 17 November 1993 [1.12] provided a wide-ranging review of social policy in the Union, the *acquis communautaire* (legal attainments) and the areas where further action was needed. Government departments, social partners, the European Parliament, the Economic and Social Committee and other organisations and individuals were invited to respond to assist the Commission in preparing the next phase of the Union's social policy.

The Green Paper sought views on the objectives, targets and measures that would be acceptable to member states and social partners in the areas of the labour market, social protection and exclusion, equal opportunities and training, thereby providing a clear indication of the wide range of issues which were considered to fall within the Union's competence. It also demonstrated that the Commission wanted to be seen to take account of the opinions expressed by other social actors. While the Green Paper stressed that high standards of social protection would be needed to underpin economic competition, it was intended as a stocktaking exercise rather than a prescription for future action. The White Paper on 'European Social Policy – a Way Forward for the Union', published on 27 July 1994 [1.13], went on to set the scene for European social policy through to the end of the decade by providing a comprehensive statement of policy directions and goals. The document described the 'vital part it [social policy] had to play in underpinning the process of change' by building on the achievements of the past and putting forward new proposals for the future, with the aim of ensuring that the people of Europe benefit from 'the unique blend of economic well-being, social cohesiveness and high overall quality of life which was achieved in the post-war period' [1.13, p. 1]. Policy was to be broadly based, meaning that, although jobs were to remain at the top of the agenda, it should also extend to categories of people who were not in work, with a view to establishing 'the fundamental social rights of citizens as a constitutional element of the European Union' [1.13, p. 53], a goal which the Community Charter did not espouse.

CONCEPTUALISING EUROPEAN SOCIAL POLICY

The preceding sections go some way towards answering the questions why and how the Union has progressively but cautiously extended its intervention in social affairs, providing an indication of the philosophy underlying social policy and the possible interconnections between European and national levels. This relationship is explored in more detail in subsequent chapters with reference to specific policy areas. In concluding this chapter, an overview is provided of what can be considered as the distinguishing characteristics of European social policy towards the end of the twentieth century.

Although a number of policy statements have been made over the years about the importance of the social dimension of the Community, such as that quoted above by Jacques Delors, there is little concrete evidence that European social policy is perceived by the Council as other than a handmaiden to economic objectives. In the mid-1980s Ivor Richard, a former Commissioner for Social Affairs, aptly summed up what would seem to have been the prevailing attitude in the Community at that time regarding the reciprocal relationship between economic and social policy: 'A good economic policy may be a major requisite for an efficient and adequate social policy, but a good social policy can be a powerful support for a good economic policy' (Richard, 1985, p. 203). If social affairs have been placed on the Union's agenda, consultation procedures initiated and laws drafted to establish workers' rights, nowhere is the economic motivation difficult to find. Just as the French had insisted on provision for equal pay between men and women in the EEC Treaty to prevent the distortion of competition, the principle of guaranteed access to adequate social protection in the Community Charter of 1989 was also justified on economic grounds.

Although the Council of Europe's Social Charter served as a model for the Community Charter, the central focus in the latter was unambiguously on economic forces. The terms in which the Charter was couched clearly indicated that it was almost exclusively concerned with workers and with rights derived from employment. The development of a large European internal market based on free trade and economic progress dictated the priority given to economic objectives and the labour market orientation. The eligibility of workers, or former workers in the case of older people, to social protection was therefore logically dependent on employment status rather than on citizenship rights. Some provision was made in the Community Charter for those excluded from the labour market and without 'adequate' resources to gain access as of right to social and medical assistance and to benefit from social welfare services. Unlike the Council of Europe's Social Charter, however, reference was made to the fact that they were unable either to enter or re-enter the labour market, implying that social and professional integration was paramount.

While regulatory instruments were approved by the Council of Ministers in June 1988 under Article 130b of the SEA to enable the operation of the Structural Funds, the Community Charter did not contain proposals for implementation. Rather, it invited the Commission to submit possible initiatives, with a view to adopting the necessary legal instruments for implementing rights which fell within the Community's competence. Application of the principles of subsidiarity and proportionality meant that the areas of Community competence in the social field were not easy to identify or demarcate. Although the concept of a social plinth seemed to offer a promising solution in the debate over the standards to be set, the Charter did not give any clear guidance on how to define a minimum level of provision. In addition, the seemingly arbitrary distinction between areas where qualified majority voting or unanimous voting would apply served to obscure policy objectives.

In the absence of a commitment to a well defined interventionist role, it could be argued that European social policy may not have been developed further because, apart from the case of migrant workers, the Union did not really need its own common social policy. Mark Kleinman and David Piachaud (1993, pp. 8–9) have suggested that, if the Community were to remain no more than simply a customs union, it would have no need for a social policy. A common social policy is more readily justified in the context of economic integration, as advocated for example by Jacques Delors or Ivor Richard, but at best in a secondary role. Were the Community to become a political union or federation, the case for a centralised social policy aimed at redistributing resources to the member states most in need would undoubtedly be much stronger on both humanitarian and democratic grounds.)

⭐By the mid-1990s, new challenges were facing the Union as a result of slow economic growth and persisting long-term unemployment, population ageing, the increasing cost of providing social protection and the development of a welfare dependency culture. The aim of the 1993 Green Paper on European social policy was to seek a response to these challenges. According to Pádraig Flynn, the Commissioner responsible for Social Affairs and Employment, the Green Paper was premised on the understanding that the Union was committed 'to ensuring that economic and social progress go hand in hand' [1.12, p.7], a more modest statement than those of his predecessors. The 1994 White Paper on European social policy echoed the Commissioner's words [1.13, p. 2], but it adopted a more forceful tone, stressing that high social standards were a key element in the competitive formula and a factor contributing to the efficiency of European society. The Commission was signalling its intention to make every effort to ensure that the social dimension maintained a high profile through to the end of the century.)

Box 1 Official documents relating to the social dimension of the European Union

PRIMARY LEGISLATION

1.1   Treaty establishing the European Coal and Steel Community (ECSC), signed in Paris on 18 April 1951.

1.2   Treaty establishing the European Economic Community (EEC), signed in Rome on 25 March 1957.

1.3   Treaty establishing the European Atomic Energy Community (EAEC), signed in Rome on 25 March 1957.

1.4   Treaty of 8 April 1965 establishing a Single Council and a Single Commission of the European Communities (the Merger Treaty).

1.5   Single European Act (SEA), signed in Luxembourg on 17 February 1986 and at the Hague on 28 February 1986, came into force on 1 July 1987.

1.6   Treaty on European Union (EU), signed in Maastricht on 7 February 1992, came into force on 1 November 1993;

Agreement and Protocol on Social Policy, concluded between the member states, with the exception of the United Kingdom.

CHARTER

1.7 Community Charter of the Fundamental Social Rights of Workers, adopted in Strasbourg on 9 December 1989 by the member states, with the exception of the United Kingdom.

SECONDARY LEGISLATION

1.8 Council Resolution of 21 January 1974 concerning a social action programme (*OJ* C 13/1 12.2.74).

1.9 Communication from the Commission concerning its action programme relating to the implementation of the Community Charter of basic social rights for workers (COM(89) 568 final, 29 November 1989).

1.10 Communication from the Commission to the Council and the European Parliament on the principle of subsidiarity (SEC(92) 1990 final, 27 October 1992).

1.11 Third Report on the Application of the Community Charter of the Fundamental Social Rights of Workers (COM(93) 668 final, 21 December 1993).

1.12 Green Paper on European Social Policy. Options for the Union (COM(93) 551, 17 November 1993).

1.13 White Paper on European Social Policy – a Way Forward for the Union (COM(94) 333, 27 July 1994).

OFFICIAL PUBLICATIONS BY THE COMMISSION OF THE EUROPEAN COMMUNITIES (CEC)

1.14 CEC (1992) 'First Report on the Application of the Community Charter of the Fundamental Social Rights of Workers', *Social Europe 1/92*.

1.15 CEC (1993) 'Second Report on the Application of the Community Charter of the Fundamental Social Rights of Workers', *Social Europe Supplement 1/93*.

2 Harmonisation of Social Policies

Under the section on social policy provisions, Article 117 of the Treaty establishing the European Economic Community (EEC) [1.2] introduced the principle of harmonisation of social systems across the six original member states. Neither the Single European Act (SEA) [1.5] nor the Maastricht Treaty on European Union [1.6] replaced or amended the original wording, which presented the agreement of member states over 'the need to promote improved working conditions and an improved standard of living for workers, so as to make possible their harmonisation while the improvement is being maintained'. Such a development was expected to 'ensue not only from the functioning of the common market, which will favour the harmonisation of social systems, but also from the procedures provided for in this Treaty and from the approximation of provisions laid down by law, regulation or administrative action'.

The intention in the Treaty was to remove barriers to mobility and ensure that no one nation would be at a competitive advantage or disadvantage because of its social policies. The founder members – Belgium, France, the Federal Republic of Germany, Italy, Luxembourg and the Netherlands – had developed social protection systems which can be considered as variants of a 'continental' model of welfare, based on corporatist rights and derived from income-related insurance contributions. This shared tradition did not mean that harmonisation would be easy to achieve, since each country had its own particular brand of social provision in terms of both the principles underlying the system and the policy-making process itself. The new members that joined the Community in later years brought with them different welfare models. The social protection systems in the Anglo-Saxon/Nordic countries – Denmark, Ireland and the United Kingdom – that became members in 1973, had developed in line with the principle of universal coverage of risks funded from taxation. The southern European countries, sometimes described as the Latin rim, that joined the Community in the 1980s (Greece in 1981 and Portugal and Spain in 1986) had much more limited welfare systems and still relied heavily on family, community and religious support in dealing with social problems.⟩

⟨While the goal of harmonising social protection was made more pressing by the development of economic union and the need to ensure freedom of movement within an enlarged Community, as envisaged with the completion of the internal market by 1993, over the years doubts were expressed increasingly about the feasibility or even desirability of harmonisation. Although the Community Charter of the Fundamental Social Rights of Workers used the term in three contexts [1.7, points 3, 8 and 9], the Agreement on Social Policy, concluded by eleven of the twelve member states and annexed to the Maastricht Treaty [1.6], made no reference to harmonising social protection systems across the Union.⟩

In the previous chapter, the focus was on the development of social policy at European level and on the policy-making framework. In this chapter the problem of how to deal with differences in national welfare systems is examined as a possible contributing factor in the shift away from the original aim of using approximation to achieve harmonisation of social protection across member states. Firstly, the concepts of co-ordination, co-operation, cohesion, mutual recognition and convergence are introduced and located in relation to the changing focus of interest in the social dimension of the Union. Differences in national welfare systems, which are deeply embedded in national cultural traditions, are then explored with reference to the concept of welfare models or regimes. Finally, the possibility of spontaneous convergence occurring as a result of welfare pluralism is considered as an alternative to the legislative route.

PROGRESS TOWARDS HARMONISATION OF NATIONAL SOCIAL POLICIES

⟨The EEC Treaty carried conflicting messages about harmonisation of social policy. The establishment and functioning of the common market were founded on the principle that provisions should be approximated (Article 100). Approximation as laid down by law, regulation or administrative action was intended to affect the establishment and functioning of the common market and thereby to favour 'the harmonisation of social systems', as advocated in Article 117. From the outset social policy was, however, primarily a matter for individual member states to determine, except in the case of migrant workers

(Articles 51 and 121). The Commission was required in Article 118 to 'act in close contact with Member States by making studies, delivering opinions and arranging consultations both on problems arising at national level and on those of concern to international organisations', but it was under no compulsion to propose legislation. It has been argued that Article 117 did no more 'than direct attention to the need to consider the removal of artificial restrictions which have grown up over the years as part of national policies', and that the close collaboration referred to in Article 118 'did not imply the necessity for subsequent action' (Collins, 1975, pp. 22–3). Rather, the EEC Treaty could be seen as 'broadly educational and promotional' (Collins, 1975, p. 31), leaving member states to define their own approaches to social policy.

The co-ordination of national systems, with the intention of safeguarding social security arrangements for migrant workers and their dependants, figured amongst the very first regulations adopted by the Council of Ministers in 1958 (see Chapter 9). Elsewhere the Treaty was less prescriptive about how harmonisation, or approximation, of social systems was to be achieved. Article 122 required the Commission to report annually on social developments within the Community and gave it the ill-defined brief of drawing up reports on 'particular problems concerning social conditions'.

In this section the goal of achieving harmonisation is examined more closely within the wider context of European social policy by charting the progressive shift towards the concept of convergence of social protection systems.

From harmonisation . . .

Harmonisation of social protection implies that member states should work together and adapt their own social security systems to bring them into line with one another through a change in the substance of national laws. It goes further than co-ordination, which involves a linkage of separate legal systems at supranational level and an acceptance of certain common principles and standards without changing the content, so as to minimise loss of rights by migrant workers (Holloway, 1981, pp. 11–22), but it falls short of unification (as applied in Germany), which requires a fundamental reshaping of existing systems.

Controversy over the desirability and feasibility of harmonisation under the terms of the EEC Treaty continued almost unabated for more than thirty years, with individual member states taking up entrenched positions. [The French Government argued that, if the overriding aim of the Community was to avoid distortion of competition by evening out labour costs, harmonisation of social protection, particularly in terms of funding, was a desirable objective and even a precondition for fair competition. The economic argument was used by other countries against harmonisation. For the Germans, indirect labour costs were seen as only one of a number of factors determining competitiveness. Others, such as the taxation system, geographical location, labour productivity, the climate of labour relations, had to be taken into account and needed to be kept roughly in balance. According to this line of reasoning, any attempts to harmonise national social security arrangements at European level might even upset the balance, thereby obstructing competition]

Not only did member states fear that social dumping (see Chapter 1) would become a widespread practice but also that 'welfare' or 'social tourism' might develop if some countries offered more attractive living and working conditions than others (see Chapter 9). Summarising the obstacles to closer integration, Abram De Swaan (1990, p. 9) has argued that the welfare state is essentially exclusive and anti-international and that national welfare systems are kept apart by two contradictory concerns: firstly, the fear that the national arrangements of individual member states might have to be extended or reduced and, secondly, the likelihood of differences in benefits provoking welfare tourism, as labour becomes mobile in order to take advantage of higher social benefits in another member state. Welfare tourism describes the process whereby older, unemployed and poor people may be induced to seek refuge in the countries and regions within the Union with the most generous systems of social protection. According to this line of reasoning, measures to encourage harmonisation would serve to prevent welfare systems from becoming a bargaining counter between member states]

Jos Berghman (1990, p. 12) has suggested that the German argument against the need for close harmonisation of social protection systems may have been valid when the EEC Treaty was signed but was less applicable by the 1990s. Trends towards harmonisation of monetary and fiscal policies and the greater diversity between the twelve member states, as compared with the original six, according to the same author, created a new set of conditions where harmonisation of social security systems could, in fact, help to restore the overall balance. This view has been supported by Danny Pieters (1991, p. 183) on the grounds that marked differences in the funding of social security, as well as direct or indirect subsidies, can distort competition. As other elements of labour costs and other factors determining competitiveness converge following the completion of the Single European Market (SEM), for example through approximation in the area of fiscal and employment law, improvement in infrastructures and standards of education and training, Pieters argues that it becomes imperative for national social security systems to be harmonised. By 1992, however, the view of the Commission was that harmonisation of social protection systems was no longer on the agenda. Rather, the Commission recognised 'their diversity, the fact that they are firmly anchored to specific cultures, traditions and models'\(Quintin, 1992, p. 9).

— In that the Maastricht Treaty on European Union required closer involvement of social partners in the legislative process, it went some way towards reinforcing the dynamics of social cohesion in Jacques Delors' sense of the term (see Chapter 1). Had monetary union followed its intended course, it could have been a factor encouraging harmonisation of the social dimension. The danger existed, however, that the strengthening of Economic and Monetary Union (EMU) might have a negative influence on social protection by increasing the likelihood of 'social devaluations' (Chassard, 1992, p. 18). As EMU made it more difficult for countries to devalue their currencies, social devaluations, it is argued, might be used instead to reduce wage costs.

Irrespective of whether harmonisation is desirable, few instances can be cited of cases where social legislation designed to bring about harmonisation at European level has been successful in raising the actual standard of social protection. Directives derived from Article 119 of the EEC Treaty, such as 79/7/EEC 'on the implementation of the principle of equal treatment for men and women in matters of social security' [6.3], are often quoted as an exception (see Chapter 6). They afford an example of the effectiveness of Community provisions in promoting policy changes at national level and in bringing about closer integration across member states. In this case, the Community used directives to impose common principles on different national systems so as to avoid one member state gaining a competitive advantage over another without, however, attempting to align systems across the Community.

. . . through social cohesion and mutual recognition to convergence

When Jacques Delors became President of the Commission in 1985 in the period leading up to the signing of the Single European Act (SEA), he was faced with a dilemma over the best way of introducing a social dimension (see Chapter 1). He was aware that legislation requiring harmonisation would be opposed by member states unwilling to adapt national systems but, without legislative controls, states would not be bound to respond. Delors' plan represented a compromise. He rejected the idea that the social dimension implied uniformity or unification and instead advocated 'coherence' (Delors, 1985, p. xviii). His plan involved a social dialogue, whereby unions and employers would become the initiators of policy in the social field, rather than the Commission.

The SEA confirmed the shift away from harmonisation towards respect for national systems. While still referring to the 'harmonisation of conditions', the new Article 118a stressed that directives should be adopted setting out 'minimum requirements for gradual implementation, having regard to the conditions and technical rules obtaining in each of the Member States'.

The more pragmatic and less legalistic approach was pursued during the preparatory phase of the Community Charter of the Fundamental Social Rights of Workers in the late 1980s. In an analysis of the climate of opinion at that time, the European Institute of Social Security (1988, p. 9) argued that, after more than thirty years of operation, the Community was no longer seeking to modify systems. Instead, it was directing its efforts towards encouraging national policies for social protection to converge over a number of precisely defined common objectives without encroaching on systems which have developed from quite different traditions.

The Community Charter took some account of this change in approach. The term 'harmonisation' was used in the context of freedom of movement with reference to the 'harmonisation of conditions of residence in all Member States' (point 3); the duration of paid leave was to be 'harmonised' (point 8); and measures were to be taken to achieve 'further harmonisation of conditions' for safety at the workplace (point 19). Member states undertook, however, to recognise national differences in social protection systems. Reference was made, for example, to the need to act in accordance with national practices (point 8) and with the arrangements applying in each country (point 10).

The action programme for the implementation of the Community Charter stated that the diversity of national practices was to be retained as a positive input, but that a balance should be sought between economic and social measures with a view to protecting the competitiveness of business. Member states were given the responsibility of guaranteeing the social rights embodied in the Charter and implementing the necessary social measures to ensure the smooth operation of the internal market, but the Commission was invited to submit initiatives with a view to the adoption of appropriate legal instruments. To reconcile these conflicting objectives, the intention was to observe the principle of subsidiarity, whereby the most appropriate minimum level of involvement by the Union – whether it be harmonisation, co-ordination, convergence, or co-operation – is applied (see Chapter 1). In other words, the Commission should intervene only where necessary and where measures cannot be better put into effect at national level in such a way that the rules established do not constrain member states.

Rather than engaging in endless discussions in an attempt to reach agreement over regulations, which would be legally binding and the strongest form of action possible (see Appendix 1), the Community seemed to be working increasingly towards a situation of mutual recognition of systems (European Institute of Social Security, 1988, p. 50), which had been successfully applied elsewhere, for example to educational qualifications (see Chapter 3). Mutual recognition implied that national systems are respected and not called into question.

In the new European Union established by the Maastricht Treaty, member states were encouraged to co-operate and co-ordinate their efforts in order to bring about greater economic and social cohesion. The Treaty emphasised the importance of cohesion as the means of promoting 'economic and social progress which is balanced and sustainable' (Article B). The Structural Funds were identified as the main instrument available to compensate for possible losses arising as a result of economic integration and to enhance social cohesion (Hannequart, 1992).

In the Agreement on Social Policy, annexed to the Maastricht Treaty, neither harmonisation nor approximation was mentioned. Instead, Article 1 referred to the need to promote 'proper social protection', taking account of the 'diverse forms of national practices'. Article 5 established the limits of the Commission's role which was simply to 'encourage cooperation between the Member States and facilitate the coordination of their action in all social policy fields under this Agreement'. Elsewhere in the Agreement care was taken to ensure that member states should not be prevented from taking any measures under their own initiative (Articles 2 and 6). In addition, the

Commission was required to consult management and labour before submitting proposals in the social field (Article 3).

(Like the Community Charter, the Agreement on Social Policy did not set out any clear goals in the social area. Article 2 of the Treaty of Rome was substantially amended: references to approximation of economic policies and closer relations between members states were dropped.

Instead, the objective was to promote, amongst other things, 'a high degree of convergence of economic performance, a high level of employment and of social protection, the raising of the standard of living and quality of life, and economic and social cohesion and solidarity among Member States'.

At the time when the Maastricht Treaty was signed a Council Recommendation was being prepared 'on the convergence of social protection objectives and policies' [2.1]. On the basis that differences in social security cover might act as a serious brake to the free movement of workers and exacerbate regional imbalances, particularly between the north and the south of the Community, the Council proposed that 'a strategy be promoted for the convergence of Member States' policies in this field, underpinned by objectives established in common, making it possible to overcome such disadvantages' [2.1, p. 49]. The Community's strategy was to be flexible in nature, progressive and non-binding [2.2, p. 7]. The *de facto* convergence which was said to be occurring as the result of common trends leading to common problems was to be further promoted by establishing common objectives as a guide for national policies, founded on the principles of equal treatment and fairness as the means of avoiding all forms of discrimination and disadvantage. The Recommendation did not clarify how these principles were to be operationalised, stating only that social protection systems were to be adapted and developed as necessary and administered with maximum efficiency and effectiveness.

The bland tone of the Agreement on Social Policy and the fact that the Recommendation was not a binding legal document provide a further indication of the lack of commitment to a strongly interventionist social policy founded on the harmonisation of social protection systems. The Council appeared to be admitting that legislation on the harmonisation of social protection had not proved to be an effective instrument for achieving standardisation across the Union. The Agreement and Recommendation left the way open, however, for co-operation and co-ordination based on mutual recognition of systems and tolerance of diversity, which was expected to result in convergence of national social protection systems.

RECOGNISING NATIONAL DIVERSITY

The 1994 White Paper on European social policy [1.13] confirmed that future development in this area should be premised on respect for national diversity. Like the Council Recommendation, it dismissed total harmonisation as an objective and reiterated the aim of seeking convergence of goals and policies, on the grounds that co-existence of different national systems would enable 'progress in harmony towards the fundamental objectives of the Union' [1.13, p. 5]. According to the Recommendation, it was to be left to member states to 'determine how their social protection schemes should be framed and the arrangements for financing and organizing them' [2.1, p. 50]. Many of the problems associated with adopting a common stance and the reasons for the resistance to harmonisation in the social area can be attributed to the different starting points of member states and also their awareness of what they stood to lose if a uniform system, guaranteeing a minimum level of provision, was universally applied. In this section the debate over harmonisation is examined with reference to the convergence thesis and the concept of models of welfare or welfare regimes within the context of the Union.

The convergence thesis revisited

The debate about the feasibility of harmonisation and the likelihood of convergence of social protection systems as a result of economic change is not confined to the European Union. In the 1960s and 1970s, proponents of convergence theory were arguing that welfare states in industrial societies were a logical development from industrialisation and that attitudes towards social problems were converging as similar conclusions were being reached about how to resolve them.

The convergence thesis was countered by other writers who criticised it for being too deterministic and for oversimplifying patterns of development in social policy. Instead, critics such as Ramesh Mishra (1977, pp. 33–42) have stressed the persistence of diversity in welfare patterns in advanced industrial societies and the influence of technology as only one amongst a number of factors shaping social policy, as for example in the mix between state and occupational welfare provision. In the early 1980s Peter Flora and Jens Alber (1981, pp. 60–3) reviewed the argument that diffusion of welfare systems had occurred as some countries imitated and adopted innovative pioneering institutions from elsewhere. They found that internal socio-economic problems and political mobilisation also had to be taken into account. None of these commentators was, however, referring specifically to the European Community nor to the possible influence of social policy emanating from Brussels on the convergence of different welfare systems.

Models of welfare

(Concurrently with the debate over convergence, several attempts have been made to identify typologies which might help to describe and explain the diffusion of different patterns of welfare and their diversity. In the 1960s, again without reference to the EEC, Richard Titmuss (1974, pp. 30–2) had developed a conceptual approach to the analysis of welfare in which he distinguished between three models: in the residual model, social welfare institutions came into play when the private market and the family broke down, thereby limiting state intervention to marginal and deserving groups; according to the industrial achievement-performance model, social welfare institutions were adjuncts of the economy, and social needs were met on the basis of merit, work performance and productivity; under the third, institutional redistributive, model, social welfare was seen as a major integrated institution in society, operating to provide universalist services outside the market.)

↑ Residual, industrial and institutional interpretations thus represented very different conceptions of welfare: minimum, targeted provision, performance-related and optimum universal provision. The residual concept of social policy has also been extended to describe welfare as a 'residual luxury' supported by economic surpluses (Heclo, 1981, p. 403). When in the 1970s an economic surplus could no longer be assured, welfare states were criticised as a drain on resources.

In the early 1990s renewed interest in analysing models of welfare as an alternative to convergence theory led to several proposals for typologies based on the different ways in which welfare is organised in relation to social structures, political interests and market forces. The three welfare regimes proposed by Gøsta Esping-Andersen (1990) for the capitalist nations were widely discussed and provoked a number of alternative suggestions. Liberal welfare states, according to Esping-Andersen, could be exemplified by the Anglo-Saxon countries. As in Titmuss's residual model, in the absence of a class alliance, selective welfare was targeted at the poor, a dual system of private and occupational services provision was available for the middle classes, and an attempt was made to minimise direct intervention by the state in order to give free rein to market forces. As in the industrial achievement-performance model, Esping-Andersen's conservative corporatist regime could be applied to countries such as Germany, where a conservative central government had developed systems of occupational social insurance welfare, shaped in no small measure by the influence of the Church, in an effort to ensure support from the working and middle classes. Esping-Andersen's social democratic regimes corresponded to the institutional redistributive model, as represented by Scandinavian countries, especially Sweden, where the welfare state, responding to the solidarity of the working and middle classes, provided universalist services, premised on equal opportunities and full employment.

‒ Applying this analysis to unwaged care work, which Esping-Andersen neglects to do, Peter Taylor-Gooby (1991b, p. 97) has shown how the social democratic regime has gone furthest in socialising care, whereas conservative corporatist regimes tend to consider caring as part of the informal sector of the economy to be performed primarily by women. In liberal regimes caring is commodified in that it is largely left to individuals to resort to market forces and make their own provision.

According to Esping-Andersen's (1990, p. 74) classification, among member states in the European Union, Belgium, France, Germany and Italy rate high on conservative attributes, with Ireland and the Netherlands obtaining a medium score. Denmark and the Netherlands rate high on social democratic criteria, with Germany and the United Kingdom in the medium band. None of the member states is found to record a high degree of liberalism. If the United Kingdom is given a medium rating in this category, so too are Denmark, France, Germany, Italy and the Netherlands. The southern European member states were not included in Esping-Andersen's analysis. Proponents of the logic of industrialism thesis might argue that Greece, Portugal and Spain will in time develop the same level of welfare provision as their more advanced and wealthier Mediterranean neighbours. Since they already rely heavily on social insurance mainly funded by employers' contributions well above the European average, as illustrated in the next section, there is a strong case for expecting their systems to develop in line with the continental model.

WELFARE STATES IN THE EUROPEAN UNION

In this section consideration is given to the different models of welfare which have characterised member states in the three waves of membership in the 1950s, 1970s and 1980s, in order to test the argument that, at the very least, the expansion of the Community complicated the harmonisation process and made prospects for achieving convergence more distant, but possibly more necessary.

During the 1980s and into the early 1990s *per capita* spending on social protection increased by more than 40 per cent across the Union. Figure 2.1 summarises trends in social spending over the 1980s in

Figure 2.1   Trends in social protection spending in member states (as % of GDP, 1981–91)

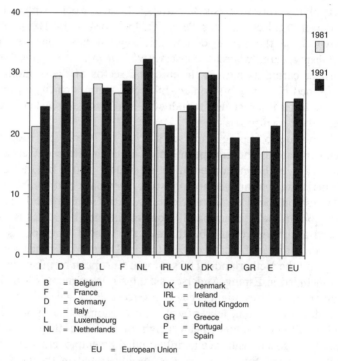

B	=	Belgium
F	=	France
D	=	Germany
I	=	Italy
L	=	Luxembourg
NL	=	Netherlands

DK	=	Denmark
IRL	=	Ireland
UK	=	United Kingdom
GR	=	Greece
P	=	Portugal
E	=	Spain

EU = European Union

Sources: Eurostat, 'Social Protection in Europe: Trends from 1980 to 1989', *Rapid Reports: Population and Social Conditions*, no. 4, 1991, table 2; Eurostat, *Basic Statistics of the Community: Comparisons with the Principal Partners of the Community*, 30th edn, 1993, table 3.31.

relation to Gross Domestic Product (GDP), using data derived from the European System of Integrated Social Protection Statistics (ESSPROS). Only five countries – Belgium, Denmark, Germany, Ireland and Luxembourg – reduced their spending on social protection during this period, while expenditure increased most rapidly in the member states which started from the lowest base, namely Greece, Portugal and Spain, bringing them closer to the European average.

Figure 2.2 shows how social protection is financed across member states: two countries – Denmark and Ireland – rely heavily on state subsidies, whereas employers make the largest contribution in France, Italy and Spain and employees in the Netherlands. During the 1980s the trend was to reduce the burden on employers and increase the contributions of the state and employees, but the changes were not enough to provoke any real convergence between funding mechanisms.

Figure 2.2 Social protection receipts in member states in 1991 (in %)

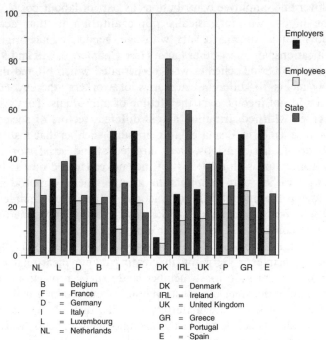

B = Belgium	DK = Denmark
F = France	IRL = Ireland
D = Germany	UK = United Kingdom
I = Italy	
L = Luxembourg	GR = Greece
NL = Netherlands	P = Portugal
	E = Spain

Source: Eurostat, *Basic Statistics of the Community: Comparisons with the Principal Partners of the Community*, 30th edn, 1993, table 3.35.

The legal basis and administrative structures of the different national systems of social protection are briefly summarised in Appendix 2, grouped according to the same three waves of membership of the Union. These thumbnail sketches also provide a reference point for the analysis of different areas of social policy in subsequent chapters.

Continental welfare states

The founder members of the EEC shared a certain similarity of approach to welfare in that their social protection systems were mainly derived from the Bismarckian statist corporatist model, in accordance with the principle that workers are guaranteed benefits and a substitute income related to their previous earnings through a contractual insurance scheme (Clasen and Freeman, 1994). This 'continental' insurance model was based on the assumption that employment qualified individuals for welfare benefits as well as wages, and that benefits were funded primarily, if not exclusively, by employer and employee contributions as part of labour costs.

The model was intrinsically non-egalitarian in that access to employment is known to vary with age, gender, ethnic origins and qualifications, amongst other factors (see Chapters 6, 7, 8 and 9). Over the postwar period schemes were perpetuated which offered different arrangements to different categories of workers, thereby ensuring distribution of income over the lifetime of individuals. They were less concerned with redistribution across different sectors of society. The original schemes in Bismarckian Germany, such as that instituted in 1889 for old age pensions, were targeted at industrial workers and provided compensation for loss of income, calculated on the basis of earnings, rather than a minimum income, thereby reproducing in retirement the inequalities of income earned from employment. Provision for public sector workers was particularly generous and therefore constituted another source of inequality.

Belgium, France, Italy, Luxembourg and the Netherlands followed a similar principle to Germany in creating employment-related social insurance schemes. In most member states social protection was first introduced in the areas of industrial injuries and occupational diseases, followed by sickness and maternity benefits, then old age, survivors' and invalidity benefits, and lastly unemployment benefits, which have tended to remain at the margins of social insurance systems, and family allowances. The provision of health care was also based on insurance contributions, although Italy operated a national health service. In addition, all six EEC founder members developed some form of non-contributory minimum social assistance as a safety net subsidised by the state from general taxation (see Chapter 8).

These six countries not only display commonality in the underlying principles and organisational structures of their social protection systems, they also have in common that their spending on social welfare, as a proportion of GDP, is generally higher than in the other member states, particularly in the Netherlands, as shown in Figure 2.1. Although they all share several of the broad characteristics of the continental welfare model, their social protection systems are far from being uniform either structurally or in terms of their funding arrangements: the social costs of labour are, for example, likely to be much higher in France and Italy where contributions fall heavily on employers. While the Italian national health service shifts some of the burden to the state, reforms in the early 1990s were moving in the direction of a partial withdrawal of the state in favour of market and voluntary sector solutions. When social assistance is organised at regional or local level, considerable variations in coverage are likely to arise not only between but also within countries, as illustrated in particular by the case of Italy, where important disparities occur between north and south.

Nordic and Anglo-Saxon welfare states

The states that joined the Community in 1973 – Denmark, Ireland and the United Kingdom – shared a general conception of social protection closer to what can be described as the citizenship or welfare model. According to the Beveridge scheme for social welfare in Britain and to the Scandinavian, or social democratic (Esping-Andersen, 1990), model which developed in Denmark, the right to a pension, health care and family allowances was granted on the basis of social citizenship. The implication was that employment provided a living wage, whereas welfare benefits were distributed through taxation to all citizens on equal terms whatever their employment status.

The social security systems in these three countries continue to be distinguished from the 'continental' model by their preference for fiscal resources and the universal provision of health care rather than insurance contributions and income-related benefits. In Denmark, however, emphasis was placed on income maintenance, whereas in Ireland and the United Kingdom the aim has been to ensure subsistence by providing low flat-rate payments or means-tested social assistance, which may help to explain the difference in the overall level of spending on social protection in relation to GDP.

The southern European welfare model

Greece, Portugal and Spain, which joined the Community in the 1980s, were characterised by less advanced and less coherent social security systems compared with most of the earlier members. They continued to rely heavily on traditional forms of support through family and kinship networks and the Church and discretionary provision at local level. Social protection was broadly based on corporatism, as in the continental model, with employers carrying the major burden of the cost of providing benefits, but in Spain and Portugal health care was largely provided by the state and funded from taxation. In the early 1990s a relatively high proportion of the population were still not covered by social insurance, and neither Greece nor Portugal had a general social assistance scheme. While most other member states were trying to contain public spending, in all three countries the state was bearing an increasing share of the cost of funding social protection as coverage was extended across the population.

CONVERGING OR DIVERGING WELFARE REGIMES

The social protection systems in the countries considered within these three groupings (continental, Nordic/Anglo-Saxon and southern European) share a common core both in terms of the risks they cover and the general administrative arrangements set up to deal with them. Closer scrutiny, however, reveals numerous differences within and between groupings in the legal status of social protection, funding mechanisms, the distribution of responsibilities and the population groups covered by contributory and non-contributory schemes. Each country has developed its own peculiar brand of social protection as a result of a long process reflecting idiosyncratic socio-economic, political and cultural traditions, which would seem to give the lie to the thesis of the logic of industrialism. These differences are examined in more detail in subsequent chapters with reference to specific areas of social policy.

In line with convergence theory it could be argued that disparities in systems might be due to the stage of socio-economic development reached by each country. Accordingly, the southern European countries might be expected to learn from and imitate their more advanced northern neighbours. While there is some evidence to suggest that innovatory schemes may be used as models, as was the case with the Bismarckian and Beveridgian social security schemes, the recessionary conditions in which Greece, Portugal and Spain were developing their social protection systems when they joined the Community were very different from those of the 1960s and 1970s, even if the Structural Funds contributed to some upwards levelling. In the economic climate of the 1980s and early 1990s the examples which seemed most likely to be imitated were those of countries which were showing most success in controlling social spending)(Belgium and Germany).

(All welfare regimes have adapted over the postwar period in response to changing socio-economic and political circumstances. Most countries in the Union have developed a mixed economy of welfare or welfare pluralism, in which the insurance model has become predominant. A certain amount of involuntary or spontaneous, rather than intended or planned, convergence may therefore be taking place under the influence of market forces, which would seem to have been driving social policy in most member states. The actual welfare mix continues, however, to depend on the political context in which it occurs and the human and social processes involved in policy development at national level. Just as industrial technology and state intervention in social affairs were not considered sufficiently powerful to bring about convergence of social policy in the past (Mishra, 1977, p. 40), the economic factors which seem to be a major force behind welfare pluralism may not necessarily suffice to overcome differences in national welfare state ideologies.)

(Evidence for the development of a mixed economy of welfare is present in all member states. The corporate welfare systems, based on employers' and workers' contributions and income-related benefits, did not replace all the existing occupational schemes, which continued to provide supplementary cover for contingencies such as old age for some groups of workers. Private insurance has been retained as yet another layer of protection for the recipients of high incomes in several member states. Over the postwar period means-tested social assistance benefits have become an increasingly important aspect of welfare in countries which began with a compensatory employment-related insurance system. In Belgium, France, Germany and Italy, for example, means-tested non-contributory old age assistance schemes have been introduced to cater for the income needs of older people and other groups not eligible for occupational schemes (see Chapter 7). The underlying principle that rights are derived from employment is still in evidence in schemes like the *revenu minimum d'insertion* (RMI) in France where benefits are dependent upon the willingness and ability of the destitute to undertake some form of employment or social training as a means of returning to the formal labour market (see Chapter 8).

In countries, such as the United Kingdom, which initially founded their welfare systems on universal state provision of health care and flat-rate benefits for other contingencies, policy makers have not sought to prevent schemes from developing for earnings-related payments and occupationally based pensions and private health care, which enable more highly qualified people in better paid jobs to gain access to additional benefits. Occupational schemes have been extended in countries with both insurance and assistance based systems to all sectors of the working population, with the exception of Denmark, where the basic old age pension has remained particularly generous.

In the early 1990s in Denmark universality continued to depend on a high degree of involvement of public sector institutions, although here too pressure was increasingly being exerted by public opinion and government to reduce the tax burden and turn to market and civil society solutions. By contrast, in the southern European countries, the state has been increasing its contribution to the public provision of welfare.

Convergence towards corporatism as the dominant model of welfare pluralism inevitably leads, it has been argued, to dualisation within societies (Abrahamson, 1992, p. 10). The employment insurance model of welfare has been attacked for reinforcing differentiation, segregation and polarisation. Although such a model might be expected to serve the economic interests of the SEM, at the social level it has been interpreted as a retrograde step, since it is premised on social exclusion. While the market can be expected to take care of workers in regular employment, the less privileged groups in society are likely to be further marginalised. Convergence towards the employment-centred model of welfare can therefore be criticised on ideological, moral and political grounds for moving member states further away from a more redistributive conception of welfare citizenship.

Box 2 Union documents relating to the harmonisation of social policies

SECONDARY LEGISLATION

2.1 Council Recommendation of 27 July 1992 on the convergence of social protection objectives and policies (92/442/ EEC) (*OJ* L 245/49 26.8.92).

OFFICIAL PUBLICATIONS BY THE COMMISSION OF THE EUROPEAN COMMUNITIES (CEC)

2.2 CEC (1992) 'The Convergence of Social Protection Objectives and Policies', *Social Europe Supplement 5/92*.

3 Education and Training

Most references in the Community's and Union's Treaties and Charter to action in the area of social protection are confined to provisions for workers under labour law and in social security systems where the basis for entitlements is derived primarily from employment. When the Treaty establishing the European Economic Community (EEC) was signed in 1957 [1.2], member states were concerned with social provisions only in so far as differences in national systems might impede freedom of movement for workers within the Community or distort competition. For the EEC founder members, education and training were therefore of only indirect interest: attention was focused on recognition of qualifications and on co-operation in vocational training rather than on harmonising educational systems (Articles 57 and 128).

When social policy is defined in a broad sense as the collective provision of particular services or as government interventions with the aim of shaping society in some way (Kleinman and Piachaud, 1993, p. 3), covering both non-economic and economic objectives (Titmuss, 1974, p. 29), education and training can be considered as legitimate areas for intervention at European level. As the social remit was gradually extended (see Chapter 1), education became an area where the Union developed its own policy agenda, by formulating an agreed set of objectives and organising administrative measures for their implementation, albeit with due regard to the principles of subsidiarity and respect for diversity.

In this chapter, the place of education and training is first located within the wider context of European social policy, including a review of the lengthy process of negotiation leading to the mutual recognition directives. Union initiatives on education are then examined, followed by a comparison of the arrangements for education and training across member states. In conclusion consideration is given to the possible impact of the Union's actions in this area of policy on national systems.

'EDUCATIONAL SPACE' IN THE EUROPEAN UNION

The interests of the Union have been primarily bound up with economic concerns, as shown in previous chapters. If the Council of

Ministers progressively turned its attention towards education and training, the aim was to improve the quality and skills of the labour force and consequently to further the goal of economic cohesion. The issue of competition was also relevant in that employers were expected to seek to poach well qualified labour and to compete in offering the most favourable terms of employment in an effort to attract appropriate skills in areas of labour shortage (see Chapter 9). Since the 1970s another labour market-related reason for interest in education and training has been the growing problem of unemployment, particularly amongst young people (see Chapter 8). In this section the development of policy for education and training is considered with reference to the Union's primary legislation and directives for the mutual recognition of qualifications.

Vocational training in the EEC Treaty

Although Article 118 of the EEC Treaty gave the Commission the task of 'promoting close cooperation between Member States' in the area of basic and advanced vocational training amongst others, the subject of education was not explicitly addressed. Article 128 provided for the establishment of a 'common vocational policy capable of contributing to the harmonious development both of the national economies and of the common market'. The first phase of a programme for the exchange of young workers was launched in 1964, setting a pattern for a series of initiatives designed to encourage mobility during training. Under the section on the right of establishment, Article 57 empowered the Council to 'issue directives for the mutual recognition of diplomas, certificates and other evidence of formal qualifications' in order to make it 'easier for the self-employed to take up and pursue activities in another member state'.

Education and training in the Community social action programme

When, ten years later, in 1974 the Commission signalled an interest in the social dimension of Europe through its social action programme (see Chapter 1), education was placed on the agenda. A Council Resolution of 9 February 1976 'comprising an action programme in the field of education' [3.1] identified a number of priorities, including improved facilities for education and training, closer relations and closer co-operation between member states in education, training and higher education, improved possibilities for the recognition of qualifications and periods of study, the exchange of information and free movement of teachers, students and researchers.

The programme also addressed the questions of unemployment amongst young people, the educational needs of the children of migrants, the preparation of young people for work and the smooth transition from education to working life, equal opportunities in access to all forms of education, the combating of illiteracy and teaching of Community languages. Subsequently European Social Fund (ESF) rules were recast to give priority to the under-twenty-fives, and a range of measures were introduced which had implications for employment. The programme thus prepared the way for the development of a number of actions over the following decade.

Education and training in the Community Charter

While the final stages of the Community Charter of the Fundamental Social Rights of Workers [1.7] were being negotiated, the Commission issued a Communication 'on education and training in the European Community', setting out medium-term perspectives for education over the period 1989–92 [3.4]. It provided a clear statement of the Community's objectives and initiatives in this area. In the introduction the Communication spoke of the need to create an 'educational space for mobility and interchange', analogous to Jacques Delors' 'social space' (see Chapter 1). The same document stressed the broad consensus reached over the pivotal role that education and training would be called upon to play in the 'overall development strategy of the Community', spearheading the Community's commitment to invest in people. The Communication suggested, moreover, that human resources could provide 'an essential bridge between economic and social policies' [3.4, p. 1].

The Commission's views on the subject were, to some extent, incorporated into the Community Charter, which, like the EEC Treaty with regard to education and training, stressed the importance of removing barriers to the mobility of workers (point 2) and reiterated the need to eliminate obstacles arising from the non-recognition of qualifications (point 3). Emphasis was placed on the right of workers to vocational training throughout their working lives (point 15). Vocational training was mentioned in five of the twelve sections of the Charter, indicating the priority being given to this area of social policy in so far as it had immediate relevance for workers. The right was affirmed of every worker to training and retraining throughout working life and without discrimination on grounds of nationality. The aim was to help workers improve or extend their skills, particularly in the light of technical developments (point 15). Under the heading of protection of children and adolescents, the rights of young people included a minimum working age which 'must not be lower than the minimum school-leaving age and, in any case, not lower than 15 years' (point 20). Young people were to be entitled to 'initial vocational training of a sufficient duration to enable them to adapt to the requirements of their future working life', and such training was to take place during working hours (point 23).

The right of men and women to equal treatment was to extend beyond access to employment, remuneration, working conditions and social protection to equality in access to education, training and career development (point 16). The section on health protection and safety at the workplace included measures to cover the need for training (point 19), and disabled persons were to be entitled to vocational training where appropriate 'aimed at improving their social and professional integration' (point 26).

Applying the Community Charter's provisions on education and training

Rather than formulating further directives to implement the policies on education and training outlined in the Community Charter through legal mechanisms, the Commission issued a Memorandum 'on higher education in the European Community' [3.5]. The purpose was to deal with the problem of co-ordinating the many programmes which had been launched in the area of education and training, some dating back to the 1970s. The Memorandum was aimed at establishing an overall framework of reference for locating and managing all Community initiatives and actions in the context of a common vocational training policy, focusing on the development of human resources as an essential component in economic, social and political advancement. The European dimension of higher education was stressed, as was the need to extend opportunities for international exchange schemes to young workers.

While the economic motivation of encouraging freedom of movement of workers continued to dictate policies on education and training, the concept of an educational space was gaining acceptance. Emphasis was gradually shifting towards more qualitative objectives, with mobility being presented as a source of mutual enrichment and cultural interchange rather than an end in itself. The 1991 Memorandum clearly set out the Community's policy objectives for post-compulsory education and training and the 'wider responsibilities of higher education institutions for maintaining, developing and transmitting the cultural heritage of Europe and its Member States and for mobilising the creativity of people to advance the boundaries of knowledge, in the humanities as well as in science and technology' [3.5, pp. 1–2]. A number of factors were identified in the same document as influencing higher education in the Community: the increasing pace of European integration and labour mobility following the completion of the internal market and the advance towards monetary and political union; the impact of scientific and technological advances on economic and daily life; the enlargement of the Community and increasing opportunities for co-operation, partnership and mutual support both within Europe and on the world scene. All these changes were expected to have an impact on the level and mix of skills required by the workforce, and thus on education and training, if skill shortages were to be avoided and competitiveness was to be maintained.

On the basis of this and other documents, by the early 1990s two main dimensions of the Union's policy objectives in this area could be identified. From the economic point of view, the aim was to promote quality education, vocational training and retraining designed to ensure the supply of multiskilled and polyvalent workers able to operate on a European scale and to adapt to meet changing needs. From the social perspective, the Union was seeking to 'secure equality of opportunity for young people to develop their talents and skills without regard to their financial means, social class, gender, ethnic origin, or geographical location of residence' [3.5, p. 8]. While the Commission was not attempting to harmonise the content and duration of education and training systems across member states, it did consider that a likely practical effect of its actions, as for example over the mutual recognition of qualifications, would be 'to stimulate movements towards convergence in the training for particular professions' [3.5, p. 6].

Education and training in the Maastricht Treaty

Unlike many other areas of social affairs, the Maastricht Treaty [1.6] addressed the issue of education and training directly rather than relegating it to the Protocol and Agreement on Social Policy (see Chapter 1). One section in the main body of the Treaty was devoted to social policy, education, vocational training and youth (Title VIII). The wording of Article 123 of the EEC Treaty on the ESF was revised by adding a reference to vocational training and retraining as the means of helping workers to adapt to industrial change, and Articles 126 and 128 were replaced by new texts which set out the Commission's commitment to encouraging quality education through co-operation between member states. They reaffirmed the principle of subsidiarity: individual member states were to retain responsibility for the content of programmes and the organisation of their educational and vocational systems; cultural and linguistic diversity were to be respected. The aims expressed were wide ranging: to develop the European dimension in education through language teaching and dissemination; to encourage the mobility of students and teachers, including the recognition of qualifications and periods of study in another country; to promote co-operation between educational institutions; to develop the exchange of information and experience on common issues; to encourage the exchange of young people and socio-educational instructors; and to encourage distance learning. Action programmes were also introduced to encourage co-operation between member states. As in other areas of social policy, the Treaty did not seek to impose legislative reform on member states but rather to make recommendations, which are the European Council's least binding policy instrument (see Appendix 1).

Vocational training policy was intended, in addition, to ease the process of adaptation to industrial change, improve initial and continuing training, in order to assist entry and re-entry into the labour market and access to vocational training, and stimulate co-operation amongst training establishments or between them and firms (Article 127).

When the terms of the Community Charter are read in conjunction with Articles 126 and 127 of the Maastricht Treaty, it is clear that education and training policies, while being firmly on the agenda, were being handled with the usual caution which characterised the Council's approach to social affairs. The Union continued to be concerned primarily with promoting co-operation between member states through programmes aimed at encouraging mobility and the exchange of information. According to the Maastricht Treaty, the intention was not to interfere with national education systems nor to use the legislative channel to bring pressure to bear on member states to persuade them to harmonise systems. The key verbs in the Treaty on the subject of education and vocational training were 'develop, encourage, promote, facilitate, improve, stimulate', whereas the

Community Charter, which was not legally binding on member states, was more prescriptive: under point 15 it stated that 'Every worker. . .must be able to receive such training. . .there may be no discrimination. . .. The competent public authorities. . .should set up continuing and permanent training systems. . .'.

The Maastricht Treaty provided a legal framework allowing the Union to propose co-operative actions in the area of education. A Green Paper on the European dimension of education [3.6], issued shortly before the Treaty came into force, was quick to seize the opportunity to stimulate discussion about future action, by identifying areas where the Union could complement the efforts of member states and bring added value to the development of quality in education. The measures proposed reflected the Union's priorities in the mid-1990s: promotion of mobility and exchanges between young people, training of teachers, development of language teaching and distance learning, promotion of innovation in teaching and the European dimension of education. The 1994 White Paper on European social policy further demonstrated the Commission's commitment to investing in education and training as 'one of the essential requirements for the competitiveness of the Union as well as for the cohesion of our societies' [1.13, p. 15], justifying continued action at European level.

Mutual recognition of qualifications

As in other areas of social policy, over the years the focus of interest in education shifted progressively from harmonisation to co-operation, but not before much effort had been expended comparing the content and level of qualifications across the Community in an attempt to reach agreement over transferability between member states. The overall shift in education and training policy did not mean that the original aim of achieving mutual recognition of qualifications had been forgotten; rather it was extended from the self-employed to cover all levels of vocational training. The Community Charter reiterated the initial objective as stated in the EEC Treaty by proposing that 'obstacles to mobility arising from the non-recognition of diplomas or equivalent occupational qualifications' should be eliminated (point 3).

Although the completion of the internal market in 1993 was heralded as marking the advent of a new era of enhanced mobility of human capital and labour, harmonisation and convergence within the European Union, most of the measures resulting from the Single

European Act (SEA) of 1986 [1.5] with reference to recognition of qualifications had already been initiated before that date. A large number of directives relevant to the harmonisation of the professions had become statutory before 1986. Since 1964 about sixty sectoral directives have been adopted, ensuring the mutual recognition of conditions for access to particular occupations. In many occupations, the directives sought to enable recognition of work experience acquired in another member state. Between 1964 and 1982 directives were issued covering industry and crafts, the retail trade, personal services, such as restaurants, bars and hotels, food industries and drinks production, wholesale trade in coal, trade in toxic products, itinerant activities, insurance agents and brokers, transport agents and hairdressers. Occupations involving the transport of goods or passengers by road were granted freedom of establishment and freedom to provide services.

For other occupations, as in the health professions for example, a more complex set of measures were needed to cover the conditions under which the relevant occupation could be exercised. Two directives were required for each occupation: the first to co-ordinate and harmonise training, covering both quality (content) and quantity (number of years of study and hours of courses); the second to establish the automatic recognition of diplomas conforming to Community standards. The standards imposed were minima, leaving each country to determine additional expectations but without requiring that they should be met. The directives were binding but, in order to leave room for flexibility, they did not go into the details of education and training. Co-ordination and mutual recognition directives were issued between 1976 and 1985, covering doctors, nurses, dentists, veterinary surgeons, midwives, accountants, architects and pharmacists. Seventeen years of negotiations were needed before architects with specified diplomas were granted the right to establishment and to exercise their profession in another member state in 1985. Where important differences existed between the types of education concerned, compensatory requirements could be imposed. Professionals in regulated activities were given the right to establish themselves in another member state, subject to fulfilling the requirements of the host country by undertaking a period of adaptation or undergoing aptitude tests (Séché, 1988). Lawyers were, for example, authorised to plead cases jointly with a lawyer from the host country and to provide some legal services, but an additional diploma was required before they could set up business in another country.

These lengthy and abortive attempts at harmonisation for individual professions progressively gave way to a more global approach, as exemplified by Council Directive 89/48/EEC 'on a general system for the recognition of higher-education diplomas awarded on completion of professional education and training of at least three years' duration', which came into force in 1991 [3.2]. The Directive applied to all diplomas not covered by sectoral directives involving higher education and training of at least three years. The same principle was applied in the supplementary Directive, 92/51/EEC, issued in 1992 [3.3], which extended recognition to other post-secondary qualifications and training courses previously excluded.

Whereas equivalence is generally understood to refer to a detailed comparison of the individual course elements constituting a programme of study, recognition involves a more global evaluation of the whole of a student's education, taking account of the function and overall level of academic study for the purposes of admission to further study or employment. The directives were intended to operate on a case-by-case basis, relying upon mutual confidence between member states and assuming comparability between levels of education and training. By the early 1990s the necessary steps had thus been taken at the legislative level to comply with formal provisions for the mutual recognition of qualifications as stipulated in the EEC Treaty, the Community Charter and the Maastricht Treaty.

UNION INITIATIVES ON EDUCATION AND TRAINING

Statements from the Council and the Commission on vocational training have emphasised the importance of the European dimension in training through the broadening of the understanding of other cultures. A number of programmes have been established since the mid-1980s to encourage mobility of students and researchers in Europe with a view to providing opportunities for exposure to different languages and cultures as part of the learning experience.

Mobility of scholars within Europe is not a new idea. Of all institutions, universities have one of the longest traditions of co-operation dating back to the Middle Ages, when they shared a *lingua franca* (Latin) and the itinerant scholar was a common phenomenon. Yet, over the centuries national higher education systems have tended to diverge, with the result that today they display quite marked differences in their aims and objectives, structures, programmes and qualifications. Having formally recognised that 'Blanket harmonisation or standardization of the educational system is entirely undesirable' [3.4, p. 4], the Union has taken as its objective 'to improve the overall quality of educational provision by bringing the different systems into a long-term process of contact, cooperation and concertation and by avoiding unnecessary divergences which would otherwise impede the free movement of persons and ideas' [3.4, pp. 4–5]. More specifically co-operation is seen as essential in developing a commitment to lifelong learning based on quality and solidarity. One means of achieving closer co-operation has been by devising arrangements whereby educational reforms and restructuring within member states are carried out in full awareness of experience elsewhere.

The aim of improving opportunities for vocational training has led to a number of programmes to encourage the mobility of students, with the explicit objectives of promoting shared democratic values, increasing the understanding of the multicultural dimension of the Community and preparing young people for European citizenship [3.4, p. 5]. As Director of the Task Force for Human Resources, Education, Training and Youth, Hywel Jones (1990, p. 9) presented education as the 'binding force for cooperation and partnership in all other sectors', stressing the importance of 'mutual understanding' and the 'ability to work together' which these programmes were intended to stimulate. Patrick Venturini (1989, pp. 29, 38), a member of the Lacroix Group of advisers to the Commission, has described a students' Europe as one of the 'Beacons for a European Social Area'.

The programmes launched over the years can be divided into four main categories which broadly cover the objectives set out in the Maastricht Treaty: programmes for collecting and disseminating information about education and training arrangements across the Union so as to provide a better understanding of other national systems; programmes designed to encourage mobility of students and young people and promote co-operation between educational institutions in different member states, with a view to extending knowledge of Europe and its languages and adding a European dimension to education and training; programmes designed to provide work experience and vocational training in another national setting in order to enhance social and economic integration and promote co-operation between educational institutions and industry; programmes concerned with the need to adapt to new technologies and extend opportunities for collaboration in research and development.

Information on education and training

In 1975 the Council established a special agency, the European Centre
for the Development of Vocational Training (Cedefop), as an
information network to increase and improve the circulation of
information in the area of education policy. The agency was originally
located in Berlin. Then, following a decision by national governments
in 1993, it was moved to Thessalonika. The Eurydice information
network was set up a few years later and came into operation in 1980,
with the responsibility for developing a data bank on education and
training.

The Council recognised the diversity of education systems in member
states but wanted to ensure that it would not become an obstacle to the
free movement of people. Cedefop was charged with providing
information in all the Community languages, involving a process
which was both costly and laborious. The decision in the 1980s to
pursue the recognition of vocational qualifications for occupations
through a more general directive similar to that for professional
occupations can be seen as a means of avoiding the problems
associated with trying to document and standardise different practices
in qualifications and training.

Despite the efforts of Cedefop and Eurydice to underpin the
programme of educational co-operation within the Community, in its
Communication on education and training [3.4, p. 15], the Commission
noted that national governments were continuing to implement major
educational reforms without systematic reference to practices in other
member states and without adequate consideration of the implications
for different systems. The Commission therefore recommended that
arrangements should be made to ensure a regular flow of information
on experience across the Community and that a forum should be
provided for co-ordinating discussion of policy issues, with technical
assistance from Eurydice.

Mobility and co-operation between institutions

In the late 1980s several programmes, such as the European Community Action Scheme for the Mobility of University Students, Erasmus,
named after the sixteenth-century humanist scholar and priest Desi-
derius Erasmus, were designed to foster co-operation without requiring
harmonisation. Awarding bodies were called upon to recognise
formally the period of training in another member state, but each

country remained free to decide on the content and organisation of its own programmes in respect of the principle of subsidiarity as reaffirmed in the Maastricht Treaty. In 1984 a network of National Academic Recognition Information Centres (Naric) had been established, subsequently co-ordinated by the Erasmus bureau, to provide information on the recognition of qualifications across member states and of periods of study in other member states or countries in the European Free Trade Association (EFTA). The European Community Course Credit Transfer System (Ects) was set up in 1989/90 to enable students to undertake all or part of their higher education in another member state.

The aim of the Youth for Europe programme was to extend opportunities provided by Erasmus to countries or categories of young people that were under-represented in student exchanges or whose language was less widely spoken. The Lingua programme was proposed by the Commission as a response to the realisation that foreign languages should be an essential part of European education and training and that inadequate knowledge of languages was a major obstacle to mobility as well as a handicap in international trade. The Trans-European Mobility Scheme for University Studies (Tempus) extended exchanges to Central and Eastern Europe from 1991.

When they were introduced, Erasmus, Lingua and Youth for Europe were promoted as the Community's 'flagship' programmes [3.4, p. 3]. The target set for student mobility, that 10 per cent of all students should enjoy a period of training abroad, had not been reached by the time the new action programme, Socrates, was launched to replace Erasmus and Lingua when they expired in 1994. In all member states except Luxembourg, the proportion of foreign students from non-European countries was greater than that from within the Union [3.10, table 2]. Despite the efforts of the Commission, the main obstacles to greater intra-European mobility were still identified as admission restrictions, language, recognition problems, practical, administrative and financial problems as well as inadequate information [3.5, pp. 25–7].

Work experience, training and co-operation between education and industry

The Exchange of Young Workers Programme was one of the earliest Community actions, dating back to 1964, in compliance with Article 50 of the EEC Treaty which invited member states to encourage the

exchange of young workers within the framework of a joint programme. The Community's programme for the Vocational Training of
Young People and their Preparation for Adult Working Life (Petra),
set up in 1988, was another response to this particular need. It involved
placements or exchanges for young people undergoing training and a
network of transnational partnerships and initiatives for young people.
A European Network of Vocational Training Programmes for
Women (Iris) was established the same year to meet the specific needs
of women. It aimed to develop a methodology on women's vocational
training as well as evaluation tools. A further impetus was given to
equal opportunities for women in education and training under the
provisions of the Community Charter; the New Opportunities for
Women (Now) initiative, which began operating in 1990, was intended
to offer member states opportunities for co-funding actions (see
Chapter 6).

New technologies and training

Several action programmes were created in response to the need of the
workforce to master technological change through a partnership
between education and industry. A programme in the Field of
Vocational Training and Technological Change (Eurotecnet) was
formalised in 1990, and the programme on Co-operation between
Universities and Enterprises regarding Training in the Field of
Technology (Comett), another of the Community's flagship programmes, was launched in 1986. In its first year of operation Comett
funded 1320 projects and some 2400 students. Both programmes
recognised the blurring of the boundaries between jobs under the
pressures of technological change as well as the need to introduce
young people to new technologies, not only while they are in full-time
compulsory education but also once they begin initial training. In 1991
an action programme for the Development of Continuing Vocational
Training in the European Community (Force) was established to
encourage information exchange and good practices.

Drawing on the experience gained from implementing these earlier
programmes, in 1995 the Commission launched a new initiative on
vocational training, called Leonardo. The programme was designed to
rationalise and streamline existing actions and improve their effectiveness on the basis of a common vocational training policy. In keeping
with the principle of subsidiarity and in recognition of the diversity of
systems, the action programme took account of the need to ensure that,

within a common framework of objectives, member states would be free to choose means appropriate to their situation. The measures proposed were intended to support national systems, arrangements and policies, innovative actions for the training market and the development of a European dimension in vocational training. Together the Union's programmes represent a substantial input of resources. Most of the schemes have proved to be administratively onerous to operate. Their success is difficult to evaluate, particularly in cases where the intention has been to heighten awareness of other cultures. In quantitative terms the total number of beneficiaries is probably small in relation to the number of potential clients and the target figures: for example, an estimated 200 000 students took advantage of the Erasmus programme between 1987 and 1994 [3.8, p. 13]. If the number of students undertaking part of their studies in another member state has increased consistently over the years, so too has the total student population in the Union. Although the opportunity to spend some time training or studying in another member state may seem attractive, in a recessionary climate and when public spending is being cut back, it is not always easy to find suitable placements and accommodation for applicants; language barriers and cultural differences have continued to present major obstacles, highlighting the need for trainees to be properly prepared for the experience. These problems do not seem to have deterred the Union from continuing to pursue its longer term aim of supporting action programmes designed to promote a more coherent policy for human resources, education, training and youth.

TRENDS IN EDUCATION AND TRAINING IN MEMBER STATES

Although directives on the mutual recognition of vocational and professional qualifications involved examining their content, European policy on education and training has not sought to influence national systems of education, except indirectly by exposing educators and trainers to different approaches through the exchange and mobility programmes described in the previous section. The Maastricht Treaty deliberately ruled out all attempts to harmonise national legislation or to interfere with national practices in this area (Articles 126 and 127). The non-interventionist stance may be attributed to two factors in particular: firstly, member states have resisted supranational legislation in areas where they consider national sovereignty to be paramount; secondly, the experience of seeking to harmonise qualifications had shown how difficult and counterproductive it would be to attempt to standardise educational systems. In this section, some of the main trends in education and training arrangements across member states are examined in order to determine whether national policies in this area are showing any signs of convergence.

National educational systems

In keeping with the spirit of European policy, all member states have invested heavily in the education and training of their young people. The proportion of the population aged between five and twenty-four in education rose steadily during the 1980s, reaching 71 per cent by 1990/ 91 across member states [3.10, table 1], despite a fall in the number of pupils at primary school level due to lower birth-rates, which had affected all member states to a greater or lesser extent (see Chapter 5). The largest increase was in higher education, due partly to the effect of the postwar baby boom and the lengthening of the period of study in response to labour market conditions (job shortages and growing demand for qualifications). To a great extent it was also explained by the increase in the number of female students continuing their education. With longer schooling, the sex ratio was therefore changing. Whereas at primary level boys outnumbered girls in all member states, mainly because more boys are born than girls, by the upper secondary level this was no longer the case, except in Germany, Greece, Luxembourg and the Netherlands. In higher education, women outnumbered men or had reached parity with them in Denmark, France, Greece, Luxembourg, Portugal and Spain. Germany and the Netherlands showed the largest discrepancy between the sexes in favour of men at this level.

Differences remain between member states in the length of compulsory schooling [3.9]. In 1990 compulsory schooling began at the age of five in Belgium, Luxembourg, the Netherlands and the United Kingdom, or in the year in which the child turned five in Greece, and at the age of six in all other member states, except Denmark, where children began their schooling at the age of seven. In Belgium, Denmark, France and Italy, however, 85 per cent or more of children aged between three and the age when compulsory schooling began had places in pre-school establishments [6.16, table 3]. In Luxembourg a pre-school year was compulsory for children aged five to six. The minimum age for leaving school was fifteen in Belgium, Germany, Greece, Ireland, Luxembourg and Portugal, and sixteen in other countries except Italy and Spain where it was fourteen, which meant that these two countries did not satisfy the requirements of the Community Charter (point 20). As a result of differences in starting and leaving ages, the minimum length of full-time compulsory schooling varied from eight years in Italy and Spain to eleven years in the Netherlands and the United Kingdom. In three countries children were routinely expected to complete further years of general education or vocational training, either full time or part time after the minimum school-leaving age: one more year in the Netherlands, two more in Belgium and three in Germany.

Although a Council Directive recognises qualifications based on three years of higher education after the school-leaving certificate as being equivalent throughout the Community, differences in the arrangements for upper secondary level education and training, in combination with disparities in the structure and content of university higher education, make it difficult for employers to interpret qualifications obtained in another member state. While British students routinely graduate after three years and leave higher education by the age of twenty-one or twenty-two with a qualification which is recognised in the United Kingdom as an indication of general intellectual and academic ability, it is far from unusual for students in France, Germany, Greece, Italy, Portugal and Spain to complete study for very specialised higher education qualifications at or after the age of twenty-four, particularly if a period of compulsory national service has to be intercalated.

Lynne Chisholm (1992, pp. 131–78) has suggested a classification of education systems according to the stage at which pupils select or are selected for important transition routes which determine later participation rates. Amongst the countries in northern Europe, the British education system is characterised by early selection and low participation rates in further and higher education, whereas Belgium and the Federal Republic of Germany exemplify early selection and high participation systems. France and the Netherlands select later and retain slightly lower proportions of each age group in education and training, although the rates in France are particularly high in older age groups (Debizet, 1990, p. 332). Denmark provides an example of late selection and high participation.

Vocational training and national labour markets

Much larger proportions (70–80 per cent) of eighteen to twenty year-olds in the non-university sector are likely to be in vocational education and apprenticeships in Germany, Italy, the Netherlands and Denmark, whereas only a small proportion (17–20 per cent) of students at upper secondary level in Ireland, Belgium and the United Kingdom take this route (OECD, 1993, table P.13). The labour market in Germany, in particular, has gained a reputation for the high respect in which it holds vocational qualifications. The Germans have a detailed regulatory framework for apprenticeship training, and the demand for vocational training is so strong that about 60 per cent of each age cohort qualifies through the dual system, which covers part-time attendance at vocational schools. In France and Britain access to jobs is influenced by other considerations, such as the company culture or seniority (Drake, 1994).

Many attempts have been made to construct typologies portraying the relationship between the labour market and education. According to a model proposed by the Centre d'Études et de Recherches sur les Qualifications (Céreq) in France, adapted by Keith Drake (1994), the linkage between schools, firms and labour markets takes different forms: it may be market led and industry based as in Italy and the United Kingdom; it may be training led and school based as in Belgium, Denmark, France and the Netherlands; or it may be training led and industry based as in Germany. Drake argues that these interlinkages were the result of elaborate historical trade-offs between social partners, central and regional government, different pressure groups and taxpayers and workers themselves, each with their own objectives and time horizons. The result is that opportunities for young people may differ significantly according to the social and economic environment of the country or region in which they live. The effectiveness of initial vocational and educational training will also be influenced by these conditions, implying that training arrangements need to be country specific, if not region specific.

Much of the comparative research undertaken in the 1980s on vocational education and training seemed to lead to the conclusion that Britain was trailing behind countries such as France and Germany in terms of the effectiveness of its training when measured by economic performance indicators. Britain, in particular, was criticised for its poor record on intermediate skills (Ryan, 1991, pp. 2–3). As more emphasis was placed on qualifications, the implication was that it would become increasingly difficult to find a job without a recognised qualification, and workers from the United Kingdom would be at a particular disadvantage in the European market place. Approaching the topic from a different angle, Robert Lindley (1991, p. 193) has used Dutch evidence to question the assumption that skill shortages were developing as a result of inadequate training. In the Netherlands the output of qualifications appeared to have increased more rapidly than the skill requirements of jobs, leading to the possible threat of over-qualification and what he described as 'educational crowding-out'. Lindley thus gave the lie to exaggerated claims about the 'burgeoning job content of the economy as a whole and the need for educational levels to rise to keep pace with the increasing sophistication of the modern world of work' (Lindley, 1991, p. 194).

The phenomenon of 'diploma inflation' has also been identified in several member states. The tendency in most countries is to over-produce graduates and under-produce technicians. The 'downward filtering' (Lindley, 1991, p. 203) of able people and the placing of graduates in what were previously non-graduate jobs have not, however, led to any major readjustment in education and training (Drake, 1994). Increasingly the focus has been shifting towards the recognition of the possibility of over-qualification at the top end as it continues to be difficult to attract young people into technical studies. Vocational education has, at the same time, become more general, while what were previously general courses may have assumed a pre-vocational character [3.7, p. 105]. Despite concern about the under-valuing of technical education and long standing efforts to promote the study of technical subjects, particularly amongst women, the debate continues about the aims of education: whether it should offer vocational training or provide basic competencies and broadly based qualifications. The reply would seem to vary both between and within member states.

Employers' groups do seem to have a common view of what they want from compulsory schooling and vocational training. They are looking for general transferable skills as well as more specific technical abilities and competence in languages, expressed in terms of

commitment to quality; ability to communicate effectively; knowledge of one or more foreign languages; the desire to use and develop technologies; general grasp of the importance of the economic environment in which firms function; problem-solving capacity; willingness to adapt to change; ability to work in a team and to relate to others; and an understanding of economics and of the labour market. (Jones, 1990, p. 12)

These objectives would seem to correspond fairly closely to what is being sought by policy makers at European level, as a response to socio-economic and demographic change. While all national governments in member states are undoubtedly being driven by the same momentum, the extent to which they have translated these objectives into provision for education and training is still subject to quite marked variations from one country to another.

THE IMPACT OF EUROPEAN POLICY ON NATIONAL EDUCATION AND VOCATIONAL TRAINING SYSTEMS

Since the signing of the EEC Treaty in 1957, the Community has progressively broadened its social remit. In the area of education, policy objectives have been extended to accommodate the changing needs of the economy and of society at large. The ageing of the population and the demands of the labour market for more workers with a high level of knowledge and skills and the ability to adapt to technological change have stimulated action programmes designed to ensure that national education systems are equipped to respond to not only initial training requirements but also the need for constant upgrading and updating of qualifications throughout working life. The growing emphasis on the importance of being able to operate across national and cultural boundaries has given a new impetus to the European dimension of education 'perceived as a practical economic necessity apart from its desirability on cultural and political grounds' [3.5, p. 40]. Within this context, the recognition of qualifications for academic and professional purposes can be interpreted as a necessary support for freedom of movement, which was a primary aim of the original Treaty.

As in other areas of social policy at European level, it is difficult to evaluate the success of policies for education and training or to assess their impact on national policy making. The Commission has clearly defined its role in this area: it sees itself essentially as a 'catalyst and facilitator of cooperative and common action' [3.5, p. 41], working in accordance with the principle of subsidiarity and respecting diversity of provision. Although tangible results have been achieved in terms of the mutual recognition of qualifications and the increase in the number of students and young people who have had the opportunity to spend periods in other member states and who might not otherwise have done so, the evidence is that the mobility of workers has not expanded commensurably, suggesting that acceptance of qualifications may not be the key factor in relocation of labour as originally believed (see Chapter 9).

The impact of European policy on the harmonisation of education and training systems may also be much less than anticipated. It has been argued that, because the process of mutual recognition of qualifications involved close scrutiny of the structuring of occupations, it provoked a certain amount of convergence of concepts (Merle and Bertrand, 1993, p. 42). Some procedures have been called into question, for example the *numerus clausus* imposed in higher education subjects such as medicine in different member states, the professional qualifications required for practice or the mix of qualifications and work experience. As in other areas of European social policy, the growing importance of the principle of subsidiarity and the reluctance of the Union to legislate have encouraged a shift towards the idea of identifying common European standards, as in health and safety at work, which can serve as reference points, irrespective of differences in national educational systems.

Awareness of educational and training practices in other member states has undoubtedly been enhanced, but here too it is not possible to demonstrate that greater cross-cultural knowledge and mutual recognition have necessarily resulted in the convergence of education and training systems. The proportion of the population participating in higher education has most certainly been growing throughout the Union, and educational opportunities for women, in particular, have improved, but there is no convincing evidence to show that these changes can be attributed to the Union's legislation and action programmes.

By the mid-1990s a consensus did seem to have emerged amongst member states, as reported in the White Paper on European social policy, over the need for better co-ordination between education and vocational training systems and for closer association of the social partners with the design and delivery of training. The Commission reaffirmed, however, 'that national qualification systems should be developed along convergent, but not harmonised, lines at the level of the Union so as to underpin the free movement of persons on a transparent and practical basis' [1.13, p. 15].

Box 3   Union documents relating to education and training

SECONDARY LEGISLATION

3.1   Council Resolution of 9 February 1976 comprising an action programme in the field of education (*OJ* C 38/1 19.2.76).

3.2   Council Directive 89/48/EEC of 21 December 1988 on a general system for the recognition of higher-education diplomas awarded on completion of professional education and training of at least three years' duration (*OJ* L 19/16 24.1.89).

3.3   Council Directive 92/51/EEC of 18 June 1992 on a second general system for the recognition of professional education and training (*OJ* L 209/25 24.7.92).

3.4   Communication from the Commission to the Council on education and training in the European Community. Guidelines for the medium term: 1989–92 (COM(89) 236 final, 2 June 1989).

3.5   Memorandum from the Commission on higher education in the European Community (COM(91) 349 final, 5 November 1991).

3.6   Green Paper from the Commission on the European dimension of education (COM(93) 457 final, 29 September 1993).

OFFICIAL PUBLICATIONS OF THE COMMISSION OF THE EUROPEAN COMMUNITIES (CEC) AND EUROSTAT

3.7   CEC (1989) *Employment in Europe 1989.*

3.8   CEC (1994) *Le Magazine*, no.1.

3.9   CEC/Eurydice and Cedefop (1991) *Structures of the Education and Initial Training Systems in the Member States of the European Community.*

3.10   Eurostat (1993) 'Pupils and Students in the Community in 1990/91', *Rapid Reports, Population and Social Conditions*, no. 9.

4 The Improvement of Living and Working Conditions

The emphasis in the Community's and Union's Treaties and Charter on workers' rights and the need to create conditions that would facilitate freedom of movement of labour between member states explain why issues concerned with the equalisation of living and working conditions have always been high on the policy agenda. As with social security, disparities between member states in the treatment of workers could be seen not only as a factor inhibiting mobility but also as a source of unfair competition. The objective of achieving harmonisation at the same time as the improvement of living and working conditions therefore featured in the Treaty establishing the European Economic Community (EEC) [1.2] and recurred in subsequent Treaties and in the Community Charter of the Fundamental Social Rights of Workers in 1989 [1.7], albeit with the emphasis on working conditions.

In the countries of the EEC founder members, industrial accidents and occupational diseases were amongst the first contingencies to be covered by national employment insurance. Since industrial health problems had long been a concern of the original member states, the Community's role in industrial welfare was primarily to stimulate interest in co-ordinating action which would remove barriers to the mobility of goods, services and labour. Although the rights of workers to a decent standard of living and to a high level of protection at the workplace have continued to be given priority, progressively the areas encompassed under the general heading of living and working conditions have been clarified and widened to include health and safety at work, working hours, employment contracts, conditions governing collective redundancies and bankruptcies, the environment and public health.

As the Union's remit was extended (see Chapter 1), the improvement of living and working conditions remained firmly on the policy agenda. This area of policy has not, however, attracted the same level of public attention or been contested to the same extent as topics like the harmonisation of social protection systems or equal treatment of men and women (see Chapters 2 and 6). Although the Union's approach has tended to remain cautious for reasons which will become more apparent in the course of this chapter, living and working conditions do provide a good example of the way in which policy can be moved forward at European level through the legislative process, action programmes and information campaigns. In this chapter, after examining the development of policy in this area, particularly with reference to health and safety at work, work-time arrangements and public health, comparisons are made of practices in individual member states, with a view to assessing the extent to which European policy may be encouraging member states to adopt common standards.

COMMUNITY POLICY ON LIVING AND WORKING CONDITIONS

The 1951 Treaty establishing the European Coal and Steel Community (ECSC) [1.1] set a number of precedents for the six original member states. Article 3(e) stated the aim of promoting improved working conditions and an improved standard of living for workers in the coal and steel industries while also seeking harmonisation. The 1957 Treaty establishing the European Atomic Energy Community (EAEC) [1.3] devoted ten of its 225 articles to health and safety. Articles 30–9 set out the basic standards to be observed for the protection of the health of workers and the general public against the dangers of ionising radiations, and they stipulated the legal procedures for ensuring they were harmonised and respected. This section examines the development of the themes of health and safety in the Treaties and the Community Charter.

Living and working conditions under the EEC Treaty

Several references were made in the EEC Treaty to the need to improve living and working conditions, although no clear guidance was given about how equalisation between member states should be defined and achieved. Article 117 stated 'the need to promote improved working conditions and an improved standard of living for workers, so as to make possible their harmonisation while the improvement is being maintained'. The authors of the Treaty seemed confident that the development they were calling for would automatically ensue from the functioning of the common market, both through harmonisation of social systems and from procedures for approximation of provisions as laid down by law, regulation or administrative action (see Chapter 2). Amongst the tasks assigned to the Community, Article 2 of the Treaty referred to 'an accelerated raising of the standard of living'. One of the objectives set for the European Social Fund (ESF) was to improve employment opportunities for workers and to contribute to the raising of their standard of living (Article 123).

The areas identified in Article 118 of the Treaty for close co-operation included labour law and working conditions, prevention of occupational accidents and diseases, occupational hygiene, the right of association and collective bargaining. Article 120 dealt with the equivalence of paid holiday schemes. Although the key aspects of working conditions were thereby recognised as social policy issues, the Treaty did not specify the standards to be achieved, nor did it set a timetable for implementation.

Notwithstanding these limitations, in the field of industrial welfare, economic interests provided a powerful incentive for Community action in the early years of the EEC. Common standards of protection against industrial hazards were needed to prevent any one country from gaining a competitive edge and to avoid a situation where migrant workers might be treated differently from one member state to another. In the 1960s studies were commissioned on topics such as occupational diseases, industrial safety, the influence of human factors in the prevention of accidents and the health and protection of women and young people. Study programmes were organised to enable senior management to visit other member states with the intention of alerting them to practices elsewhere, and safety consciousness raising exercises were initiated. A series of directives and recommendations were drafted in an attempt to standardise practices and to protect and compensate workers in the areas of industrial medical services and diseases, paying special attention to young workers and working mothers in industry. Substantial progress was made during the 1960s in reaching agreement over safety standards, creating a useful basis for future legislation.

Action programmes to improve living and working conditions

Industrial health and safety was already under consideration in 1974 when the Commission presented its social action programme (see Chapter 1). In the same year the Council set up an Advisory Committee on Safety, Hygiene and Health Protection at Work. Its brief included issues such as training, research, data collection, provision in sectors subject to special hazards and for groups of workers at risk, as well as the harmonisation of regulations for products and processes. The Commission extended its interest to medical research and common action on emerging health problems such as bad environmental conditions and stress. An environmental protection programme was prepared at the same time as the social action programme in response to growing public concern about pollution from noxious materials and in recognition of the fact that pollutants do not respect national borders.

In 1976 the Commission signalled its commitment to this rapidly developing policy area by setting up the European Foundation for the Improvement of Living and Working Conditions, in Dublin. The Foundation was assigned the task of monitoring progress, undertaking analyses, studies and research. It was also made responsible for disseminating knowledge on a systematic and scientific basis concerning the consequences of economic development, diminishing natural resources and environmental quality, and persistent social and regional disparities in living and working conditions. Its brief included advising Community institutions and other policy-making bodies in member states on objectives and guidelines for action.

Living and working conditions in the Single European Act

The next landmark in policy for the improvement of living and working conditions was the Single European Act (SEA) of 1986 [1.5]. The new Article 118a advised member states to 'pay particular attention to encouraging improvements, especially in the working environment, as regards the health and safety of workers'. It reiterated the aim of harmonising conditions, but introduced the important principle of qualified majority voting for decisions on legislative action in this area (see Chapter 1). Article 100a confirmed that health, safety, environmental and consumer protection were to be governed by qualified majority voting and added that 'a high level of protection' was to be taken as a base.

While facilitating the legislative process, Article 118a limited the scope for Community intervention so as to avoid imposing administrative, financial and legal constraints which might adversely affect small and medium-sized undertakings. In addition member states were not to be prevented from maintaining or introducing their own more stringent measures to protect working conditions. Article 118b of the

SEA also referred to the need to develop the dialogue between management and labour at European level, which had been one of the planks of Jacques Delors' negotiating platform (see Chapter 1) and was to be given further attention in the Community Charter, together with a number of other issues concerned with improving working and living conditions.

The SEA coincided with a spate of action in the area of public health, even though the Community had no authority in this field. In 1987 the Commission launched the 'Europe against Cancer' programme which aimed to reduce mortality from cancer. The main thrust of policy was the promotion of co-operation in the field of research and dissemination of information about the most effective national practices. The programme contained actions for prevention, information, education and training and led to a ban on smoking in public places, rules on the maximum tar content of cigarettes, the labelling and advertising of tobacco products [4.9].

Living and working conditions in the Community Charter

Despite the action programmes of the 1970s, the Community had been reluctant to intervene in the industrial bargaining process. Delors' attempt to launch the social dialogue was slow to gather momentum, but labour relations increasingly came to the fore, even if the input of the social partners to Community policy tended to lack 'purpose and rigour' (Teague and McClelland, 1991, p. 20).

By the late 1980s, worker participation and consultation over changes in working conditions and work organisation and issues concerning working and living conditions were high on the collective bargaining agenda, as illustrated by the Community Charter of the Fundamental Social Rights of Workers of 1989. Several articles in the Charter focused on the improvement of living and working conditions, presented as an important element in policies for equalising opportunities and promoting mobility. The Charter provided a firm statement of the Community's objectives in this area:

> The completion of the internal market must lead to an improvement in the living and working conditions of workers in the European Community. This process must result from an approximation of these conditions while the improvement is being maintained, as regards in particular the duration and organisation of working time and forms of employment other than open-ended contracts, such as

fixed term contracts, part-time working, temporary work and seasonal work. [1.7, point 7]

The reference in the EEC Treaty to maintaining 'the existing equivalence between paid holiday schemes' (Article 120) was made more specific and was extended in point 8 of the Charter which laid down the right of workers to a weekly rest period and to annual paid leave, stipulating that the duration 'must be harmonised in accordance with national practices while the improvement is being maintained'.

In accordance with the general aim of improving living and working conditions, Community policy on health protection and safety at the workplace was also set out in point 19 of the Charter, which stated that: 'Every worker must enjoy satisfactory health and safety conditions in his working environment. Appropriate measures must be taken in order to achieve further harmonisation of conditions in this area while maintaining the improvements made'. It required that account should be taken of 'the need for the training, information, consultation and balanced participation of workers as regards the risks incurred and the steps taken to eliminate or reduce them'. As in the area of social protection, the terms used to define levels of provision, 'satisfactory' and 'appropriate', were cautious, but, as in point 3, with reference to freedom of movement and conditions of residence, and point 8, on rest periods and annual leave, the objective of achieving harmonisation was made explicit (see Chapter 2).

Under a section on the protection of children and adolescents, the Charter set out restrictions on working hours for young people and the prohibition of night work under the age of eighteen (point 22). In recognition of the different practices adopted across the Community and in accordance with the subsidiarity principle, an exception could be made where national legislation provided otherwise.

The Community Charter thus confirmed the general aims set out more than thirty years previously in the EEC Treaty, presenting work organisation and the employment contract as major components in the improvement of living and working conditions and areas where the Community was competent to act.

Implementation of the Community Charter's provisions

Although the Charter did not have binding force, it did authorise the Commission to submit proposals for initiatives under the terms of the Treaties with a view to adopting the legal instruments needed for effective implementation, within the context of the completion of the Single European Market (SEM).

The action programme implementing the Community Charter [1.9] demonstrated the capacity of the Commission to bring forward proposals for action in this area within the constraints of national and sectoral interests. It included a series of quite specific proposals for binding instruments in fields where safety is a cause of concern. Framework Directive 89/391/EEC 'on the introduction of measures to encourage improvements in the safety and health of workers at work' was issued in 1989 [4.1]. It covered all sectors of activity and all workers except the self-employed and domestic servants. Employers were required to take a much more proactive stance. Their obligations were clearly set out: not only were they required to ensure health and safety of workers in every aspect of work and to develop a health and safety policy, they also had the duty of assessing and recording risks, informing and consulting workers, providing training and taking preventive measures. Workers were given the right to make proposals relating to health and safety and to appeal to stop work if in danger. They had the duty to follow instructions from employers regarding health and safety and to report on potential dangers.

Following the Framework Directive, ten proposals were made for improved conditions for specific categories of workers. Council recommendations on occupational diseases were updated, and a regulation was proposed on the establishment of a health, hygiene and safety agency. The year March 1992 to March 1993 was designated 'European Year of Safety, Hygiene and Health Protection at the Workplace'. It was a response to the realisation that, despite the efforts made in this area and the problem of collecting reliable data, of approximately 120 million workers in the Community about 10 million suffer an industrial accident or occupational injury every year [1.12, p. 65]. The aims were to alert member states to the importance of the social and economic aspects of problems relating to safety, hygiene and health at work and to make workers, employers and young people more aware of the risks at the workplace and the action needed to deal with them.

The Commission was able to take advantage of the provisions of Article 118a of the SEA to bring forward legislation which had made little progress during the 1980s. Directive 93/104/EC 'concerning certain aspects of the organization of working time' [4.8] provides a good example of how qualified majority voting can be exploited in the case of health and safety at work to introduce contentious legislation.

During the 1980s an attempt by the Commission to formulate a directive requiring the extension to part-time workers of the rules governing full-time workers had not been adopted. A draft proposal brought forward in 1990 covering other aspects of working time was more successful. It was aimed at protecting workers against excessively long working hours and against an organisation of working time which could be detrimental to their health and safety [4.2]. It raised the issue of the harmful effects of practices introduced under the banner of flexibility. Directive 93/104/EC, which was eventually adopted in November 1993, laid down a set of minimum provisions not only for daily and weekly rest periods, but also for conditions relating to shift work, night work and health and safety protection for workers subject to changes of rhythm in their working hours. The minimum daily rest period was set at twelve hours for a twenty-four-hour period, and minimum paid holidays at four weeks. The definition of night work was extended to cover workers who occasionally worked at night, and provisions were made for health assessments. The Commission's concern to avoid creating problems for individual firms or sectors of activity with special needs, for example because their activities are subject to seasonal fluctuations, meant that a number of possibilities were left open for derogation, and consultation procedures were strengthened. Employers and representatives of workers were not to be prevented from concluding collective agreements on the organisation of working time, so long as equivalent compensatory rest periods were granted.

The Commission had also been trying since the early 1980s to have proposals adopted on a related topic, atypical work, in its efforts to resolve the problems created by the rapid growth in the number of workers not covered by a standard open-ended full-time employment contract. The interests of atypical workers were dealt with in an indirect way by two Council directives in 1991. In Directive 91/383/EEC [4.3] a proposal was put forward as a measure for health and safety at work aimed at improving the working conditions of workers with a fixed duration employment relationship or a temporary employment relationship. Directive 91/533/EEC [4.4] made provision for a form of proof of an employment relationship as a means of improving the transparency of the labour market in a context where more flexible forms of employment, such as part-time, distance working, home or teleworking, had become widespread and were tending to marginalise large sectors of the labour force. The purpose of the directive was to make clear to all workers for whom they were working and the essential conditions of the employment relationship. A proposal for a directive concerning the protection at work of pregnant women or women who have recently given birth was also brought forward under Article 118a as a health and safety measure and within the meaning of the Framework Directive. Directive 92/85/EEC [4.6] covered not only exposure to agents liable to damage health but also the contentious issue of leave arrangements, duration of work and employment rights, which might have prevented the passage of the proposal had it been subjected to unanimous voting.

Since the focus was on workers, the Charter did not refer to public health. In 1991, however, the Commission launched a 'Europe against AIDS' programme aimed at containing and combating the spread of the disease throughout the Community. A Resolution of the Council and the Ministers for Health the same year drew attention to the importance of health policy choices [4.5], urging member states to work together to identify common problems and, if appropriate, develop common solutions, thereby preparing the ground for the higher profile which was to be given to public health in the Treaty on European Union.

Living and working conditions in the Maastricht Treaty

The Maastricht Treaty on European Union, and the Agreement on Social Policy signed in 1992 by all member states except the United Kingdom [1.6], set out further details of European policy in the area of living and working conditions. The Union's activities listed in Article 3 of the Treaty included 'a contribution to the attainment of a high level of health protection' (paragraph o). Under a new Title X on public health, Article 129 stated the Union's aim of ensuring 'a high level of human health protection by encouraging cooperation between the Member States and, if necessary, lending support to their action'. The area where action was to be promoted at European level through research, health information and education included major health scourges such as drug dependence. The Union was not, however, prescriptive: it offered to assist member states by taking any useful initiatives to help them co-ordinate policies and programmes rather than instigating legislative action of its own. The Treaty proposed adopting incentive measures but explicitly excluded 'any harmonisation of the laws and regulations of the Member States'. In a Communication 'on the framework for action in the field of public health' [4.7], published two years after the Resolution on health policy choices, the Commission reiterated the need for member states to identify common objectives and goals and set out the legal bases for action at European level, again stressing the importance of respecting the principles of subsidiarity, transparency and proportionality. With the completion of the SEM, the signing of the Community Charter and the Treaty on European Union, together with agreement over the relevant action programmes, and particularly the Framework Directive on health and safety at work, the Union's competence in the broad area of living and working conditions had become far reaching. The introduction of qualified majority voting in the SEA for issues concerning health and safety at work and the improvement of the working environment meant not only that member states would more easily be able to implement the measures thought necessary but also that attempts could be made to use Articles 100a and 118a to push forward proposals in the social field which were likely to be rejected if unanimous voting was applied.

WORKING CONDITIONS IN MEMBER STATES

The Commission's numerous directives and recommendations have established high target standards for the provision of health and safety at work, which member states are expected to meet. If all the measures that have been proposed were implemented, it has been suggested that the standard of protection in member states would exceed that in the United States (Springer, 1992, p. 104). Despite the emphasis constantly given in the Treaties and Charter to the need for approximation of both preventive measures and compensation for workers suffering from the adverse effects of industrial accidents and diseases, standards of health and safety at work are still subject to considerable variation from one country to another. A major problem facing the Union is how to ensure that member states with relatively poor provision for health and safety at work are able to raise their standards so that they approximate to those found in neighbouring countries. The let-out clause for small and medium-sized undertakings contained in 118a of the SEA and Article 2 point 2 of the Agreement on Social Policy annexed to the Maastricht Treaty meant that countries such as those in southern Europe, where commerce and industry had continued to be largely dominated by small firms, were likely to maintain lower levels of protection from industrial hazards, reinforcing the concept of a two-speed Europe and the distinction between core and periphery.

In this section the focus is on national policies for the improvement of working conditions, and more particularly measures concerned with health and safety at the workplace and work-time organisation, in an attempt to assess the extent to which they are compatible with the Union's requirements or provide an explanation for some of the difficulties experienced in trying to reach agreement at European level.

Health and safety at work

The momentum for policy on health and safety at work has come largely from the member states in northern Europe, where insurance schemes to protect workers against the consequences of industrial accidents were established before the end of the nineteenth century. Since the southern European countries that joined the Community in the 1980s – Greece, Portugal and Spain – did not share the same long tradition of protecting workers from industrial hazards, they have had difficulty in conforming with the high standards set.

In some member states, namely Greece, Italy, Luxembourg and Portugal, provision was made for the control of health and safety at work in the national constitution. Basic occupational health and safety principles were set out in national legal codes in France, Germany, the Netherlands and Spain. In Belgium protection was provided in the civil code for all individuals both at the workplace and outside work. In Denmark, Ireland and the United Kingdom individual rights were established in civil or common law. All countries except Spain obliged employers to provide healthy and safe working conditions.

In several member states the scope of existing legislation already went beyond what was required by the Framework Directive: Ireland and the United Kingdom, for example, included the self-employed, and legislation in Greece, the Netherlands and the United Kingdom offered protection for third parties. Most countries already had statutory provision for consultative procedures at the workplace for health and safety: elected worker's councils in Germany, Italy, Luxembourg and the Netherlands; health and safety committees in Belgium, France and Portugal; elected safety representatives in Denmark and the United Kingdom. Only Greece, Ireland and Spain did not have such a high level of statutory provision [4.11, pp. 109–14].

Work-time organisation

Agreement amongst member states was more easily reached over technical standards than over the deployment of human resources. The growing problem of unemployment since the mid-1970s, the diversification of forms of work resulting from technological change and the decline in the number of workers in manufacturing and agriculture in favour of the services, as well as the increasing proportion of women in the workforce, gave a new impetus to policies designed to deal with the impact of greater flexibility of working patterns. European legislation on the organisation of working time and atypical work affords some interesting examples of the shift of emphasis in policy and resistance to change associated with disparities in existing practices between member states.

Statistics on conditions of employment provide an indication of the reasons why, in the 1980s, some member states were more or less eager than others to encourage harmonisation of working arrangements with a view to reducing competitive advantage. Temporary contracts were, for example, most common in Greece, Portugal and Spain, and least common in Belgium, Italy, the United Kingdom and especially Luxembourg [4.13, table 5.13]. As a proportion of all employees, women were more likely than men to be on temporary contracts in all member states except Greece. In Belgium, Luxembourg and the United Kingdom, women made up well over 50 per cent of all workers on temporary contracts [4.13, table 5.15].

In the late 1980s working hours also varied markedly from one member state to another, according to economic sector [4.13, table 5.4]. Workers in agriculture in Luxembourg, Ireland, the United Kingdom and Portugal usually worked almost fifty hours a week. The maximum number of working hours for industry was found in the United Kingdom, followed by Portugal. The United Kingdom also had the highest figure in the services, followed this time by Germany. Gender differences varied from one member state to another: women in full-time employment in Portugal, Germany and the United Kingdom were found to have the longest working hours. The lowest working hours overall were found in Belgium for men and in Italy for women. The disparity between the lowest and the highest weekly working hours was 6.9 for men and 4.0 for women.

No clear relationship emerged, however, between length of working hours and legislation on the duration of working time. At the beginning of the 1990s, in Greece, Ireland, Italy, the Netherlands and

Portugal legislation fixed the standard working week at forty-eight hours, and the standard working day was eight hours in Germany. Belgium, Luxembourg and Spain set a maximum for the working week at forty hours. In France the legal average working week was thiry-nine hours but it could be extended up to forty-eight hours if an industry-wide agreement existed. In Denmark the thirty-seven-hour week was established by collective bargaining. In the United Kingdom, which had no general legislation on working hours, the duration and distribution of working time were a matter for negotiation between employers and workers [4.11, p. 39].

The overall distribution of working hours showed important variations when part-time work was added into the calculation. In the early 1990s part-time work was particularly widespread in Denmark, the Netherlands and the United Kingdom [4.13, table 5.7]. The term 'part-time' may be something of a misnomer in that part-time hours were in some cases close to full-time hours: in Luxembourg men employed part time worked 35.1 hours, and in Portugal and Italy close to thirty hours. For women, part-time hours ranged from 16.7 on average in the Netherlands to 23.1 in Italy, indicating a greater disparity both between countries and between men and women than for full-time work [4.13, table 5.12].

With regard to night work, another area where the Union has sought to intervene, two patterns were identified in member states in the early 1990s: in Belgium and the Netherlands night work was generally forbidden but with derogations for a number of activities. Elsewhere night work was generally permitted, unless expressly prohibited [4.11, pp. 40–2). In several cases restrictions on night work applied to women: in Belgium, Germany and Greece. In others the prohibition applied only to pregnant women: in Italy, Luxembourg, the Netherlands and Portugal. Elsewhere the ban on night work had progressively been lifted for all adults.

The Community Charter made explicit reference to weekly rest periods and annual paid leave (point 8), areas where practices again vary. In all member states except the United Kingdom, weekly rest periods have been introduced into legislation. In most cases employees who work on a Sunday have the right to take a compensatory day of rest in the following week or may be given financial compensation [4.11, pp. 45–6]. In the early 1990s Denmark and the United Kingdom had no legislation governing the number of public holidays; elsewhere the number ranged from six in the Netherlands to fourteen in Spain. Paid annual holidays were governed by legislation everywhere except in the United Kingdom. The number of days ranged from fifteen in Ireland to thirty in Spain [4.11, p. 49].

Issues involving the organisation of work time have been a concern of the Union for two main reasons: firstly, working time is a factor in production capacity and can therefore create competitive advantage or disadvantage, as for example through the excessive concentration of annual paid leave; secondly, by adapting working time the Union has been seeking a solution to the problem of unemployment. Attitudes towards the restructuring of work time are, however, far from being uniform across member states or amongst the social partners. A report commissioned in 1988 showed that, although at least two-thirds of full-time workers would prefer to continue working full time, a larger proportion (at least 24 per cent) of workers in Italy, Portugal, Spain and the United Kingdom would prefer part-time work [4.10, p. 14]. In Denmark, Germany, the Netherlands and the United Kingdom, few part-time workers said they would prefer full-time work, whereas part-time workers in Greece and especially France expressed their preference for full-time status. Although attitudes towards shorter working hours and flexible daily and weekly schedules were generally supportive and suggest there may be some potential for extending part-time work and for restructuring work-time patterns, many socio-economic and political factors, such as national employment contexts and the social policy arrangements in each member state, may determine what is acceptable to the social partners.

The slow progress made by proposals from the Commission for reorganising working time and resolving anomalies in working conditions may be explained by the problems involved in trying to reach agreement when national work-time practices and collective bargaining processes differ markedly. Whereas in some member states decisions regulating employment contracts are taken by central government and become an integral part of labour law, as in France and in countries with a Latin tradition, in others with a stronger contractual tradition, such as Denmark and the United Kingdom, negotiations may be decentralised either at branch or enterprise level. Germany and the Benelux countries probably lie between the two extremes. Other national traditions, in particular those associated with differences in welfare regimes (see Chapter 2), may also determine reactions to proposals which have as their objective to avoid distortion of competition by aligning working conditions. Some member states are, for example, likely to be reluctant to support the institutionalisation of new forms of work-time organisation in the cause of international solidarity when the impact on their social protection systems would be to produce higher labour costs.

LIVING CONDITIONS IN MEMBER STATES

Directives aimed at improving living and working conditions have focused primarily on issues concerned with the workplace and more generally the working environment. Industrial health and disease were areas where the Union could move relatively quickly in adopting common policies, whereas public health and wider environmental concerns were less obvious targets for intervention at European level. In this section public health is considered as a component of policies for the improvement of living conditions.

Whereas harmonisation of social security systems, as advocated in the EEC Treaty (see Chapter 2), was progressively abandoned in favour of the principle of co-operation, public health, as opposed to health and safety at work, is an area where action was not a priority for the Community. Given the very marked differences in national public health systems between member states (Berthod-Wurmser, 1994), it is not difficult to understand why, when reference is made to public health, as in the Maastricht Treaty, the principle of subsidiarity has been advocated.

All the health schemes of the EEC founding members, except Italy which had a mixed system, were based on employment insurance contributions, which gave workers entitlement to income-related sickness benefits in cases where they were prevented by ill health or disability from pursuing their economic activity. Both workers and their dependants had the right to medical treatment. Provision has also been made for health care for pensioners, the unemployed and other categories without a regular income from employment. The member states that joined the Community in the 1970s – Denmark, Ireland and the United Kingdom – had state-run national health services, financed from taxation, to which all residents had access on the basis of need. Of the countries which became members of the Community in the 1980s, Greece and Spain had a mixed system close to that of the continental model but strongly subsidised by the state, whereas Portugal provided health care through a national system on the basis of residence. By the 1990s in all member states virtually the whole population was covered for health care through a nation-wide health service, in return for insurance contributions, through private insurance or social assistance schemes.

Other differences affect access to health care within the Union. Three countries – Belgium, Greece and France – required a qualifying period for benefits. Although patients had a free choice of medical practitioner in all countries, in Belgium, France, Luxembourg and Portugal they paid for treatment and were then partially reimbursed. In all but Italy and Spain patients contributed to the cost of medicines. Belgium, Germany, France, Ireland and Luxembourg each levied a daily charge on patients in hospital. Doctors may be salaried employees as in Greece, they may be paid solely on a capitation basis, as in Ireland and Portugal, or according to the services provided, as in France, Germany and Luxembourg, or by a combination of arrangements in the other member states (Berthod-Wurmser, 1994, pp. 138–9).

In addition to differences in institutional arrangements, patterns of provision and the cost of health care differ markedly from one member state to another. The number of doctors per 1000 inhabitants varied from 1.4 in the United Kingdom to 3.9 in Spain in the early 1990s, and the number of hospital beds ranged from 4.3 in Spain to 11.8 in Luxembourg (Berthod-Wurmser, 1994, p. 168). Household expenditure on medical care and health expenses as a proportion of final household consumption per inhabitant was considerably lower in countries with a national health service, ranging from 1.4 per cent in the United Kingdom and 2.1 per cent in Denmark to 12.5 per cent in the Netherlands and 14.2 per cent in Germany [4.14, table 2.8].

Whatever the administrative arrangements and the sources of funding, all member states have in common the growing cost of health care provision and their efforts to reduce spending in this area [4.12, pp. 97–109]. The member states with public health services have attempted to contain costs by exercising tight budgetary control over the supply of services, generally leading to greater efficiency. Alternatives to expensive health treatment have been encouraged, focusing on community care for older and disabled people (see Chapter 7). The insurance-based systems, which tend to be more expensive to operate, have tried to curb expenditure by measures such as controlling the price of drugs or introducing charges for hospital beds

In some respects, it seems surprising that the Union has not devoted more attention to standardising public health practices across member states. Intervention could have been justified both on the grounds of ensuring access to a satisfactory level of social protection for migrant workers and as a means of avoiding distortion of competition, since health care represents the largest proportion of spending on social protection, apart from old age, in all member states and the largest proportion overall in Germany, Ireland and Portugal [4.12, table 2]. The Union has been active through health programmes to encourage co-operation in combating health scourges such as AIDS, cancer, drug and alcohol abuse, and to promote healthy lifestyles through health education, as advocated in Article 129 of the Maastricht Treaty. Here too, differences persist between member states in the incidence and recording of certain diseases: in the late 1980s, for example, Luxembourg and Belgium recorded the highest mortality rates for cancers amongst men and Denmark for cancers amongst women, with Greece, Portugal and Spain showing the lowest rates for both sexes [4.13, table 8.16]; in the early 1990s France had the highest incidence of AIDS in the Union, with almost six times as many cases as in Greece in relation to population size (United Nations, 1993, table 21). Although the Union is empowered to act in these areas by adopting incentive measures, any harmonisation of the laws and regulations of member states is explicitly excluded.

TOWARDS CONVERGENCE OF WORKING CONDITIONS AND LIVING STANDARDS

One of the pessimistic conclusions which have been drawn from analyses of the pressures working for and against social Europe is that the social dimension of the Union would be 'a fragmentary arrangement, with the Community presence confined to specific segments of the labour market' (Teague and McClelland, 1991, p. 21). Matters relating to health and safety at work or the working environment provide a good example of what have come to be regarded as legitimate areas for public intervention, whereas the restructuring of working hours and arrangements for the social protection of part-time workers or public health have not commanded the same level of acceptance, except in so far as they affect the health and safety of workers or can be catered for by action programmes targeted at very specific problems. Where policy objectives do not coincide with values which are widely shared across member states, the Union is unlikely to be able to exert its influence or to attempt to shape national policies.

Health and safety at work have been described as the 'most active aspect of EC social policy in the employment field' (James, 1993, p. 135). The quantity of legislation on the subject would seem to confirm that the Commission has been more active in this area of social policy than in any other and has sought to set standards across the Union. If the terms 'approximation' and 'harmonisation' are used in the Community Charter with reference to living and working conditions and health and safety at the workplace, whereas they are absent from the paragraphs on social protection, it may be, at least in part, because the principle of standardising procedures for protecting workers has proved to be much less contentious and possibly more attainable than, for example, the setting of targets for public health. The Union was able to build on national precedents for health and safety at work and, since the SEA came into force in 1987, to play a central co-ordinating role, progressively bringing national legislation into line with Council directives and recommendations. The 1989 Framework Directive was particularly noteworthy in that it probably went further than national legislation in its requirements that employers should adapt working conditions to meet individual needs. Even though agreement may be more readily reached amongst member states in this area, there is no guarantee that all member states will be able to conform immediately with the standards set or that arrangements and systems will converge.

The importance attributed in the 1994 White Paper on European social policy [1.13] to high labour standards in making Europe competitive was reminiscent of earlier policies for upwards harmonisation, although the Commission recognised that no clear consensus existed between member states over the level at which such standards should be set. It favoured consolidation rather than new legislation but stated its intention to take a firm line on issues such as working time where it was ready to consider making proposals for further directives based on Article 118a if agreement between social partners could not be reached [1.13, pp. 21–5].

By contrast, the raising of living standards has not been presented as a desirable objective, as exemplified by the approach to policy on public health. In the White Paper the Commission adopted a responsive stance focusing on multi-annual programmes and limiting its action to facilitating co-operation between member states [1.13, p. 41]. Although national systems may continue to diverge in their financial and managerial arrangements, paradoxically the need to ensure coverage of the whole population while containing costs may have resulted in the development of some common objectives which could lend themselves to common solutions.

Box 4   Union documents relating to living and working conditions

SECONDARY LEGISLATION

4.1   Framework Directive 89/391/EEC of 12 June 1989 on the introduction of measures to encourage improvements in the safety and health of workers at work (*OJ* L 183/1 29.6.89).

4.2   Commission proposal for a Council Directive concerning certain aspects of the organization of working time (COM(90) 317 final, 3 August 1990) (*OJ* C 254/4 9.10.90).

4.3   Council Directive 91/383/EEC of 25 June 1991 supplementing the measures to encourage improvements in the safety and health at work of workers with a fixed-duration employment relationship or a temporary employment relationship (*OJ* L 206/19 29.7.91).

4.4   Council Directive 91/533/EEC of 14 October 1991 on an employer's obligation to inform employees of the conditions applicable to the contract or employment relationship (*OJ* L 288/32 18.10.91).

4.5   Resolution of the Council and the Ministers for Health of 11 November 1991 concerning fundamental health-policy choices (*OJ* C 304/5 23.11.91).

4.6   Council Directive 92/85/EEC of 19 October 1992 on the introduction of measures to encourage improvements in the safety and health at work of pregnant workers and workers who have recently given birth or are breastfeeding (*OJ* L 348/1 28.11.92).

4.7   Commission Communication on the framework for action in the field of public health (COM(93) 559 final, 24 November 1993).

4.8   Council Directive 93/104/EC of 23 November 1993 concerning certain aspects of the organization of working time (*OJ* L 307/18 13.12.93).

OFFICIAL PUBLICATIONS BY THE COMMISSION OF THE EUROPEAN COMMUNITIES (CEC) AND EUROSTAT

4.9   CEC (1991) 'Europe against Cancer. Public Health: Initiatives and Texts Adopted in 1990', *Social Europe 1/91*.

4.10 CEC (1991) 'Working Time, Employment and Production Capacity. Reorganisation/Reduction of Working Time', *Social Europe Supplement 4/91*.

4.11 CEC (1992) 'The Regulation of Working Conditions in the Member States of the European Community', vol. 1 'Comparative Labour Law of the Member States', *Social Europe Supplement 4/92*.

4.12 CEC (1993) *Social Protection in Europe*.

4.13 Eurostat (1991) *A Social Portrait of Europe*.

4.14 Eurostat (1993) *Basic Statistics of the Community. Comparison with the Principal Partners of the Community*, 30th edn.

5 Family Policies

Family policy affords a good example of the general principle that national governments should be left to determine how their social protection systems are framed, financed and organised. Three reasons may help to explain why, until the late 1980s, the Commission was particularly reluctant to intervene in family affairs. Firstly, and perhaps more so than in the case of policy for the young, older people or health, views on the objectives of family policy are divided along ideological lines both within and between countries. The resulting diversity of practices is such that the Commission may have been loath to take on the daunting task of seeking to co-ordinate policies to improve the well-being of families. Secondly, some governments have considered family life to belong to the private domain and therefore to be forbidden territory for explicit state intervention. Thirdly, and perhaps most importantly, the welfare of families has been given low priority because social protection in the Union and in most member states is centred on workers' rather than citizenship rights. The social security systems of most of the founder members of the European Economic Community (EEC) were strongly influenced by the Bismarckian statist corporatist model of welfare, with its guiding principle that workers should be guaranteed benefits and a substitute income calculated from their previous earnings in return for the payment of employment-related insurance contributions (see Chapter 2). By the end of the 1980s most member states had a mixed economy of welfare but were converging towards corporatism, as reflected in the Charter of the Fundamental Social Rights of Workers of 1989 [1.7], which was primarily concerned with the rights of workers derived from employment status (see Chapter 1). The Community Charter, like the 1974 social action programme [1.8], did take some account of the status of women as mothers by recognising that parents needed support to enable them to reconcile family and employment responsibilities, but again on the understanding that employment status was paramount. Because family policy was not considered to be of immediate relevance to economic concerns, it was placed very low on the political agenda.

Since the Community's and Union's Treaties, Charter and action programmes have only rarely addressed the subject of family policy directly, the approach in this chapter differs from that adopted elsewhere in the book. Firstly, the limited references to family policy in official documents are briefly reviewed. More lengthy consideration is then given to the ways in which member states have conceptualised family structure and family policy and to an analysis of the policy-making process and national policy-making styles. Finally the possible impact of public policy on families is examined. Measures for reconciling family and professional responsibilities are treated in the next chapter as an issue concerning women's rights.

EUROPEAN FAMILY POLICY IN EMBRYO

The Union's focus on employment-related rights and benefits and the Commission's reluctance to intervene in national welfare systems meant that member states largely continued to develop their own policy agendas in areas, such as family policy, that were not directly affected by European legislation. The Council of Europe's Social Charter of 1961, which served as a model for the Community Charter, was much less inhibited in its approach to family welfare. It openly recognised the social importance of the family, stating that: 'The family as a fundamental unit of society has the right to appropriate social, legal and economic protection to ensure its full development'. The duties of the state towards individual family members, whether or not the family unit was legally constituted, were clearly set out: 'Mothers and children, irrespective of marital status and family relations, have the right to appropriate social and economic protection' (Council of Europe, 1988, part I, paragraphs 16 and 17).

Despite the early reference in the 1974 social action programme to the objective of ensuring 'that family responsibilities of all concerned may be reconciled with their job aspirations' [1.8, p. 2], the measures taken in the 1970s centred on women's rights to equal pay and equal treatment (see Chapter 6). In 1983 the European Parliament formulated a Resolution 'on family policy in the European Community', stating its view that 'family policy should . . . become an integral part of all Community policies', and calling on the Commission to draw up an action programme and to introduce a comprehensive family policy, and, where appropriate, to harmonise national policies at Community level [5.2, p. 117]. The Council did not respond with any formal action. Then, prompted by a series of worrying reports on demographic trends, in 1989 the Commission drafted a Communication 'on family policies', in which it reviewed the changes occurring in society and pointed to the essential role assumed by the family 'in the cohesion and the future of society' [5.3, p. 12].

Four areas of common interest were identified: the means of reconciling work and family life and sharing family responsibilities; measures to assist certain categories of families; consideration of the most deprived families; and the impact of Community policies on the family, in particular the protection of children during childhood [5.3, p. 3].

Action at Community level was justified, according to the Commission, not on the basis of ideology, but on the grounds that the family played an important economic role, serving as a 'touchstone between generations' and as a route to equality between men and women. The Commission noted that action would have to be pragmatic in order to 'respect the special features of different national policies already created and the varying socio-economic contexts in which such policies operate' [5.3, p. 15]. The Council responded formally by reiterating most of the proposals made in the Communication, although it substituted the theme of equal opportunities for the reconciliation of professional and family life [5.4].

A concrete result of the Council's Conclusions was the establishment of a network of twelve national experts in 1989, known as the European Observatory on National Family Policies, to monitor demographic trends, collect information on the situation of families and on measures taken relating to families in member states, with a brief to report back annually to the Commission. By the end of the 1980s the Community had legitimised its interest in family policy. Little progress had been made, however, towards defining a 'comprehensive' European family policy as requested by the European Parliament in 1983.

The only mention of the family in the Community Charter was in the context of measures 'enabling men and women to reconcile occupational and family obligations' in the section on equal treatment for men and women under point 6. The Agreement on Social Policy, annexed to the Maastricht Treaty [1.6], referred only obliquely to family matters, again under the equality heading (see Chapter 6). The Council Recommendation 'on the convergence of social protection objectives and policies' [2.1] was more explicit. Not only did it set out the aims of removing 'obstacles to occupational activity through measures to reconcile family and professional responsibilities' and of integrating individuals who wished to enter the labour market after bringing up children, but it also advocated developing targeted benefits for categories of families in need [2.1, p. 52]. While the 1994 White Paper on European social policy did not make any proposals for developing a European family policy by the year 2000, it stressed that the Union needed a broadly based social policy which took account of family life [1.13, p.1].

CONCEPTUALISING FAMILIES AND FAMILY POLICIES

The reluctance of the Council to intervene directly in family affairs, together with the lack of consensus over the role of governments and the possible objectives and instruments of family policy, has meant that no wholly satisfactory and generally accepted operational definition of family policy has been formulated at European level. The concept of the family itself as defined for statistical purposes in studies of changing family structure over time differs from the institutional definitions used to assess the legal status of family members and entitlements to social protection, which tend to place more emphasis on relationships within 'households'. Cutting across these variations in definition, national differences further complicate the picture. In line with the Union's interest in demographic trends (Article 7 of the Agreement on Social Policy requires the Commission to draw up annual reports on the demographic situation in the Union) and the possible impact of social protection measures on the family, the focus in this section is on changing family structures and their implications for institutional definitions of the family as a benefit category.

Changing family structures

The Council Recommendation 'on the convergence of social protection objectives and policies' identified changing family situations as one of the comparable trends across member states which may lead to common problems, justifying the formulation of common objectives [2.1, p. 49]. Changes in family structure may, for example, affect the ability of families to provide support for their members. The premises on which welfare states were based in most countries are, it is argued [5.8, p. 119], being undermined as the intergenerational balance is upset and the stability of marriage and family unity are increasingly disrupted. Analysis of change in family structure is used in this section as an indication of the extent to which common trends can be discerned and of the way that traditional assumptions about social protection are being called into question.

Since 1973, when the Council of Ministers adopted Directive 73/403/ EEC [5.1] on the harmonisation of census dates and the standardisation of information, data have been collected by Eurostat on the number of marriages, age at marriage, its duration, the number of births to women belonging to a particular generation, total period fertility rates (the number of births to women during the reproductive period of their lives), age at childbirth, household size and structure. Attempts have been made to standardise data so that they can be used to quantify patterns of family building and structure, record changes over time and compare trends between countries (Baldwin, 1991). Progressively, in recognition of changing family patterns and the growing interest in demographic trends across the Union, data collection has been extended to take account of factors which are more difficult to record, either because of social taboos or because information is not readily available or reliable, as for example on the number of extramarital births, lone parenthood and cohabitation, where the definitions used in individual member states often diverge.

According to Eurostat, for demographic purposes the family, or what is also referred to as the family unit, can be a couple, with or without children, or a single parent with children [5.10, p. 30]. Data collected in national censuses generally focus on private households rather than families, defined as a group of persons living together and taking their meals together, whether or not they are related. Several families may make up a household, just as an individual living alone can also be considered as a household unit.

Initial scrutiny of harmonised demographic data on member states, as illustrated in Figures 5.1–5, would seem to suggest that the major family and household indicators are converging. This appears to be the case for fertility patterns. From the mid-1960s, as effective means of contraception became more widely available, and legislation was enacted in most member states to enable the whole population, at least in theory, to have access to birth control, total period fertility rates declined steeply, albeit without removing the differences between member states (Figure 5.1). Although Ireland, where abortion was still illegal, continued to record the highest total period fertility rate in 1991 while Italy had the lowest, a position held by Greece in 1965, the gap between the most and the least prolific nations narrowed from 1.73 to 0.81. In the countries of southern Europe which reduced their fertility rates relatively late, the proportion of one-person households remained smaller, whereas in Denmark it rose to a particularly high level (Figure 5.2).

Figure 5.1 Total period fertility rates in member states (1965–91)

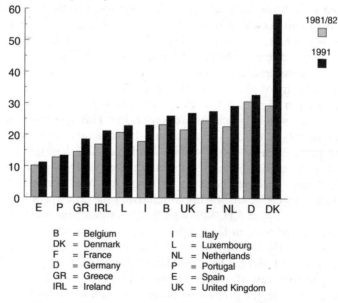

Source: Eurostat, *Demographic Statistics 1994*, table E-10.

Figure 5.2 One-person households in member states (as % of households, 1981/82–91)

B	= Belgium	I	= Italy
DK	= Denmark	L	= Luxembourg
F	= France	NL	= Netherlands
D	= Germany	P	= Portugal
GR	= Greece	E	= Spain
IRL	= Ireland	UK	= United Kingdom

Source: Eurostat, *A Social Portrait of Europe*, 1991, table 2.7; Eurostat, *Basic Statistics of the Community: Comparison with the Principal Partners of the Community*, 30th edn, 1993, table 3.13.

Over the same period the number of births outside marriage increased rapidly in all member states, but again at differing rates, with the net result that, by the early 1990s, the gap between the countries with the highest and lowest rates, Denmark and Greece respectively, had widened to over 400 points (Figure 5.3). This trend did not follow marriage rates closely: although marriage became less frequent in all member states over the period in question, rates fell most steeply in Greece, followed by Denmark, Germany and the Netherlands. Ireland maintained its position with the lowest marriage rate, where it was joined by France, while Portugal reached the top of the scale (Figure 5.4). The relationship between marriage and divorce also differs from one country to another. Between 1965 and 1991, despite the doubling in the divorce rates in most member states, the north continued to be distinguished from the south where divorce was harder to obtain (Figure 5.5). Here the United Kingdom and Denmark displayed the highest rates, and no data were available for Ireland, where divorce was still illegal.

Figure 5.3   Extramarital births in member states (per 1000 live births, 1965–91)

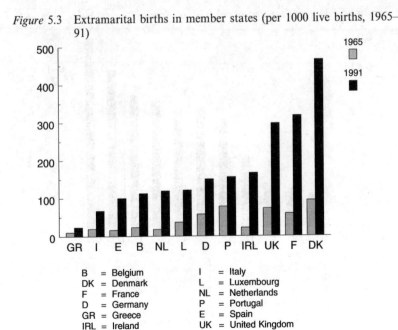

Source: Eurostat, *Demographic Statistics 1994*, table E-4.

Figure 5.4   Marriage rates in member states (per 1000 population, 1965–91)

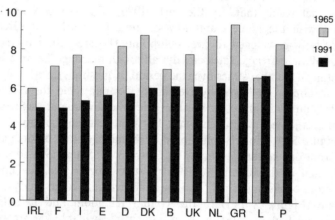

Source: Eurostat, *Demographic Statistics 1994*, table F-3.

Figure 5.5   Divorce rates in member states (per 1000 population, 1965–91)

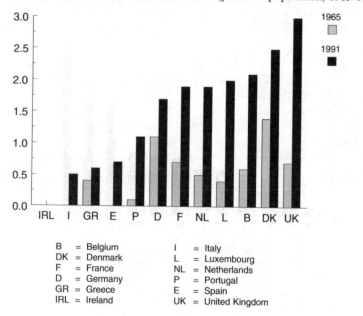

B	= Belgium	I	= Italy
DK	= Denmark	L	= Luxembourg
F	= France	NL	= Netherlands
D	= Germany	P	= Portugal
GR	= Greece	E	= Spain
IRL	= Ireland	UK	= United Kingdom

Source: Eurostat, *Demographic Statistics 1994*, table F-31.

Comparisons of the number of single-parent families, or lone-parent families as they have come to be called, and of cohabitation rates in Europe are unreliable, because these two phenomena are often conceptualised and measured differently from one society to another and because they form particularly unstable and heterogeneous categories. Yet they have become an important focus of attention for policy makers and therefore need to be recorded. Lone-parent families can be comprised of divorcees, separated or widowed spouses or unmarried parents. Whereas a century ago lone parenthood was most likely to be the result of bereavement, and unmarried motherhood was a condition which went unrecorded in census statistics, by the 1990s lone parenthood was much more likely to be the outcome of divorce, separation or extramarital births.

A standardised definition used in the Community context and adapted by Jo Roll (1992) for a report on lone-parent families in the twelve member states has yielded results which are more readily comparable. A lone parent is identified as not living in a couple (either married or cohabiting); he/she may or may not be living with other people but is living with at least one child under eighteen years old (Roll, 1992, p. 10). Data for the late 1980s, using a standardised definition, placed the United Kingdom and Denmark at the top of the scale with 15 to 17 per cent of families composed of a lone parent and child; Greece, Italy and Spain recorded the lowest rates with between 5 and 7 per cent.

The number of cohabiting couples is equally, if not more, difficult to assess, in this case mainly because of the unreliability of responses to survey questions on the subject. Despite the lack of comparable data, since the 1970s extramarital cohabitation is known to have become increasingly prevalent amongst the younger generations. It was a well established phenomenon in Denmark by the early 1990s and was developing quickly in the Netherlands and France, followed by Germany and the United Kingdom, whereas it was much less widespread in the southern European member states (Kiernan and Estaugh, 1993, pp. 61–2). In Denmark, France and the United Kingdom cohabitation was accompanied by a high level of extramarital births, whereas in Germany and the Netherlands marriage was still the main context for childbearing.

The similarity in the general direction of the trends shown by this batch of demographic indicators does not imply that the pace of change has been the same throughout the Union. The family building patterns established in northern Europe in the early 1960s were followed in the

1970s in France, Germany and the United Kingdom, and in the 1980s by the southern Mediterranean countries, which had joined the Community in the third wave of membership. In some cases by the early 1990s the north was being overtaken by the south, as demonstrated by fertility rates; in others it was generally displaying much higher rates, for instance for divorce, the number of extramarital births, single-person households and lone-parent families, which are all indicators of the breakdown of what is generally considered as the 'complete' family. The picture of family structure which emerges from these data is not unequivocal, making it difficult to identify a common European family model which could be the target of a common family policy.

The legal rights of families

Statistical representations of family structure are determined to some extent by institutional frameworks which set the legal parameters of the family. The definitions used for demographic and institutional purposes are not, however, identical. Differences do matter for family policy, as for example when marital status or legal recognition of paternity may determine eligibility for tax relief and social security entitlements.

In most member states the normative institutional framework is embodied in the national constitution. In France, Germany, Greece, Ireland, Italy, Luxembourg, Portugal and Spain, the constitution recognises the family as a fundamental social institution and undertakes to afford it protection. The Portuguese constitution goes furthest in setting out concrete measures which the state pledges to implement in order to protect the family and respond to its needs (Steindorff and Heering, 1993, pp. 136–7).

Despite strong opposition in countries with a powerful Catholic lobby, many changes in family structure have gradually been given official recognition, even if they are not always written into codes of law. From the 1960s legal frameworks were being changed to reflect the fact that the husband was no longer the undisputed head of the family and its sole or main breadwinner. Parental responsibility for children has been increasingly shared between married partners, and the breakdown of marriage is legally endorsed.

The situation is less clear cut in the case of unmarried cohabiting couples. The legal rights of unmarried couples were first recognised formally in the 1970s in Denmark, which was soon followed by France (Steindorff and Heering, 1993, p. 139). By the late 1980s cohabiting couples in both countries, and also in Italy, could officially register their partnership. At the other extreme, in Ireland, unmarried cohabitees had no legal rights, and in several member states the issue had not reached the political agenda.

Practices regarding the attribution of paternity and the sharing of parental responsibility in unmarried couples also differ markedly from one member state to another (Meulders-Klein, 1993). In France paternal recognition is a discretionary right of the father; in Denmark and Germany it is compulsory to establish paternity by recognition or legal decision; elsewhere paternal recognition is subject to consent of the mother alone and/or the child, or in the United Kingdom at the request of the child. In most cases parental authority for children born outside marriage is exercised *de facto* by the mother, but in Belgium, Italy and Spain little if any distinction is made between married and unmarried parents in this respect, and the rules depend on whether or not they are living together.

Once paternity is established, the way is open for defining the responsibilities of parents towards one another and towards their children as well as their relationship to state support. The legal rights and responsibilities of married and unmarried parents are not always closely matched by provisions in tax and social security law. In many countries, with the shift from the family to the individual as the basic unit for taxation, the distinction has been removed between married and unmarried households; the situation of married couples has been brought into line with that of unmarried couples rather than the reverse. In four member states, Denmark, Ireland, the Netherlands and the United Kingdom, no tax relief is granted for children [5.6, vol. 1, pp. 48–53]. France is, by contrast, an example of a country where the tax system is family centred, and generous tax relief is given for children from the first child and at a higher level for three or more children. A lone parent and his/her children are also considered as a family unit if they are receiving family allowances. Children can only be offset against one of the partners in unmarried couples, but the first child gives entitlement to twice the amount of relief allowed for the first child of a married couple up to a ceiling. In addition France, like Belgium, Greece and Spain, allows tax relief for childcare costs.

The benefit family

Variations between countries in the way the family is defined and taken into account in legal statutes on parentage, tax law and social security benefits reflect not only the principles underlying national family policies but also differences in the socio-economic and political contexts in which they are implemented. While tax law represents the interests of adults, social security and social assistance schemes have long been concerned with the well-being of children. Family allowances (the term used in French-speaking and southern European countries) and child benefits (the term used in northern Europe) are paid irrespective of the marital status of parents on a universal basis, but progressively they have been targeted at low-income and lone-parent families: by the early 1990s Germany, Greece, Italy, Portugal and Spain had introduced income-related adjustments, and Denmark, Germany, Greece, France, Ireland and the United Kingdom paid supplements for lone-parent families on low incomes [5.9, table X]. Family policy may thereby be losing its distinctive universal character and merging with the wider concept of social welfare.

As in statistical data, the definition of a dependent child applied in assessing entitlement for child benefit varies from one country to another, reflecting differences in policy orientations and factors such as family size, the rank of the child or the length of education. In the early 1990s in the United Kingdom the rate was higher for the first child than for subsequent children. Only France did not pay family allowances for the first child, but rates were progressive for larger families in France, Greece, Ireland and Luxembourg. Portugal imposed the lowest age limit: benefits were paid for all children up to the age of fifteen and extended up to twenty-five for those who continued in education. In Germany, Ireland and the United Kingdom, children up to sixteen were considered as dependants for the purpose of child benefit, and up to seventeen in the Netherlands. The age limit was extended to twenty-seven in Germany, eighteen in Ireland, twenty-four in the Netherlands and nineteen in the United Kingdom for those still in education, and unemployed children could receive benefit up to the age of twenty-one in Germany. Seven countries – Belgium, Denmark, France, Greece, Italy, Luxembourg and Spain – routinely paid benefits up to the age of eighteen. Denmark, Italy and Spain made no age concessions for children continuing their education after the age of eighteen, unlike Belgium (twenty-five), France (twenty), Greece (twenty-two) and Luxembourg (twenty-seven) [5.9, table X].

Before statistics began recording a steep rise in the incidence of extramarital births, cohabitation and lone parenthood, most countries already had provisions for lone parents as a result of divorce or bereavement, and unmarried mothers were also catered for, primarily in order to ensure that their children would not suffer financially from having only one parent. By taking lone parents, and particularly lone mothers, into account both as a statistical category and as social welfare beneficiaries, the *de facto* situation of a growing number of lone parents has been given legitimacy, and they have been identified as a target group for social work and special benefits, usually because of their low incomes (Lefaucheur, 1991).

The attitude of the state towards cohabitation and lone parenthood is ambivalent and problematic, which may help to explain why all EU member states are progressively moving towards a situation where individual rights, and particularly those of children, are being given precedence over the rights of the family as a legally constituted unit. Attention has focused increasingly on the needs of children and their legal rights to protection, whatever the relationship between their parents, and attempts are being made, as with the Child Support Act of 1991 in the United Kingdom, to ensure that fathers fulfil their responsibilities towards their children after separation. The International Convention on Children's Rights adopted by the General Assembly of the United Nations in 1989 confirmed the joint responsibility of parents for their children, not in response to claims for greater equality between the sexes but rather in support of the needs of children.

DEFINING AND MAKING FAMILY POLICY

Because definitions of the family are many and varied, it is equally, if not more, difficult to reach agreement over how to define family policy. In the 1970s in a seminal study of policies for families in fourteen countries, four of which were members of the Union by the early 1990s, Sheila Kamerman and Alfred Kahn (1978, p. 3) proposed a wide-ranging definition: 'everything that government does to and for the family'. The report by the European Observatory on National Family Policies covering 1989–90 [5.5, p. 9] took a similarly broad definition of family policy, describing it as 'measures geared at influencing families', but excluded unintended outcomes for the family of measures implemented in other areas. Family policy might be considered as the range of objectives and measures which policy makers pursue in order to ensure the effectiveness of the family as a social institution. In this section different approaches to family policy making are examined, with reference to organisational structures and objectives and the instruments used for implementation.

Policy-making styles

Various attempts have been made to categorise countries according to their family policy-making styles. Kamerman and Kahn (1978) distinguished between countries which had explicit and implicit family policies. By explicit they meant comprehensive family policies, as exemplified in their sample by France, the non-EC Scandinavian countries, Hungary and Czechoslovakia. Countries with an explicit but more narrowly focused family policy, according to their definition, included Denmark and Germany, as well as Austria, Poland and Finland. Countries without an explicit family policy and which went so far as to reject the idea of such a policy were illustrated by the United Kingdom, Canada, Israel and the United States.

Another version of this categorisation has been applied to the member states of the European Union by Franz Schultheis (1990, p. 74), but without identifying the countries belonging to each grouping. He described a few countries as having a long tradition of explicit, far reaching and legitimated family policy making. In this category policy has often been anchored in a specific and autonomous branch of social security, generally based on redistributive principles, characterised by a high degree of socio-political control over family affairs and seeking to respond to a wide range of needs. In a second grouping, Schultheis placed countries which have pursued more implicit family policies, taking account of family needs but without creating an autonomous area of policy. The measures used have been more selective and may have lacked overall coherence. In a third grouping were countries described as having a negative family policy. Their governments were reluctant to intervene in family life, claiming not to have a family policy, but at the same time pursuing actions which were likely to have an impact on families.

The policy-making environment is an important component in understanding why and how policy objectives are formulated and implemented and thus provides an indication of the appropriateness of classification systems such as these for member states. One yardstick of the interest that governments have in family policy is whether or not they appoint ministers with responsibility for family affairs, the relative importance of these ministers within governments and how family policy is funded and organised.

In most member states responsibility for family allowances and child benefits either rests with a ministry for social affairs, social security or social welfare, as in Belgium, France, Ireland and the United Kingdom, or it comes under a joint ministry with employment, as in Germany, Italy, the Netherlands, Portugal and Spain. In Denmark it falls within the orbit of the Ministry for Taxes and Duties as well as Social Affairs, and in Greece it is covered by the Ministry for Labour. Only Germany (at Federal level) and Luxembourg had a designated ministry for family affairs in 1993 [5.9, table I]. Most French governments over the postwar period have had at least a junior ministry with responsibility for the family, often attached to social affairs. In Belgium, France and Luxembourg specialised agencies administer family funds.

The ways in which family allowances or child benefits are funded and distributed provide a further indication of national approaches to the policy-making process in this area. In most member states where social security systems have been based on the insurance principle (see Chapter 2), family allowances were conceived as part of the wage package, and employment-related contributions were the main or sole source of funding. In a few cases employees do not contribute, as in Belgium, France, Italy and Luxembourg, and in the last three countries various subsidies have been introduced to relieve the burden on employers. In Greece, Portugal and Spain employers and employees share contributions, and the state provides subsidies in Greece and Spain. Funding is solely or mainly from the state in Denmark, Germany, Ireland, the Netherlands and the United Kingdom, thereby breaking the direct link with employment [5.9, table II].

These examples suggest that the method of funding cannot in itself be interpreted as a reliable indication that the state in a particular country has a more or less well developed or generous family policy. Nor does the fact that in some countries benefits are considered as an integral part of social security and are funded by employers, and in a few cases employees, demonstrate non-involvement on the part of the state. Often it reflects the origins of family allowances as a supplement to wages, a tradition which was not entirely broken when social security systems were established.

Policy objectives

One of the reasons suggested at the beginning of this chapter to explain why the Union had not developed its own family policy was the problem of reaching a consensus over objectives. The aims and consequences of family policy can, like other areas of policy, be manifest or latent, direct or indirect, mutually consistent or inconsistent. Over the postwar period governments in member states formulated their own policy objectives in line with their political ideology, their approach to policy making and as a response to their interpretation of the needs of families in the context of a changing economic and socio-cultural climate.

Few countries, if any, can be said to have pursued wholly coherent family policy objectives. Inconsistency may be explained to a large extent by the potential conflict of needs with which policy makers have to deal. Policies formulated in other areas, such as health, education or employment, are likely to have an impact on the family and may also lead to conflicts over objectives. For example, policies which are intended to preserve traditional family structures may be in conflict with others which are aimed at the pursuit of equality of opportunity (Land and Parker, 1978, with reference to the United Kingdom). Policy for families can thus give rise to divisions of opinion over fundamental issues which may have unintended as well as deliberate effects on individuals and families. Given that resources are never infinite, choices have to be made which may involve moral judgements. These conflicts of interest raise a number of questions. Should policies concentrate support on families which conform to traditional family types, that is married couples and their legitimate offspring, or should they recognise and institutionalise new family forms, such as cohabitation and lone parenthood? In other words should they try to stem change or keep pace with it? Within this same framework should policy makers seek to influence family size or the timing of childbirth? Should family policy be universally applied to all families or should it operate as a form of social solidarity and, by being selective, help only families most in need? Should attention be focused on individuals rather than on the family unit? Should women be encouraged to stay at home to look after young children or should the state provide facilities which enable women to combine employment outside the home with child-rearing?

Over the postwar period three main policy objectives have been pursued by member states, reflecting the different rationales underlying their welfare regimes and their attempts to deal with these questions: income distribution, pro-natalism and equal opportunities. Some member states have pursued all these objectives, albeit with different emphases depending, amongst other things, on the political ideology of the governments in power.

Most countries have sought to use family policy as a means of redistributing income, either horizontally from individuals or couples without children to those with children, or vertically from those on high incomes, to those with low incomes often targeting families most in need. In many cases both horizontal and vertical redistribution have been pursued, but increasingly emphasis has been placed on helping children at risk in line with the child-centred approach of policy in the 1990s. Efforts to contain costs in an economic context where young people remain dependent on their parents until a later age may also encourage targeting of benefits.

Some countries have been concerned about population growth and have sought to provide incentives to encourage couples to have larger families. France and Belgium have pursued this objective in their family policies over the postwar period and have not been reluctant to make their pro-natalist aims explicit. The United Kingdom and, until the late 1980s, the Federal Republic of Germany are examples of countries which deliberately avoided formulating policies that might be interpreted as encouraging population growth because of its expansionist connotations.

Another area of growing interest, which is closely related to family policy, and in some countries, for example Denmark and France, considered as an integral part of it, is the welfare of women. Provision is therefore being made to protect their rights as mothers and workers, either simultaneously or sequentially, their access to the labour market and the promotion of equal opportunities in employment and within households through a more equitable distribution of labour (examined in Chapter 6).

Irrespective of their other aims, an objective increasingly shared by EU member states is the desire to make policy more accountable, efficient and open to public scrutiny, resulting in tighter regulation and greater control at national level [5.7].

Policy instruments

Whatever the differences and fluctuations in the objectives of family policy in member states, many of the instruments used are the same. Similar policy measures may therefore be found to achieve different objectives, or they may be adapted to suit the specific conditions pertaining from one country to another. Policy instruments may also be used without reliable evidence as to their effectiveness.

When they referred to explicit policies Kamerman and Kahn (1978) meant deliberate measures or instruments such as childcare, child allowances, tax benefits, income maintenance and some housing policies, specifically aimed at the family, as well as policies which have an impact on the family even if their agreed goal is not family well-being. The European Observatory on National Family Policies excludes this last category from family policy measures, although it has chosen to monitor policy areas, such as housing, which are not necessarily incorporated into family policy. In its reports the Observatory aims, in addition, to cover measures concerned with the protection of women's health at the workplace if they are designed to support women as mothers but, if their aim is to protect women as individual citizens and workers, they belong to health policy and are discounted. Implicit family policies, according to Kamerman and Kahn, are concerned with government action which has indirect or unanticipated consequences for the family, as for example immigration policy. A study commissioned by the German Bundesministerium für Familie und Senioren of family policy in the twelve member states examined all these areas, except immigration, and also looked at education and training, caring for older people and measures to combat poverty (Neubauer *et al.*, 1993). An international comparison of child support by the Social Policy Research Unit in York (Bradshaw *et al.*, 1993b) included tax allowances in respect of childcare, housing, health care and services reducing the costs of schooling and pre-school care.

When these areas are taken into account, all member states are found to be implementing both explicit and implicit measures, even if they do not claim to be pursuing deliberate family policies, but the extent and nature of state involvement varies considerably from one member state to another, as shown above in the case of family allowances or child benefits, provisions for lone parents and income tax relief. Although in several countries the state provides some support for housing costs, only in France is an explicit link made between the family and housing by treating housing allowances and social housing as an integral part of family policy within social security in a scheme administered by the Caisses des Allocations Familiales. Allowances for handicapped children are not considered as an integral part of family policy in Denmark, Germany, the Netherlands and the United Kingdom. All member states are, however, taking account of changes in family structure and of the de-institutionalisation of care not only for children but also for older and disabled people (see Chapters 6 and 7).

THE FAMILY IMPACT OF PUBLIC POLICY

Demographers, political scientists, economists and sociologists, particularly in France, have long been debating whether public policy has an impact on demographic trends, and more especially on family structures. Some argue that the apparent convergence of demographic indicators, showing falling fertility and marriage rates, growing numbers of extramarital births and divorce and rising female economic activity rates in all member states, in the absence of harmonised family policies, might suggest that no direct causal link can be established between policy and family building. Many observers and policy makers reject the idea that family policy used as population policy can have an effect on demographic trends. They argue rather in favour of the redistributive effects of extensive family policy measures. From this viewpoint, fluctuations in the birth-rate are more likely to be attributable to economic factors and broad cultural and social forces.

For other commentators, disparities in demographic trends between member states can be attributed to policy differences. In this case the assumption is that policies formulated by member states are founded on the same objectives, are implemented using the same policy instruments and produce the same effect, irrespective of the societal environment.

In this chapter the political motivation underlying family policies has been shown to differ from one socio-cultural context to another. Comparisons between member states do not produce unequivocal findings about the family impact of public policy as far as financial incentives are concerned. The net result of adding together benefits and differential payments in combination with tax relief is that average incomes are increased by different amounts from one country to another. The largest increase to family income from these sources with the arrival of the first child is in Denmark, followed by Belgium. Italy shows the smallest increase. For families with two children France tops the list, followed closely by Belgium, with Denmark further behind but well in front of the other member states. Ireland makes the smallest addition to the income of families with two children. The rank order is similar with three children, but the difference between the most and the least generous contributions is even more marked: France is by far the most generous state, again followed by Belgium; Luxembourg and Denmark are trailing a long way behind, and Ireland is again distinguished by its very low figure; Portugal and Italy are consistently in the lower ranks, with Germany and Greece, the Netherlands and the

United Kingdom in an intermediate position (Neubauer, 1993, pp. 300–2). Comparable data are not available for Spain but, in the absence of universal family allowances and given the small amount of tax relief, it seems likely that Spain would rank even lower than Ireland.

When the benefits package paid to specific families of different size and composition is considered in combination with other forms of support encompassing tax allowances, housing costs, health care and educational services, a similar rank order emerges: Belgium, France and Luxembourg are found to provide the most generous child benefit packages, followed by Denmark, Germany, the Netherlands and the United Kingdom. Families in Greece, Ireland, Italy, Portugal and Spain receive the least generous packages (Bradshaw *et al.*, 1993a, p. 265).

Whereas references to the family in a country's constitution and the existence of a designated ministerial function might seem to imply that the state is seeking to adopt a high profile in family policy, this assumption is not supported unambiguously by information about the way in which transfer payments are funded and distributed. Using the whole batch of criteria analysed above, the impact of family policy in member states can perhaps best be described in terms of a continuum, with reference to the classification systems used by Kamerman and Kahn and Schultheis. Belgium, France and Luxembourg would seem to fit into the category of countries with explicit and relatively coherent family policies. When the various criteria are considered together, France emerges as a country which has consistently given a high profile to the family, fluctuating between all three types of objectives outlined above. The case for Belgium and Luxembourg is also convincing. Both countries provide universal family allowances irrespective of income and, as in France, the family unit has been a strong focus of policy. Denmark, Germany and the Netherlands could be classified as having less explicitly family-oriented policies. While Denmark has been a leader in terms of provision for childcare and parental leave (see Chapter 6), the main focus of attention is not the family unit but rather the needs of children and gender equality. Germany is committed in its constitution to supporting the family and attributes ministerial responsibilities for family affairs. Priority is given to the conjugal family, but the system for distributing transfer payments does not put Germany amongst the countries which provide the most generous help for families with children. Despite the lack of formal recognition of the duties of the state towards families, the Netherlands have supported not only conjugal families but also their offspring as a fundamental social value, although by the early 1990s a marked shift was occurring towards individualisation of rights and self-reliance, accompanied by a more diversified and pluralistic approach.

The United Kingdom is usually assigned to the category of countries which deliberately set out to reduce the power of the state by strengthening family responsibility, with the effect, it is argued, that the state may be overburdening families and creating a negative impact (Taylor-Gooby, 1991a, pp. 46–8). Comparisons which are not confined to analysing only direct forms of intervention or public policy pronouncements suggest that state support for families in the United Kingdom, while remaining implicit, may be greater than is sometimes recognised and founded on assumptions about patterns of responsibilities and dependencies within marriage and families (Land and Parker, 1978, pp. 331–2). By the early 1990s the family was on the agenda of all political parties (Wicks, 1991, p. 48), suggesting a more direct interest.

Reference is made to the family in the constitutions of Greece, Ireland, Italy, Portugal and Spain but, together with the United Kingdom, they rank as the member states which appear to have relatively less coherent or comprehensive family policies. Portugal is a country where the state recognises that it has a duty to support families but is prevented by economic circumstances from pursuing active and interventionist family policies. Intergenerational family networks therefore continue to be the main source of support. Ireland and the other southern European countries are in a similar situation: they are not disinterested in the family as a social institution, but they are not in a position financially to formulate and implement a coherent family policy. The focus in Ireland has been primarily on families in need, again probably more because of financial constraints than for ideological reasons, as borne out by the fact that governments have increasingly given greater priority to family policy as spending on social protection has increased, while almost all other member states have reduced the proportion of social spending devoted to this budgetary head [5.11, table 3]. Amidst the contrasts and conflicts resulting from rapid social change, family policy in Spain has relied on the support provided by the traditional three-generation family, while trying to cope with the developing social problems associated with lone-parent families. Greece has also retained a more traditional family structure but lacks the funds needed to ensure overall coherence in its social security protection system. Despite the commitment to the family in its constitution, Italy, like the United Kingdom, has tended to consider that family life is a private matter and has concentrated attention on families in need.

A whole range of socio-economic and political factors need to be taken into account in assessing the possible impact of family policies: in addition to economic and demographic pressures and the broader social policy framework at both national and European level, the relationships between the public and private sectors and the way citizenship and employment rights, solidarity and redistributive justice are conceptualised may all influence patterns of provision from one member state to another. Family policy therefore provides an interesting example of the complexities of the policy-making process and obstacles to policy co-ordination across the Union, making even convergence of objectives, unless very narrowly defined, seem difficult to achieve.

Box 5   Union documents relating to family policies

SECONDARY LEGISLATION

5.1   Council Directive 73/403/EEC of 22 November 1973 on the synchronization of general population censuses (*OJ* L 347/50 17.12.73).

5.2   Resolution of the European Parliament of 9 June 1983 on family policy in the European Community (*OJ* C 184/116 11.7.83).

5.3   Communication from the Commission on family policies (COM(89) 363 final, 8 August 1989).

5.4   Conclusions of the Council and of the Ministers Responsible for Family Affairs meeting within the Council of 29 September 1989 regarding family policies (*OJ* C 277/2 31.10.89).

OFFICIAL PUBLICATIONS OF THE COMMISSION OF THE EUROPEAN COMMUNITIES (CEC) AND EUROSTAT

5.5   CEC/European Observatory on National Family Policies (1991) *National Family Policies in EC-countries in 1990* (co-ordinated by W. Dumon), V/2293/91-EN.

5.6 CEC/European Observatory on National Family Policies (1992) *National Family Policies in EC-countries in 1991* (co-ordinated by W. Dumon), vols. 1 and 2.

5.7 CEC/European Observatory on National Family Policies (1994) *Changing Family Policies in the Member States of the European Union* (edited by W. Dumon).

5.8 CEC (1993) *Social Protection in Europe.*

5.9 CEC/Mutual Information System on Social Protection in the Community (1993) *Social Protection in the Member States of the Community. Situation on July 1st 1993 and Evolution.*

5.10 Eurostat (1991) *A Social Portrait of Europe.*

5.11 Eurostat (1993) 'Social Protection in Europe: Trends from 1980 to 1989', *Rapid Reports. Population and Social Conditions*, no. 4.

6 Women, Welfare and Citizenship

While family life is an area in which the Commission and some national governments have been reluctant to intervene, women's rights have long been on the Union's policy agenda, not, it is argued by some observers (for example by Buckley and Anderson, 1988, p. 10; Crawley, 1990, p. 7), from a desire to ensure equality between the sexes but as a means of promoting equal competition between member states. As in other areas of social policy, initially the motivation for Community intervention in gender issues was to avoid any one member state gaining a competitive edge, in this case by paying women at lower rates than men. The impetus for legislation is said to have come from France, which had enshrined the principle of equal rights in its postwar constitution of 1946 and wanted other member states to follow suit so that it would not be at a competitive disadvantage (Quintin, 1988, p. 71).

In the early years of the European Economic Community (EEC), interest in equality between the sexes coincided with both second-wave feminism and the development of socio-economic conditions which were conducive to women's emancipation (Buckley and Anderson, 1988). Economic reconstruction, expanding opportunities in education and changes in family structure all contributed to producing an environment in which national governments were receptive to proposals for promoting greater gender equality.

Over the years action in this area at European level has been extended to cover many other aspects of women's economic activity. The Commission has monitored the situation, initiated research and taken action against individual governments through the European Court of Justice (ECJ). In the 1960s studies and conferences were organised, and recommendations were made on the workings of Article 119 of the EEC Treaty [1.2] which dealt with equal pay. In the Community's social action programme of 1974 [1.8], implementation of the equal pay principle was one of the priority actions. By the mid-1970s the focus of attention had broadened to encompass equal treatment in access to employment, training and conditions of employment, and from 1977 the European Social Fund (ESF) was used to support training for women over the age of twenty-five. Exchange of information and experience was promoted through international activities, supported by a series of positive action programmes in the 1980s and 1990s.

Women have been more strongly represented at European level than in most national parliaments, with nearly 20 per cent of elected members in the European Parliament in 1989 and 25 per cent in 1994. They have played an active role in influencing equality legislation both informally and through the formal structures instituted as mechanisms for policy making. Following the 1984 elections, the European Parliament established a Standing Committee on Women's Rights to monitor existing directives and look into ways of extending European equal opportunities legislation, while also keeping under review the impact on women of policy decisions taken in other areas. The Committee has sought to be pro-active in its dealings with the Commission and the Council of Ministers and can be credited with having consolidated a large body of information about the situation of women in the Union and with pushing forward legislation. Another group that has played an important part in setting the agenda for women's affairs and in initiating research and action is the European Women's Lobby, which grouped together non-governmental organisations across the Community in 1991 with the aim of co-ordinating action to further women's interests at both European and national levels (Vale, 1991).

Although, as in the case of equal pay, the Union has clearly been influenced by national legislation, the impetus provided by the Commission can be considered as a strong incentive for change in individual member states. As in other policy areas, the extent and pace of change in behaviour and attitudes towards women's roles in society vary in relation to a number of factors, including the wider policy environment, the state of labour markets and national trends in family building and structure (see Chapter 5). While some degree of convergence may be occurring as a result of a common policy framework at European level, it is argued in this chapter that the situation of women in the twelve member states continues to display important differences with regard to social policy, in terms of both expectations and access to welfare. In order to gain a better understanding of the impact for women of measures promoted at European and national level, the Union's policy-making framework with regard to women's welfare is first examined in more detail. The characteristics of women's employment patterns are then considered as the context in which women exercise their rights, leading on to an analysis of the relationship between employment and family life and the influence of different welfare traditions and policy-making styles on women's access to social citizenship. In conclusion an attempt is made to assess the ways in which the welfare of women has been conceptualised in individual member states and the extent to which welfare can be described as gendered.

EUROPEAN LEGISLATION FOR THE WELFARE OF WOMEN

The attention paid to women in the Union has been primarily and almost exclusively in their capacity as workers (see Chapter 1). The various legal and other instruments used to promote women's labour market rights and equal opportunities at European level and their impact at national level are examined in this section. The most important are the EEC Treaty itself and directives derived from it, the Community Charter of the Fundamental Social Rights of Workers and the Commission's action programmes. The Agreement on Social Policy annexed to the Maastricht Treaty on European Union added some support for positive discrimination towards women, whereas the 1994 White Paper on European social policy was more explicit in targeting equality of opportunity between men and women.

Equal pay and equal treatment in the Community's and Union's Treaties and Charter

In the 1957 EEC Treaty under the chapter on social provisions, Article 119 referred explicitly and unambiguously to the right of women to equal pay, laying down the principle that 'men and women should receive equal pay for equal work'. It went on to define pay and equal pay in terms which were more specific than for any other aspect of social policy: pay meant 'the ordinary basic or minimum wage or salary and any other consideration, whether in cash or in kind, which the worker receives, directly or indirectly, in respect of his [*sic*] employment from his employer'; and equal pay meant that 'pay for the same work at piece rates shall be calculated on the basis of the same unit of measurement' and 'that pay for work at time rates shall be the same for the same job'.

Despite its insistence on the status of women as paid workers, Article 119 is considered to have been useful at European level in developing equal opportunities legislation (Crawley, 1990, p. 7). Articles 100 and 235 of the Treaty enabled the Commission to prepare directives on equal pay and treatment: Article 100 made it possible to issue directives to approximate provisions across member states, and Article 235 conferred the power to legislate by unanimous voting when action was necessary to achieve EEC objectives and provision was not made under other articles. The Treaty thus provided a framework for promoting harmonisation of national legislation to the social and economic advantage of women.

Although the Commission has attempted to bring forward proposals relating to the organisation of non-working life, the main focus of policy was clearly the rights and opportunities of women as paid workers. Point 16 of the Community Charter of 1989 [1.7] stated: 'Equal treatment for men and women must be assured. Equal opportunities for men and women must be developed.' Action was required to ensure implementation of the equality principle particularly in access to employment, remuneration, working conditions, social protection, education, vocational training and career development. Reference was also made to measures 'enabling men and women to reconcile their occupational and family obligations'.

The Agreement on Social Policy in the Maastricht Treaty [1.6] confirmed the orientation towards workers' rights by reiterating *verbatim* the terms of Article 119 of the EEC Treaty. A paragraph in circuitous wording was however added, advising member states that they should not be prevented 'from maintaining or adopting measures providing for specific advantages in order to make it easier for women to pursue a vocational activity or to prevent or compensate for disadvantages in their professional careers' (Article 6 paragraph 3). This statement has been construed to mean national governments can take positive action to counter discrimination (Cox, 1993, p. 43). The White Paper on European social policy was more explicit in recommending positive action through the development of a code of practice, professional qualifications for women and the individualisation of rights, in order to 'maximise the opportunities and reduce the dangers' for women in the face of structural economic change associated with the growth of services, new technologies and new flexibility of work organisation [1.13, pp. 31–4].

Secondary legislation on women's rights

The Union has used a range of measures to promote greater equality of treatment and opportunity for women [6.13; 6.15]. In particular, the Council has adopted several important directives, one of the most binding instruments available.

In 1975 the Commission issued its first directive in this area. Council Directive 75/117/EEC 'on the approximation of the laws of the Member States relating to the application of the principle of equal pay for men and women' [6.1] enlarged on the provisions of Article 119, in particular by clarifying and extending the meaning of the principle of equal pay to work of equal value, as assessed by job evaluation schemes. It explicitly outlawed discrimination on grounds of sex, not only where an employee feels she is being directly discriminated against because she is paid less that a man, but also where conditions are imposed which exclude or impede the progress of members of one sex and which are not essential for the job. While the Directive gives employees who feel they have grounds for complaint the right to legal redress, the concepts of work of equal value and indirect discrimination remain difficult to operationalise, and a series of judgments on cases brought before the ECJ have been necessary to clarify the position (Byre, 1988).

Subsequent directives built onto the framework provided by Article 119 and the 1975 Directive. Directive 76/207/EEC extended the principle to 'equal treatment for men and women as regards access to employment, vocational training and promotion and working conditions' [6.2]. Directive 79/7/EEC, which was adopted in 1978 and finally came into force in 1984, addressed 'the principle of equal treatment for men and women in matters of social security' [6.3]. Member states were allowed six years to implement the 1978 Directive because of its complexities and the costs involved (Luckhaus, 1990, p. 12). This Directive was supplemented in 1986 by two further Directives, 86/378/EEC [6.5] and 86/613/EEC [6.6], which extended the principle of equality of treatment to self-employed men and women. The principle of equal treatment required that there should be no direct or indirect discrimination on the grounds of sex in relation to matters such as the scope of social security schemes, conditions of access and calculation of benefits, for example with regard to retirement, in cases where a married woman's employment did not entitle her husband to benefits or occupational schemes were only open to men.

Although the three Directives removed the automatic exclusion of women from benefit entitlements earned as full-time workers, they did not cover survivors' and family benefits, and they left open the possibility of excluding the determination of pensionable age, advantages for persons who have brought up children and the granting of increases for long-term invalidity, old age, industrial accident and occupational disease benefits for a dependent wife. Another important omission was that they did not directly address the issue of part-time or unpaid work. A draft directive on voluntary part-time work first proposed in 1981 was not adopted, although cases brought before the ECJ have resulted in some recognition of women's rights as part-time workers (Luckhaus, 1990, p. 18). While, in the post-implementation phase, the ECJ was more liberal in acknowledging women's needs as part-time workers, its judgments signalled the intention not to interfere with this aspect of the organisation of family life and the division of household labour.

A proposal for a directive, issued in 1983 and amended in 1984 [6.4], addressed the question of parental leave and leave for family reasons but was also not adopted, although the Council Recommendation 'on child care', which was adopted in 1992 [6.10], included special leave for parents to look after their own children as well as encouragement for men and women to share family responsibilities for childcare and the education of children. The Recommendation was the outcome of a long process of negotiation over childcare provision within the framework of policy on equal opportunities and the reconciliation of family obligations with employment. The ground had been prepared by the European Commission's Childcare Network, which began operating in 1986. The network took as its basic premise that the inequality in the conditions under which men and women supply their labour is socially determined and that childcare affects not only women's opportunities for participation in the labour market but also their general well-being, whether or not they are in paid employment [6.16, p. 2]. Childcare was as much an issue for men as for women.

Council Directive 92/85/EEC 'on the introduction of measures to encourage improvements in the safety and health at work of pregnant workers and workers who have recently given birth or are breastfeeding' [4.6] affords another example of how the Commission handled a contentious issue by bringing forward a proposal under the Framework Directive as a health and safety measure (see Chapter 4). Essentially, the Directive sought to provide a minimum level of protection by proposing that women who are working at the time when they become pregnant, or who are registered as unemployed, are automatically entitled to fourteen weeks' maternity leave with pay and without loss of employment-related rights. Another aspect of women's working conditions was tackled in a Council Recommendation 'on the protection of the dignity of women and men at work' [6.9], which outlawed sexual harassment at the workplace.

In the 1994 White Paper on European social policy the Commission announced its intention to keep all these items on the agenda for the remainder of the decade: legislation was to be pursued on part-time work [1.13, p. 22); on the question of parental leave and career breaks the possibility of a framework directive would be examined on measures aimed at reconciling professional and family life, with a view to establishing minimum standards [1.13, p. 22]; the implementation of the Recommendation on childcare would be assessed, baseline data would be established on childcare infrastructures and services; and the issue of gender stereotyping would also be addressed [1.13, p. 33].

Community action programmes on equal opportunities for women

Directives and recommendations are one of the more tangible outcomes of the Union's activities in the area of women's rights. While legislation provides a framework for action, the Commission has been aware that the law alone cannot ensure equality of opportunity. Throughout the 1960s the Commission regularly reported on the difficulties of putting the equal pay principle into practice. One of the objectives of the 1974 social action programme was to achieve greater equality between men and women with regard not only to pay but also access to employment and vocational training and working conditions. Reference was made for the first time to the political will to adopt measures to ensure that family responsibilities could be reconciled with job aspirations [1.8, p. 2]. Subsequently the Commission registered its intention to act as a prime mover in the area of equal opportunities by initiating a series of action programmes promoting equal opportunities for women. An important feature of the programmes was their attempt to raise awareness, disseminate information and mobilise what they called 'equality partners', referring in particular to national governments and social partners [6.14, p. 1].

The first equal opportunities action programme for the period 1982–85 stressed the need to put equal opportunities into practice, by means of positive action programmes aimed at enabling women to overcome their disadvantage in relation to men [6.11]. The second action programme for 1986–90 addressed the consolidation of the legal rights of individuals and sought to promote positive action aimed at overcoming the non-legal barriers to the achievement of equal opportunities [6.12].

The Council responded to the provision made in the Community Charter by adopting a Resolution on the third medium-term Community action programme on equal opportunities for women and men for the period 1991–95 [6.7]. The programme was presented against the background of the conditions and opportunities created by the completion of the internal market and the need to develop new policies and measures taking into account the social and economic changes of the 1990s and beyond [6.14]. The Council recommended that 'better use should be made of women's abilities and gifts so as to permit their full participation in the process of European development' [6.7, p. 1]. Women's participation was, moreover, described as 'an essential factor in European economic and social cohesion'. The Council underlined the need for measures to reconcile professional and family life. As argued in the previous chapter, the justification for extending European policy to family affairs continued to focus on the status of individuals and their effectiveness as workers. However, the Resolution mentioned not only efforts to improve the status of women in society, particularly at all levels in the media sector, but also the need to promote the participation of women in the decision-making process in public, economic and social life.

The third action programme was innovatory in two other respects: firstly, in line with the principle of complementarity and subsidiarity, it identified separately measures which fell under the Commission's responsibility and those which individual member states were expected to implement; secondly, it provided for the integration of equality issues into general mainstream policy at European and national level. The New Opportunities for Women (Now) initiative for the promotion of equal opportunities in the field of employment and vocational training, particularly in less developed areas, affords an example of both these principles [6.14, pp. 12–14]. The initiative was established within the framework of the Structural Funds and involved a partnership not only between the Union and national governments but also between regional and local administrations, vocational training agents, socio-economic partners, research and information centres on women. To help women create small businesses and co-operatives or re-enter employment, Community support could extend to guidance and advice, technical assistance, such as awareness-raising actions, and the collection and dissemination of information on good practice and vocational training. As an enabling device, the Commission undertook to support the provision of childcare facilities, including the operating costs of facilities linked to vocational training centres and the training of childcare workers. It thereby extended its remit beyond the workplace into areas where previously – like some national governments – it had been reluctant to intervene, although the interest in childcare was most certainly motivated by its job creation potential [1.13, p. 33].

The impact of Union legislation on national policy making

Whereas in the previous chapter no clear picture emerged of what might be considered as a European family policy, in the area of equality between men and women at work the Union can be credited with having formulated and implemented a more coherent body of policy, with procedures for monitoring its effectiveness, incentives to ensure enactment and penalties for infringements. European policy may therefore have played a more prominent role than was the case for family affairs in shaping national legislation.

In the area of equal pay and equal opportunities, some member states have been in the forefront of change, others have kept pace with European legislation, while yet others have only gradually implemented directives, generally in response to infringement proceedings [6.13]. National equal pay legislation pre-dated European law in France where the 1946 constitution affirmed the equality principle. Work of equal value was not, however, formally defined in law until 1983. The Italian constitution of 1947 provided for the same pay for equal work while also offering protection to women workers to enable them to fulfil their family functions (Bimbi, 1993, p. 147). Several countries were introducing equal pay for work of equal value in the early 1970s when the European directives were being drafted. Ireland's Anti-Discrimination Act of 1974 included an equal pay clause. In Belgium the principle of equal pay for work of the same or equal value in the Collective Labour Agreement of 1975 was given binding force in the private sector. Luxembourg's Grand-Ducal Regulation of 1974 included an equal value clause, and the Netherlands followed suit in 1975. The United Kingdom passed an Equal Pay Act in 1970 with a five year period of voluntary compliance. The Danish equal pay law dates from 1976, but infringement proceedings were initiated against Denmark for not including the term 'equal value'. Although Germany had a Basic Law on equal rights dating back to 1949, it avoided infringement proceedings by belatedly adopting legislation on equal treatment in 1980.

Most member states also extended their legislation to cover illegal dismissal on the basis of sex and to make provision for legal redress, with the burden of proof on employers. Some established monitoring procedures through organisations such as the Equal Opportunities Commission, which was set up in 1975 in the United Kingdom, or the Equality Status Council established in 1978 in Denmark.

In most countries implementation of the 1976 Directive on equal treatment in access to employment, promotion, vocational training and working conditions, was a longer process, and infringement proceedings were initiated against all the nine earlier member states over some aspect of their national legislation. Despite the long period allowed for implementation of the 1978 Directive on equal treatment in social security, not all member states had complied by the target date of 1984.

The countries that joined the Community in the 1980s were required to bring their national legislation into line with European law which they had had no hand in drafting. In the case of equal rights and equal opportunities directives, this did not seem to present any major problems since national legislation had been moving in the same direction. Greece had already included an article in its 1975 constitution establishing equal rights between the sexes, and this principle was extended by transposing the detail of Directives 75/117/EEC and 76/207/EEC into national law which came into force in 1984. The provisions of Directive 79/7/EEC had also been progressively introduced, although self-employed and public service workers were not covered in the 1984 law. In Spain quite radical changes in women's legal status had been occurring since the mid-1970s, anticipating – albeit unintentionally – the requirements when Spain joined the Community. The Civil Code was amended in 1975 to recognise women's full legal capacity. The Spanish constitution of 1978 enshrined equality as an essential constituent element of a legally established social and democratic state. Reference was made specifically to non-discrimination based on sex in relation to work, and this principle was also embodied in the Workers' Statute and the Basic Law on Employment. On joining the Community, the Spanish Government was quick to draw up the necessary legislation in adapting its own provisions to take account of European directives. Portugal had also made profound changes to its constitution in 1976 and 1982 to grant new legal status to women. The constitution laid down the principles of equality and non-discrimination not only at work and in education but also between spouses.

Examples both from the earlier member states and the southern European countries suggest that European law was perhaps less effective as a force initiating reform at national level than as an instrument for accompanying or accelerating change. Given that directives are the outcome of a compromise reached between member states, this is to be expected. However, some cases of resistance can be identified when individual member states have felt that their own legislation was already adequate to cover the contingencies provided for in directives, or when they claimed that the social and economic cost of implementation would be unreasonable. Legislation on part-time workers, maternity and parental leave and age of retirement was opposed, and in some cases blocked, for these reasons.

WOMEN'S ACCESS TO RIGHTS AS WORKERS AND MOTHERS

Analysis of European law as it affects women shows clearly how attention has been paid almost exclusively to their rights as workers, while gradually recognising that they may need special treatment in their capacity as working mothers. A number of studies have been made of the possible impact of children on women's economic activity rates and the effect of paid employment outside the home on family building across western industrialised nations (for example Barrère-Maurisson and Marchand, 1990; Kempeneers and Lelièvre, 1991). In this section, firstly, the relative situation of women in different labour markets is examined to enable a better understanding of the implications of legislation on equal treatment and social security entitlements. A brief overview is then provided of some of the national policies aimed at helping women to reconcile professional and family life with reference to the framework provided by European law.

Women and labour markets in Europe

Comparative data reveal features and trends in women's employment patterns which are common to all member states: although women's economic activity rates have been increasing steadily across the Union since the late 1960s, everywhere they remain lower than those of men [6.19, table 02]. Even in the younger age groups, where availability is less subject to family constraints, rates for women fall consistently below those for men, indicating that, despite equality legislation, women still experience more difficulty than men in finding initial employment and in pursuing economic activity. This disparity has been interpreted as a constraint on growth and competitiveness when the contribution of women to employment in Europe is compared with that in Japan or the United States [1.13, p. 31].

In addition, there is abundant evidence to show that legislation to ensure equal pay for work of equal value and to improve women's opportunities in access to training and employment has not enabled them to enter the labour market on equal terms with men. Everywhere women are in lower paid, less secure employment than men. In all member states, women are more likely than men to be employed in part-time jobs [6.19, table 34] and on temporary contracts [6.17, appendix table 7]. In all member states, except the United Kingdom, women are more likely to be unemployed than men [6.19, table 02].

Nor has occupational segregation disappeared, as measured by the division of paid work between what are commonly accepted as men's and women's jobs. Not only do women continue to be concentrated in the least secure and least well paid sectors of employment, but the growing proportion of women in lower skilled service jobs has also made such low paid work even more female dominated. The recession and economic restructuring of the 1980s curtailed expansion of intermediate-level clerical work which might have attracted women. Although more women continued to enter paid employment, they tended to be concentrated in the caring professions and public sector employment, where working conditions were more flexible and 'women friendly', but where pay was lower than in the private sector. Analysis of the occupational segregation of employment shows that, while it may be possible to implement legislation on equal pay for the same work, it is more difficult to prove discrimination on the basis of equal value for different work or to avoid the gendering of jobs [6.17].

Commonalities in trends in working patterns for women in relation to men and the segregation of employment conceal important differences between member states. As with the demographic trends examined in the previous chapter, the extent and pace of change in women's employment rates vary from one country to another: Portugal, Denmark and the Netherlands, respectively, have seen the most rapid rise in female activity rates since the late 1970s, whereas change occurred more slowly in Ireland and the Federal Republic of Germany. Nor have the marked differences between countries disappeared: by the early 1990s, Denmark still recorded a particularly high overall female economic activity rate, followed by the United Kingdom and Portugal, where it had doubled within two decades. The gap separating Denmark from Ireland and Spain, which still showed the lowest levels, had even increased (OECD, 1991, table II).

One explanation for the high economic activity rates for women in the United Kingdom and Denmark may be the large proportion of women working part time [6.19, table 34]. Although women in the Netherlands showed particularly high levels of part-time working in the early 1990s, their overall activity rates were below the European average. Part-time work was rare in the southern European member states, including Italy, but national data may underestimate the amount since much homeworking may go unrecorded in official employment statistics. Belgium, Denmark, France and Portugal were the only member states to have full-time activity rates above 50 per cent for women with children aged under ten [6.16, table 1].

Where equal pay, equal treatment and access to social security provisions are dependent on full-time continuous working patterns, it is clear that large proportions of women in several member states are excluded from welfare rights. Even in Denmark, France and Portugal, which show the highest full-time activity rates, only between 43 and 50 per cent of women in paid employment would be eligible for full entitlement to employment-related benefits. Because of their very low full-time rates and extensive part-time working, women in the Netherlands would be heavily penalised under social security arrangements which provided for earnings-related benefits; they would therefore be reliant on a male breadwinner to ensure entitlements.

Reconciling employment and family life

Although women's increased participation in the labour force may be a contributory factor, evidence that the reduction in the birth-rate might be directly attributable to changing patterns in women's paid employment is not conclusive: economic activity rates of women in Portugal were, for example, rising steeply at the same time as their fertility rates were falling, whereas Greek women did not significantly increase their economic activity rates as they reduced their levels of fertility; in France and the United Kingdom women have maintained relatively high overall economic activity and fertility rates.

The presence of young children undoubtedly has an effect on women's employment patterns but in ways which differ from one country to another. As shown above, women in the Netherlands, Denmark and the United Kingdom are more likely to take part-time work when they have young children. Women in the United Kingdom, Germany, the Netherlands and France more often than women in other member states take a break of at least a year when they have children (Kempeneers and Lelièvre, 1991, table 26). Women in Ireland, Luxembourg and Spain, by contrast, tend to leave the labour force permanently to raise children. The ways in which these strategies relate to state provision are many and varied, and proposals from the Commission, such as those for paid maternity leave, parental and paternity leave and public provision of childcare, are likely to produce different reactions from one member state to another.

The Union has been constrained in its efforts to introduce measures, such as social security benefits for part-time workers, parental leave and leave to look after children, or state provision of childcare, by the opposition of some member states, notably the United Kingdom, which have argued against legislation in this area on the grounds that it would impinge on the private lives of individuals and also impose a heavy burden on employers. Progressively, the Union has been encouraging government intervention to assist parents in combining employment with family life. The minimalist approach adopted means, however, that individual member states can and do offer more favourable arrangements.

Maternity, parental and paternity leave

When in 1990 the Commission drafted a proposal which included provision for fourteen weeks' statutory maternity leave on full pay, as the only member state without a universal right to maternity leave for women in paid employment, the United Kingdom reacted by claiming that it would cause 'a dramatic change in entitlement to paid leave from work in the UK' [6.8, p. 1]. Under national law in the United Kingdom a working woman had no automatic right to maternity leave. She did have the right to return to work under the Employment Protection Consolidation Act of 1978 if she fulfilled the qualifying conditions. Entitlement to maternity pay, which was separate from maternity leave and was governed by the Social Security Act of 1986, was also subject to a qualifying period. The Commission's proposal was therefore expected to have important repercussions for the amount women would receive during maternity leave and on labour costs for employers. Countries which already had more generous schemes for paid maternity leave were, by the same token, keen to have these measures extended across the Union to avoid being at a competitive disadvantage. In the event Council Directive 92/85/EEC, adopted in October 1992 [4.6], stipulated that member states could make maternity pay conditional on a period of not more than twelve months' employment and set it at a level equivalent to 80 per cent of previous salary.

By the mid-1990s, all the other member states had provision for at least fourteen weeks' leave, and Italy offered up to five months. Practices differed, however, over payment: full pay was granted in Germany (with a ceiling), Greece, Luxembourg, the Netherlands (with a ceiling) and Portugal; 80 per cent or above of previous earnings was awarded in France and Italy, 75 per cent of earnings in Spain and 70 per cent in Ireland. In Belgium the rate began at 82 per cent (with a ceiling) and was reduced over time. Denmark paid a flat-rate benefit [6.18, pp. 49–51]. Most member states did not therefore need to make major changes to their arrangements to bring their practices into line with the Directive.

The proposal to harmonise provisions for paid parental leave across all member states raised similar issues for the United Kingdom, which had no statutory provision, although a number of firms had introduced career break schemes. By the mid-1990s seven countries – Denmark, France, Germany, Greece, Italy, Portugal and Spain – made formal arrangements for parental leave, with Belgium offering a more general form of leave of absence, or career break, which could be used to look after children, while the Netherlands provided for reduced working hours [6.18, pp. 54–6]. The length of leave varied from ten weeks in Denmark to three years in Germany. In some cases payment was made to parents taking leave: in Belgium, Denmark (as for maternity leave), France (not for the first child) and Germany at a flat rate and in Italy at 30 per cent of earnings.

Coverage and take-up of parental leave and career breaks vary across member states and also within countries. Even if agreement could be reached on the length of parental leave and the level of payment made to parents taking it, this form of leave is likely to continue to be conceptualised differently from one member state to another. In Denmark, relatively short parental leave has been offered to both mothers and fathers, essentially as an equality measure (Carlsen, 1993). In France parental leave is considered as a brief hiatus in employment, enabling parents to maintain their status in the labour force while their children are young, whereas in Germany paid leave is seen rather as a benefit, or maternal wage, for mothers who choose to stay at home to look after their children (Fagnani, 1992, p. 35). Differences can also be found both in practice and in the symbolic value of paternity leave. By the mid-1990s Belgium, Denmark, France and Spain made provision for paternity leave, again in line with the equality principle, and six member states provided some statutory leave to care for sick children: namely Belgium, Germany, Greece, Italy, Portugal and Spain. Provision was available under collective agreements in Denmark and France [6.18, p. 53].

These persistent disparities in arrangements for parental and paternity leave and leave for family reasons between member states may help to explain why agreement could not be reached in the mid-1980s over convergence of national systems towards the arrangements proposed in the draft directive.

Provision of childcare

By the time the Recommendation on childcare was adopted in 1992 [6.10], Denmark had by far the most extensive public provision of childcare, followed by France and Belgium. Most publicly funded childcare for children under the age of three, generally in nurseries or organised family day care schemes, was the responsibility of welfare authorities. Except for these three countries, the provision for this age group was low, with places for less than 5 per cent of children [6.16, table 3]. Pre-primary schooling or kindergartens were provided by education or welfare authorities for two to three year-olds in most member states. Provision was available for over 80 per cent of children between the ages of three and compulsory school age in Belgium, Denmark, France and Italy, and for 60 to 80 per cent of children in Germany, Greece and Spain. The best provision for children outside school hours was also in Denmark. Only in Belgium, France and Luxembourg, however, have childcare costs been found to fall below the level of benefits for families (Bradshaw *et al.*, 1993b, p. 51), and these are the countries which were characterised in the previous chapter by the comprehensiveness of their family policies.

At the other end of the scale, three member states stood out as being poor providers of publicly funded care: Ireland, the Netherlands and the United Kingdom. Ireland and the United Kingdom were also distinguished by the fact that childcare services did not give priority to the children of parents in paid employment but rather to children at risk. Ireland and the Netherlands were, with Spain, the countries with the lowest full-time economic activity rates for women with young children [6.16, table 1].

National interpretations of measures for reconciling family and professional life

When maternity leave and benefits, parental and paternity leave and childcare are considered together, it is clear that some member states have gone much further than others in supporting parents and in helping to reconcile employment with family life, albeit for different reasons and with differing effects (Lohkamp-Himmighofen, 1993). State support for the high level of labour force participation by women in Denmark is grounded in egalitarian principles. In Belgium and France public policy has been less clearly associated with a shift towards a redistribution of tasks. The sequential ordering of work and family, involving temporary part-time working, has been supported by the state in Germany, Luxembourg and the Netherlands and can be interpreted as a means of reinforcing the family as a social institution. Ireland and the United Kingdom are characterised by a low level of direct state intervention, relying on market forces and a policy of non-interference in the private sphere of family life. In Greece, Italy, Portugal and Spain policy makers began much later to concern themselves with the issue of helping couples to combine family life and employment against a background of under-developed welfare provision. The implication is that women in the last two groups of countries may experience greater difficulty in organising their daily lives because they more often have to resort to individual and private arrangements. Alternatives to state provision, such as employer's schemes and self-help groups in the United Kingdom or family and kinship support networks in the southern European member states, combined with informal paid work, are factors which may help to explain some of the relatively high female activity rates for women with young children in these countries, despite the lack of publicly provided services.

THE GENDERING OF WELFARE

Although the equality principle has been extended to cover social insurance, and social security entitlements apply beyond the workplace to family members, it has been argued throughout this chapter that the focus on paid employment has prevented the Union from adequately addressing what have been described as 'the combined sources of inequality between the sexes' (Meehan, 1993, p. 194). The failure of European policy makers to focus on the relationship between paid and unpaid work as a critical component in the equality debate has meant that, in the area of welfare, women have typically gained access to benefits as the dependants of a male breadwinner or through their own employment status. Since women are more often than men marginalised as workers, they are over-represented among the population groups which are most likely to suffer in an employment-based system of social protection. Nowhere in the member states has the unpaid work done in the home in the form of caring by women as providers of services been given the same recognition as paid work in gaining entitlements to benefits. As marginal workers, women have thus been prevented from achieving full social citizenship rights (Lewis, 1993). While legislation at European and national level may have been instrumental in narrowing differentials between men and women in terms of earnings and opportunities at the workplace, where women are employed on the same basis, in similar work or work of equal value, little change has been recorded in the division of labour in the home or in the distribution of less secure forms of paid employment, such as part-time work, between men and women.

When welfare regimes are characterised according to the way in which women gain access to entitlements (Lewis, 1992), many of the assumptions made in social policy several decades ago about men's and women's activities are found to continue to influence policy making. Despite the fact that their welfare regimes were conceptualised differently (see Chapter 2), Germany, Ireland, the Netherlands and the United Kingdom have served as examples of strong male breadwinner states. In these countries, when social security schemes were established, women were defined primarily as wives and mothers dependent on the male breadwinner. Many women have not qualified for benefits because of their precarious labour market position or, as in the United Kingdom, because they were excluded from social insurance contributions by their low earnings.

In most countries where the male breadwinner model has persisted, the assumption in policy is that women are secondary wage earners. They are not therefore compensated for their unpaid work as carers (see Chapter 7). In some cases, as in Ireland, women's home-maker role has been reinforced by social policies which actively discouraged them from taking paid work outside the home. In the Federal Republic of

Germany the attitude of the state was apparently more neutral (Ostner, 1993). While incentives were not provided for women to pursue continuous employment, and the assumption was that they would follow a sequential arrangement, leaving work when they had children, some recognition was given to their role as wives and mothers through the income tax system, which favoured the married couple (*Ehegattensplitting*), and parental leave, which could be interpreted as an arrangement encouraging mothers to stay at home.

Italy provides an interesting example from southern Europe of a process whereby the thrust of social policy fluctuated between a focus on the family as a group to be protected by the state and emphasis on individual rights. This constant shifting can be explained by the fact that women gained citizenship rights in a context of strong intergenerational support and intra-family solidarity (Bimbi, 1993). Although urban families were still organised in the 1970s around the male breadwinner/head of household, under pressure from powerful collective movements and not least from strong feminist groups, Italian social services shifted from a minimal assistance to a universal social democratic approach. As a result, women received generous protection as workers whenever they were identified as mothers. Many of the gains made have, however, militated against the interests of women, illustrating the dangers inherent in such policies: equal rights for part-timers made part-time work unattractive for employers; the erosion of wage differentials reduced the advantage of employing women, which, in combination with arrangements for extended maternity leave and leave to look after sick children, may have further discouraged employers from taking on women, possibly explaining Italy's relatively high rate of female unemployment.

In none of these countries were women supported in their efforts to combine employment with family life to quite the same extent as in Denmark and France, where, for different reasons, the male breadwinner model was 'modified' (Lewis, 1992, p. 165), and women moved closer to achieving social citizenship rights. Historically, women in France have secured a much stronger position in the labour market as full-time continuous workers (Tilly and Scott, 1987). They have also benefited as mothers from policies formulated by governments preoccupied by demographic concerns (Hantrais, 1990, 1993). As a result, they have been encouraged by state provision of childcare facilities, parental leave and other employment-related benefits and working arrangements to combine paid employment with child-rearing (Haut Conseil de la Population et de la Famille, 1987).

In Denmark women's economic activity rates have moved very close to those of men, even though they still have shorter working hours. Under the banner of equality between the sexes, the state has played a particularly active role in trying to overcome barriers to equal opportunities both at work and in the home, developing 'a mutual dependency between the private and the public sector and between the state and the family' (Siim, 1993, p. 26). As a result, women have been able to obtain social citizenship rights as individuals independently of their position in the labour market or in the family. But even in Denmark, family work still tends to be performed primarily by women and to be conceptualised as 'overtime' (Petersen, 1993, p. 44).

Despite the seeming agreement reached amongst member states over the recognition of women's social security rights as workers and the need to harmonise national laws in line with European directives, views continue to diverge about the acceptability of state intervention – and even more so intervention by the Commission – through social policies which do not have a direct impact on employment, labour markets and competitiveness. In member states which have emphasised that entitlements to benefits such as pensions or health care are on the basis of citizenship, women might therefore be expected to fare better than in states where employment is the basis for welfare entitlements. This assumption only applies for so long as the benefit system is dependent solely on taxation and provides flat-rate payments and standardised care for everyone. Most countries either already have or are moving towards a mixed economy of welfare, enabling some groups to obtain benefits over and above a guaranteed minimum rate, generally on the basis of occupational and private schemes (see Chapter 2). In such a system women, who customarily have interrupted employment patterns and work in low paid insecure jobs, are likely to continue to suffer discrimination in access to welfare, while access to a high standard of employment rights targeted specifically at women may result in them being crowded out of the job market because of the heavy demands they are expected to make on employers.

Box 6   Union documents relating to women, welfare and citizenship

SECONDARY LEGISLATION

6.1   Council Directive 75/117/EEC of 10 February 1975 on the approximation of the laws of the Member States relating to the application of the principle of equal pay for men and women (*OJ* L 45/19 19.2.75).

6.2   Council Directive 76/207/EEC of 9 February 1976 on the implementation of the principle of equal treatment for men and women as regards access to employment, vocational training and promotion and working conditions (*OJ* L 39/40 14.2.76).

6.3   Council Directive 79/7/EEC of 19 December 1978 on the progressive implementation of the principle of equal treatment for men and women in matters of social security (*OJ* L 6/24 10.1.79).

6.4   Commission proposal for a Council Directive on parental leave and leave for family reasons (COM(83) 686 final, 24 November 1983) (*OJ* C 333/6 9.12.83), amended (COM(84) 631 final, 15 November 1984) (*OJ* C 316/7 27.11.84).

6.5   Council Directive 86/378/EEC of 24 July 1986 on the implementation of the principle of equal treatment for men and women in occupational social security schemes (*OJ* L 225/40 12.8.86).

6.6   Council Directive 86/613/EEC of 11 December 1986 on the application of the principle of equal treatment between men and women engaged in an activity, including agriculture, in a self-employed capacity, and on the protection of self-employed women during pregnancy and motherhood (*OJ* L 359/56, 19.12.86).

6.7   Council Resolution of 21 May 1991 on the third medium-term Community action programme on equal opportunities for women and men (1991–1995) (*OJ* C 142/1 31.5.91).

6.8   Background Report on protection at work for pregnant women or women who have recently given birth (ISEC/B25/90, 5 October 1990) (London: CEC).

6.9   Council Recommendation of 27 November 1991 on the protection of the dignity of women and men at work (92/131/EEC) (*OJ* L 49/1 24.2.92).

6.10 Commission Recommendation of 31 March 1992 on child care (92/241/EEC) (*OJ* L 123/16 8.5.92).

OFFICIAL PUBLICATIONS OF THE COMMISSION OF THE EUROPEAN COMMUNITIES (CEC) AND EUROSTAT

6.11 CEC (1982) 'Equal Opportunities. Action Programme 1982–1985, *Women of Europe Supplement*, no. 9.

6.12 CEC (1986) 'Equal Opportunities. 2nd Action Programme 1986–1990', *Women of Europe Supplement*, no. 23.

6.13 CEC (1987) 'Community Law and Women', *Women of Europe Supplement*, no. 25.

6.14 CEC (1991) 'Equal Opportunities for Women and Men. The Third Medium-term Community Action Programme – 1991–1995', *Women of Europe Supplements,* no. 34.

6.15 CEC (1991) 'Equal Opportunities for Women and Men', *Social Europe Supplement 3/91.*

6.16 CEC/European Commission Childcare Network (1990) 'Childcare in the European Communities 1985–1990', *Women of Europe Supplements*, no. 31 (co-ordinated by P. Moss).

6.17 CEC/Network of Experts on the Situation of Women in the Labour Market (1993) 'Occupational Segregation of Women and Men in the European Community. Synthesis Report', *Social Europe Supplement 3/93* (co-ordinated by J. Rubery and C. Fagan).

6.18 European Commission/Network on Childcare and other Measures to Reconcile Employment and Family Responsibilities (1994) *Leave Arrangements for Workers with Children: a Review of Leave Arrangements in the Member States of the European Union and Austria, Finland, Norway and Sweden*, V/773/94.

6.19 Eurostat (1993) *Labour Force Survey: Results 1991.*

7 Policy for Older and Disabled People

The emphasis placed on workers' rights in the Community's and Union's Treaties and Charter signalled that European social policy was only indirectly concerned with categories of the population who did not gain entitlements to social protection as active members of the labour force. Whereas the Treaty establishing the European Economic Community (EEC) [1.2], and in later years the Single European Act (SEA) [1.5] and the Maastricht Treaty on European Union [1.6], made no reference to older or disabled people, the Community Charter of the Fundamental Social Rights of Workers [1.7], which was not legally binding, included a statement of European policy for these two potentially disadvantaged categories of former or would-be workers. As with family policy (see Chapter 5), demographic factors explain why older people have been placed on the social policy agenda. By the early 1990s one of the major challenges facing the Union was how to prepare for the demographic imbalance predicted for the twenty-first century and associated issues such as intergenerational equity and the social integration of older and disabled people. Policy makers were faced with the problems of ensuring funding for pensions and the provision of adequate and effective social services in a context where many of the premises on which welfare states had been founded were being called into question.

In this chapter the focus is primarily on the policy implications of the ageing of the Union's population and the related needs of elderly and infirm people. Consideration is given, firstly, to the development of European social policy for older and disabled people, with reference to the work of the Observatory on Ageing and Older People and the action programmes for disabled people. The social and economic problems associated with demographic ageing are then examined across member states, and national social security provisions for older and disabled people are analysed in order to determine how policy makers in member states have responded to changing needs, particularly with regard to pensions and informal caring. Finally an attempt is made to assess the possible impact of the actions at European level in this area on national policy making and on living standards within member states.

THE DEVELOPMENT OF EUROPEAN SOCIAL POLICY FOR OLDER AND DISABLED PEOPLE

Changing demographic structures have given rise to a number of policy issues which have been addressed at European level on the basis that their repercussions go beyond the realm of action of individual nations. The possible impact of these changes on the funding and provision of benefits and pension schemes, and therefore on workers' mobility and international competition, also helps to explain intervention at European level. The social and economic integration of disabled people is of interest both on humanitarian grounds and because their occupational integration into a regular working environment may represent an asset for the Union [7.10, p. 294]. In this section the various forms of action taken at European level are examined with reference to these objectives and to the policy measures that have been proposed and implemented.

Provision for older and disabled people in European legislation and the Community Charter

The concern that differences in the treatment of older or disabled people might prevent the effective operation of the common market was implicit in the EEC Treaty. Articles 51 and 121 made provision for migrant workers to aggregate entitlements to benefits during periods spent in different member states and for common measures to be implemented. Articles 117 and 118 referred to the expectation that member states would work closely together to harmonise social systems (see Chapter 2). In addition to the need to ensure that differences in social protection systems would not impede freedom of movement, another reason why older and disabled people were of indirect interest to the EEC founder members was that differences in the method of funding pensions and health care might affect the competitiveness of goods, services and manpower in countries with social insurance schemes which relied heavily on employer and employee contributions. Some member states feared they might be put at a competitive disadvantage because of their relatively high labour costs and more generous provision (see Chapter 1).

More than thirty years later, although the original reasons for EEC intervention had not disappeared, the Community Charter formally recognised the aspirations of older and disabled people for independent living. While affirming its intention to respect national systems and leave member states to make their own arrangements, the Charter made clear the obligation to ensure minimum rights for older and disabled people to help them overcome their financial and other handicaps. Points 24 and 25 stated that, at the time of retirement, every worker should be able to enjoy 'resources affording him or her a decent standard of living' and should be entitled 'to sufficient resources and to medical and social assistance specifically suited to his [*sic*] needs'. The section on disabled persons (point 26) stipulated that they should be entitled to 'additional concrete measures aimed at improving their social and professional integration', covering vocational training, ergonomics, accessibility, mobility, means of transport and housing. The shift of emphasis in policy announced in the Charter was confirmed in 1993 by a change in the name of the unit responsible for disabled people from Measures for the Disabled to Integration of the Disabled.

In the programme for the application of the Charter provision was made for action in all these areas. Although binding legislation was not considered appropriate, a proposal was issued in 1991 for a Council Directive 'on minimum requirements to improve the mobility and the safe transport to work of workers with reduced mobility' [7.6].

At least two-thirds of the disabled people in the Union are elderly. No Council directives have been issued specifically for them, but directives adopted under the aegis of equal treatment for men and women (Article 119 of the EEC Treaty) have been applied to pension rights. Directive 79/7/EEC on equal treatment in matters of social security [6.3], which was extended to occupational social security schemes and to self-employed workers in 1986 (see Chapter 6), aimed to tackle an important source of inequality by giving women greater access to social security entitlements in their own right. Women, or specifically married women, had, for example, been excluded from some state and occupational pension schemes. In 1982 a Council Recommendation set out the principles of Community policy with regard to retirement age [7.2]. The document was not concerned with gender differences, but a report from the Commission in 1992 on the application of the Recommendation raised the issue and noted that it was under examination in most member states which had different retirement ages for men and women [7.7]. Flexible arrangements for retirement were considered further in a Council Resolution in 1993 [7.8]. Broader themes relating to older people had also been placed on the agenda in the 1980s: a Resolution adopted by the European Parliament 'on the situation and problems of the aged in the European Community' [7.1] was followed in 1986 by Resolutions 'on services for the elderly' [7.3] and 'Community measures to improve the situation of old people in the Member States of the Community' [7.4].

The aim of the Council Recommendation 'on the convergence of social protection objectives and policies' [2.1], where disability was treated as 'incapacity for work', was to ensure minimum means of subsistence and social and economic integration through benefits enabling disabled people to maintain 'their standard of living in a reasonable manner in accordance with their participation in appropriate social security schemes' [2.1, p. 51]. The Recommendation provided a clear statement of the principles governing social protection for older people [2.1, p. 52]. Following on from points 24 and 25 of the Community Charter, it placed the onus on member states to guarantee a minimum level of subsistence to all older people in accordance with provisions at national and European level. They were also invited to contribute to the struggle against social exclusion of older people by giving workers the right to carry on working after minimum pensionable age, ensuring the maintenance of a replacement income throughout retirement, adapting entitlements to cover workers with incomplete careers and individualising rights, aligning provision between schemes and adapting them in response to demographic change. The aim was to prevent disparities in spending on care for older and disabled people which might impede workers' mobility between member states. The danger of welfare tourism, whereby nationals from one member state might be attracted by more generous social benefits elsewhere in the Union (see Chapter 2), is also relevant for older people, as is the concept of social dumping (see Chapter 1), whereby governments might find it financially attractive to subcontract caring to other member states with higher productive efficiency or lower labour costs (Knapp *et al.*, 1990, p. 68).

Action programmes for older and disabled people

Despite the absence of references in the Community's and Union's treaties to these disadvantaged groups and the relative lack of binding legislation, programmes for older and disabled people pre-date the Community Charter. The 1974 social action programme [1.8] had advocated measures to promote the vocational and social rehabilitation of handicapped people. Within the general context of improving quality of life for all European citizens, the Commission drew up and implemented a series of action programmes to ensure the economic and social integration of the 10 per cent or so of the population throughout the member states affected by a physical, sensorial or mental handicap. The first action programme specifically aimed at disabled people was adopted in 1981, providing support for national efforts through technical exchanges of experience in the areas of education, training, employment, social security and care systems, communications, mobility and housing. On 18 April 1988 the Council adopted a second Community action programme for the period 1988–91 under the title 'Handicapped People in the European Community Living Independently in an Open Society' (Helios), designed to promote social integration and an independent lifestyle for people with disabilities. Within the programme a computerised information system and network for disabled people in Europe was set up, under the name Handynet, containing information about technical aids and the addresses of specialist companies and organisations. A further programme was agreed on 8 October 1991 for 1992–96 with the focus on the integration of young people with disabilities into ordinary systems of education and the promotion of independent living for disabled people. It made particular reference to older people, with the overall aim of contributing to the economic and social cohesion of the Union.

Separate actions had meanwhile been adopted for older people. A programme of concerted Community actions for the elderly was established in 1991, following a Communication from the Commission 'on the elderly' [7.5]. The aim was to monitor and exchange information about demographic trends and their impact on social protection and health systems and to look at measures for improving the mobility of older people and for helping them to lead independent lives. Another more nebulous objective was to promote solidarity between generations. The positive contribution of older people to economic and social life was recognised, and the Commission undertook to ensure that their income would be protected.

Under the programme an Observatory on Ageing and Older People was set up with responsibility for providing the Commission with authoritative reports about the situation of older people in each country and the policies being pursued [7.13], and 1993 was proclaimed as the 'European Year of the Elderly and of Solidarity between

Generations', with the intention of heightening society's awareness of issues concerning older people [7.12]. The Observatory had a monitoring role similar to that of the European Observatory on National Family Policies. Its efforts were to be concentrated on four areas: 'living standards and way of life, employment and the labour market, health and social care, and the social integration of older people in both formal and informal settings' (Walker, 1993a, p. 9). The working definition of social policy for older people was couched in broad terms to include the impact of social and economic policies on older people, regardless of whether they originated from the public, private or voluntary sectors. In particular member states were to address 'the challenges resulting from present and future demographic developments and the consequences of an ageing population for all Community policies' (Walker, 1993a, p. 9).

The 1994 White Paper on European social policy [1.13] also focused on the theme of integration. The Commission proposed to draw up a code of good practice for employers and to introduce measures to eliminate discrimination against disabled people. Disabled and older people were identified as categories not to be excluded from the benefits of a more integrated Europe because they were capable of making an active contribution [1.13, p. 37].

THE IMPACT ON SOCIAL POLICY OF THE AGEING OF THE UNION'S POPULATION

All member states have had to face rising levels of public expenditure on pensions, health and social care for a growing proportion of the population, as better living and working conditions and improved social protection have contributed to greater life expectancy. A legal age of retirement has been established, generally at sixty or sixty-five, and pension schemes have progressively been extended to all categories of former workers and their spouses, further increasing the number of economically inactive older people. Despite longer compulsory schooling and the more widespread development of vocational training (see Chapter 3), the combination of falling birth-rates (see Chapter 5) and greater life expectancy and enforced retirement have shifted the balance in the dependency ratio away from young towards older people, thereby increasing the burden on the population of working age. In this section different conceptions of ageing and the differential impact of the ageing process are examined across member states.

Demographic ageing as a social problem

Between 1960 and 1990 the number of people aged over sixty in member states grew by almost 50 per cent [7.16, p. 1]. At the beginning of the 1990s, with nearly 70 million people aged sixty or over, older people represented about one in five of the population. Demographers had predicted that, from the mid-1980s, the mortality rate in member states would decline more slowly, and that, in the absence of any new waves of immigration or an unexpected rise in the birth-rate, the population in member states would cease to grow. By the year 2000 older people were therefore expected to make up more than 20 per cent of the population, rising to 25 per cent by the year 2020 (Walker, 1993a, p. 12). The consequences of demographic ageing, defined as an increase in the proportion of older people in the population, taken to mean over retirement age, have become a policy issue for the Union for a number of economic and social reasons.

Whereas high birth-rates, low life expectancy and the absence of a statutory retirement age mean that many Third World countries have large proportions of young dependants and relatively few older inactive people to support, the working population in advanced industrial societies has to meet the needs of growing numbers of older inactive people who are major consumers of social services. In this sense, all member states in the Union can be said to be suffering from the problems associated with an ageing population. Since young people are also big consumers of services, such as education, health and family benefits, any fall in the birth-rate does produce some savings in the short and medium term. In the longer term, however, the economic and social costs of an ageing population are thought to outweigh any advantages that may have accrued initially [7.9, p. 18]. The burden of supporting these two dependent population groups also falls differently: while families meet a large share of the costs of raising children, those associated with caring for older people are mainly borne by society. By the time the burden of caring for older people after the year 2000 becomes most acute, it is estimated that any savings from raising a smaller number of young people will have been expended.

Some observers (for example Bourdelais, 1993) argue that concern about the ageing of the population may, in some respects, be misguided. Statistics measuring demographic ageing in terms of the increase in the proportion of older people in the population generally assume that old age begins at sixty. They do not take account of the biological phenomenon of individual ageing. The biological or physical ageing of individuals now occurs at a much older age than it did even half a century ago: being sixty in the 1990s is very different from what it was in the 1920s or 1930s. Age when measured solely by calendar years can be misleading as an indicator of social and physical needs. The age at which older people are most likely to be suffering from disability and frailty has been delayed. At the age of sixty, men in member states can expect to live another seventeen to nineteen years and women another twenty-one to twenty-four years [7.16, table 2]. While medical advances have undoubtedly made it possible to prolong the lives of older people with disabilities, a large proportion of the population reaching the age of sixty can expect to enjoy many more years of good health.

Because of the differential impact of armed conflict and the greater incidence amongst men of health risks associated with smoking, alcohol, road accidents and industrial hazards, women are over-represented amongst older people in all member states, and they outnumber men increasingly as they get older. For the whole of the Union between the ages of sixty and sixty-nine women represent 50 to 55 per cent of survivors; after the age of eighty-five they account for almost 70 per cent of their age group [7.16, diagram 6].

The lowering of retirement age and greater longevity have created different categories of older people: the younger elderly or third age, from fifty to seventy-four, and what is sometimes referred to as the fourth age for those aged over seventy-five. The younger elderly are more likely to be in good health and able to enjoy a relatively generous pension, particularly if they contributed during their working lives to an occupational scheme guaranteeing them a high proportion of former earnings. Elderly people of the fourth age are more likely to be women contending with failing health and living alone in poor quality housing on a low income derived from a minimum state pension. An estimated quarter to one-third of those aged seventy or above have health problems requiring some assistance on an everyday basis. The proportion of severely disabled people aged over sixty-five is below 10 per cent and rises to about 30 per cent for those aged eighty or above (Alber, 1993, p. 101).

National differences in demographic ageing and retirement age

The ageing process has not taken place at the same rate or to the same extent throughout the Union [7.16, table 2]. Countries, like Germany, which began reducing their birth-rates at an early stage (see Figure 5.1), while life expectancy was increasing rapidly due to high standards of living and of health care, were amongst the first to have to grapple with the problems of a relatively large proportion of elderly dependants. Countries where the postwar baby boom continued into the mid to late 1960s, and which have maintained a higher than average, albeit declining, birth-rate, for example France and especially Ireland, will not feel the full impact of the ageing of their populations until after the year 2000. In the early 1990s Belgium, the United Kingdom, Italy, the Federal Republic of Germany and Denmark had the largest proportions of their populations aged over sixty, whereas Ireland, the Netherlands, Portugal and Spain had the 'youngest' populations [7.16, table 1]. France, Germany, Denmark and the United Kingdom had the largest proportion of people over the age of eighty. Because of national differences in life expectancy between the sexes, women constitute a particularly large proportion of people over the age of eighty in Belgium, France, Germany and the United Kingdom, whereas the gender balance is more even in Greece [7.15, table 1.26].

Differences in demographic ageing are not closely reflected in retirement age across member states. In the early 1990s the highest age of retirement, with sixty-seven for both sexes, was in Denmark, which did not have the greatest life expectancy either for men or women. In Belgium, where the proportion of the population aged over sixty years was amongst the highest in the Union, retirement age was flexible, with the possibility of leaving employment between the ages of sixty and sixty-five. In Germany, where the proportion of the population aged over eighty was the largest in the Union, legal retirement age was sixty-five in principle. Portugal equalised retirement age at sixty-five for men and women in 1994. The lowest retirement ages in the Union were in France, which had a particularly high life expectancy rate for women, and Italy, where life expectancy was above average: retirement age was at sixty for both men and women in France and for men in Italy and at fifty-five for Italian women. Despite greater life expectancy for women, different retirement ages also applied to men and women in Greece and the United Kingdom [7.14, table VII].

In the early 1980s the proportion of the workforce nearing retirement was still relatively small because the postwar baby boom generations had not yet reached the appropriate age. With the approach of the twenty-first century, countries where workers are entitled to begin drawing their pensions at a relatively low age, or where the population has been ageing most rapidly, in the demographic sense, and where the effects of the recession have eaten into reserves, are facing the problem of how to fund a rapidly growing number of pensions which will be drawn for much longer periods. By the late 1980s spending on old age was the largest item of public expenditure on social protection in nearly all member states: only Portugal, Germany and Ireland spent more on health [7.11, table 2]. In Greece and Italy old age accounted for 50 per cent or more of total spending on social benefits. Over the 1980s it had increased everywhere except Germany and Ireland. Spending on invalidity and disability was considerably lower in all member states, except the Netherlands where it amounted to more than two-thirds of the level for old age.

Since the legal age of retirement does not, in most cases, take account of the physical and mental state of the individual, except where early retirement is permitted on health grounds, the age chosen to mark the end of working life is determined more by political considerations than on the basis of fitness for work. Paradoxically, in most member states in the 1980s, statutory retirement was being set at an ever lower age on ideological grounds (as in France), and early retirement was being encouraged to release jobs, at a time when biologically, socially and economically it might have been more logical to consider postponing the end of working life.

In practice, however, statutory retirement age offers no more than a guide to the date at which individuals are normally eligible to begin drawing a state pension. Economic activity rates generally start to decline as much as ten years before legal retirement age in a process of phased withdrawal from the labour market, which again may not be a reflection of ability to work. By the early 1990s in Belgium, France, Germany, Luxembourg and the Netherlands, only one in three or four ageing workers was entitled to a retirement pension directly on leaving employment (Guillemard, 1993, p. 74). The period of economic activity has thus been reduced, creating a much larger number of individuals dependent on early and then full retirement and old age pensions for what could, in some cases, become almost as many years as they spent in employment.

FORMAL AND INFORMAL PROVISIONS FOR OLDER AND DISABLED PEOPLE

Despite the stated objective in the EEC Treaty of promoting harmonisation of national social protection systems, the Union has not used its legislative powers to eliminate some of the most marked discrepancies in formal national provision for older and disabled people. Since women's discontinuous and part-time working patterns put them at a disadvantage in systems where entitlements to pensions are based on employment record, and since they are more likely to survive to an older age than men, equal opportunities is an important issue in retirement as well as during working life. Although some convergence may have taken place over time as social security arrangements have been adapted to meet changing socio-economic conditions, major differences remain in this area of social policy. Just as several models of social protection could be identified within the Union (see Chapter 2 and Appendix 2), arrangements for old age, retirement and invalidity pensions, disability allowances and caring can be analysed with reference to different national approaches.

Income security

Continental countries which followed the corporatist or conservative model of welfare, as developed initially by Germany, based their pension schemes on the principle of income maintenance, financed by employers, employees and the state. Although Belgium, France and Italy originally established old age pension schemes using subsidised voluntary insurance, they later adopted the German occupational scheme making old age insurance compulsory. In this 'industrial achievement-performance' (Titmuss, 1974, p. 31) or 'income security' model (Ginn and Arber, 1992, p. 259), social needs are met in proportion to work performance. Basic disability allowances, invalidity and old age pensions are income related, ensuring that the workers with the highest incomes from earnings continue to receive higher benefits when they cease working. The system has the disadvantage that non-earners and many low earners are generally excluded and can only gain entitlements in their capacity as dependants (see Chapter 6).

Differences occur within the continental income maintenance model, since a full pension, which is paid as a proportion of earnings (60 per cent in Belgium, 50 per cent in France, for example), may be conditional on a minimum number of years of service. It may also be based on peak earnings, as in France, or derived from average earnings calculations as in Belgium, Germany and Luxembourg, or earnings over the final years of working life as in Italy (Walker, 1993b, p. 24). In addition to basic pensions France and Italy have developed compulsory occupational schemes, whereas they are voluntary in Belgium, Germany and Luxembourg. In countries that rely heavily on earnings-linked pension schemes, individuals who are prevented from working because of family responsibilities or disability may not qualify for full pensions in their own right nor be able to achieve the high level of income that will guarantee a substantial pension on retirement, unless they are granted special credits. This problem was recognised in the German scheme where women were conceptualised as wives and rewarded for having stayed at home to support their husbands and look after their children. Insurance credits can be claimed for periods away from the labour market in education, unemployment and sickness. They can also be gained for periods spent caring for young children, and arrangements for splitting pensions on divorce mean that women receive some compensation for loss of pension contributions (Ginn and Arber, 1992, pp. 263–6). A new compulsory state insurance, instituted in 1995 in Germany to cover the caring needs of older or disabled people, and credits for caring may further offset the financial and opportunity costs of temporary withdrawal from the labour market.

Basic security

Member states with socialist or social democratic welfare regimes initially provided a basic state pension for all citizens, regardless of their work record, funded from general taxation and with only a weak link to earnings. Denmark was one of the first member states to introduce an old age pension scheme in 1891. The Danish scheme was based on a very different principle from that in Germany: it was entirely funded from taxation with entitlements on the basis of citizenship. Means-tested services were made available according to need. The same principle was applied for invalidity pensions. Gradually over the postwar period the means-tested assistance principle was replaced by a flat-rate basic pension with a small contribution in addition to the minimum pension scheme. By the early 1990s a full flat-rate pension was paid from the age of sixty-seven to all citizens with forty years' residence. This was supplemented by a compulsory employment-related scheme for all employees working more than ten hours a week. Supplementary pensions were funded from employer and employee contributions with reduced rates for part-timers, but payments were again at a flat rate. Private occupational pensions were operated by about half of all employers and provided an additional income in retirement for about one in three pensioners. Since private schemes have been extended to most workers, the proportion of beneficiaries will increase markedly in future years as those in employment reach retirement age. The basic security model has the advantage of enabling women to draw adequate pensions in their own right, and the disregard for employment record in the universal flat-rate pension has meant that women are not penalised as in earnings-related schemes.

The 'institutional-redistributive' (Titmuss, 1974), 'basic security' (Ginn and Arber, 1992) or 'social democratic' (Esping-Andersen, 1990) model of welfare was initially followed by Britain. In his plan for pensions William Beveridge opted for a basic state contributory scheme which maintained flat-rate benefits on the grounds that the state should not be involved in income maintenance. This principle is still applied for invalidity pensions in the United Kingdom and Ireland. Subsequently, the British system moved towards the residual state welfare model described below. The Netherlands also followed the basic security model initially by instituting a first tier pension scheme based on citizenship, but they later introduced extensive private occupational pension schemes, which usually excluded part-time and low paid workers and therefore adversely affected women's pensions in a context where female part-time rates have been particularly high. In the Netherlands invalidity pensions were calculated on the basis of wages as in the income security model, but relatively generous benefits were paid to disabled and older people whose earnings fell below the general insurance level.

Residual state welfare

The British state pension scheme has tended towards the objective of alleviating poverty and thus corresponds to what has been described as 'residual welfare' (Titmuss, 1974) or a 'liberal' (Esping-Andersen, 1990) welfare regime. In such a system state provision is minimal, while the market provides for private earnings-related pensions. Compared with other member states, in the early 1990s basic state pensions in the United Kingdom were very low. Non-earners had no guaranteed income and depended on an earner or a means-tested safety net. The United Kingdom was the only member state to have created a statutory supplementary scheme: the State Earnings Related Pension Scheme (SERPS) was introduced in the 1975 Social Security Pensions Act for workers who did not contribute to occupational schemes. SERPS made very little difference to the pensions received by low income earners. For those in better paid jobs occupational and private insurance pension schemes offer more generous earnings-related benefits, and Britain is credited with having the most extensive private occupational pensions scheme in the Union.

Women have been at a particular disadvantage under the conditions of the pension schemes operated in the United Kingdom (Ginn and Arber, 1992, pp. 261–3). As shown in the previous chapter, women in the United Kingdom are more likely than in other member states to take a break in employment when they have young children and to return to work part time when their children reach school age. They more often have short part-time working hours and fall below the threshold for national insurance contributions. These disruptions to their employment histories put women at a particular disadvantage in a situation where eligibility for benefits is dependent on employment record and level of earnings. As in other member states, British women are much less likely to be in employment where they can contribute to occupational pensions. The British social security system, as conceived by Beveridge, treated women as dependants on the understanding that male earnings should be sufficient to support a wife and children (see Chapter 6). Until 1975 women could opt out of paying contributions. Yet, in the early 1990s, to be eligible for a full pension thirty-nine years of contributions were required, or twenty years for women eligible to receive home responsibility protection credits for years when they were in receipt of an attendance allowance to care for a sick or elderly person.

Ireland also developed a dual pension system, combining an old age contributory insurance pension and a flat-rate means-tested assistance pension. Within the Union, in the early 1990s, Ireland was devoting the smallest proportion of its social expenditure to old age pensions; yet, with the Netherlands, it was the member state where social assistance payments for old age reached the highest level in relation to GDP [7.11, tables 2 and 17).

Rudimentary or formative welfare

The member states which joined the Community in the 1980s – Greece, Portugal and Spain – had a much less developed system of social protection (see Appendix 2). Although their social security systems largely followed the continental model, by the early 1990s their pension schemes were still a long way from providing the level of benefits enjoyed by most older people in the northern member states, mainly because many people reaching retirement age had incomplete contributions records. For those not qualifying for a full pension the level of benefits in relation to wages could be more generous than in the countries of northern Europe since the calculation was derived from earnings in the final years of working life in Greece and Spain and peak earnings in Portugal.

Women in particular may suffer from having shorter periods of contribution to pension schemes. In Portugal they were twice as likely to be in the non-contributory pension scheme rather than the general contributory scheme and were therefore entitled to lower benefits. In Greece, however, women were entitled to retire after only fifteen years of work if they had young children. Despite this provision and the lower retirement age for women in Greece and Portugal, larger proportions of the total female working population were likely to continue working after the age of sixty than in other member states [7.16, diagram 10].

Convergence of national pension systems

Although they differed in their ideological and cultural origins and administrative structures, the pension systems in member states, like other areas of social protection, have developed a number of common characteristics. The exchange of information through the work of the European Observatory and its contribution to the development of policies on older people are expected to 'contribute to some convergence in national policies' (Walker, 1993a, p. 8). By the early 1990s most countries organised pensions in two tiers: a basic statutory scheme and a supplementary or complementary scheme (Walker, 1993b, p. 24). While earnings-related pension schemes have progressively been established throughout the Union, in response to economic and demographic factors, some form of tax-funded means-tested minimum old age and disability assistance scheme has been introduced in countries which had originally focused on occupational schemes as a way of covering older and disabled people not eligible for pensions on the basis of their employment record.

Despite some convergence towards pluralistic systems, the different starting points continue to distinguish the two main models. The extent to which different sectors of the population are covered by the various schemes depends on the ways in which policy has been shaped to take account of demographic change, socio-economic pressures and ideological factors. Statutory pension schemes, like unemployment benefits, have developed according to two distinct principles: insurance and welfare. They are either flat rate and designed to ensure a basic income, as in Denmark, Ireland, the Netherlands and the United Kingdom, or earnings related and offering a form of income maintenance, as in the other member states.

A factor which may, nonetheless, be encouraging convergence is the common concern amongst member states to contain the cost of pensions in the face of pressures from population ageing in combination with the economic recession. A number of measures have been suggested as possible solutions to the problem: increasing taxation, reducing the level of benefits, raising the actual average age of retirement, increasing labour force participation rates for women, reducing unemployment and encouraging immigration (Gillion, 1991, p. 111). As shown in other chapters, women's employment rates have generally been increasing, and the reduction of unemployment became a priority for most governments in the 1980s. Increased immigration, a reduction in benefit levels or higher taxation are politically sensitive issues, although pension schemes which rely heavily on funding from taxation, as in Denmark, are moving inexorably towards greater privatisation. Proposals to alter retirement age are equally contentious in so far as labour market exit corresponds less and less to the age of eligibility for pensions.

Already in the 1980s action was being taken to contain the cost of public pensions: by pegging uprating to prices and scaling down the supplementary pension in the United Kingdom; by changing the indexing of the general compulsory insurance scheme from gross to net earnings in Germany; or by suspending automatic indexing of pensions in the Netherlands. In 1987 Denmark abolished survivors' benefits and derived social security rights, and Greece, Luxembourg, Portugal and Spain lengthened the minimum qualifying period for pension entitlement. By the mid-1990s Italy and the United Kingdom were gradually equalising pension age at sixty-five for both men and women. France was exploring options such as extending the contribution period and basing pensions on the best twenty-five rather than the best ten years.

The impact of the solutions tried is difficult to evaluate due to differences in socio-economic and political circumstances, but they do indicate that member states are all aware of the need to prepare for the twenty-first century by ensuring that living standards for older people can be maintained at a satisfactory level, while also observing budgetary constraints.

Informal versus formal caring

A closely related issue which national governments have had to tackle is how to meet the demand for health and social care in a situation where most countries were pursuing policies focusing on community care at a time when informal care structures were being strained by changes in family and employment structures. The question of how to provide good quality care in member states arose not so much as a result of an increase in the number of frail and disabled people but rather because traditional carers had become less numerous and less available than in the past, what Jens Alber (1993, p. 104) has called the 'shrinkage of the female care taker potential', while governments were looking for ways of reducing the cost of formal caring.

Although the full impact of the reduction of family size will not be felt until after the turn of the century, by the early 1990s the general increase in female economic activity rates was already making heavy demands on women at times in their lives when they had ageing relatives requiring care. Yet, they were still expected to be the main providers of care (Ungerson, 1990; Jani-Le Bris, 1993, p. 53). Because women in the younger generations were more likely to be economically active outside the home, and in the absence of other close relatives able and willing to take on the responsibility for caring, most member states were being faced with the issues of how to ensure the most effective level of care at the lowest cost to the state, and how, if appropriate, to provide incentives for informal carers.

While provision of care services in Denmark was still recognised as a responsibility of the state, some countries continued to place a clear obligation on relatives to care for older people, and formal service provision was made only in cases where no relatives were available to meet these obligations. In France, Germany and Italy relatives have been obliged to contribute to domiciliary and residential services on a means-tested basis. In southern European countries and in Ireland family care-givers performed a duty expected of them by society, and little attention was paid to their needs. Residential care remained important in Ireland, partly because of low marriage rates. Since the 1980s most member states have been moving towards a policy of community care and de-institutionalisation. The United Kingdom, where the community care model was probably most developed, has been cited as the leader in the Union for its supportive policies towards carers (Jani-Le Bris, 1993, p. 126).

All member states have provided home care services, financial allowances in the form of social security payments and/or employment-related safeguards, but they have made different choices about how to organise and fund care (Glendinning and McLaughlin, 1993; Lesemann and Martin, 1993, p. 200). France, Germany and the Netherlands developed a welfare mix, involving a shift away from social welfare towards systems of care insurance, a practice which is likely to be extended [1.13, p. 36]. Some national governments have offered financial support for care both to informal carers and to disabled and older people (France, Ireland and the United Kingdom), while others only provided financial support to the older or disabled person (Germany and Italy). France, Germany and Italy made tax allowances in recognition of co-resident care and/or the cost of purchasing specific services, while the trend in the United Kingdom was to withdraw tax allowances towards the cost of care and dependency. Means testing of rights to financial support was stringent in Ireland and the United Kingdom and more liberal in France and Italy. Comparative studies suggested that payments to care-givers may have helped to sustain the care-giving relationship for longer than would otherwise have been the case but that they did not lower the rates of residential care (Glendinning and McLaughlin, 1993, p. 145).

Although policy and regulations are generally determined centrally, most countries have issued payments and provided services at regional or local level. Schemes that are managed locally, often by voluntary organisations, may result in very different levels of provision from one area to another, thereby accentuating the disparities both within and between member states.

THE IMPACT OF POLICY ON THE LIVING STANDARDS OF OLDER AND DISABLED PEOPLE

The centrality in European policy for older people of the problems arising from demographic ageing has led to proposals for two types of solution. The first was an attempt to tackle the problem of ageing by redressing the demographic balance, for example through incentives to encourage couples to raise more children and measures, such as parental leave and the provision of childcare, enabling women to reconcile their occupational and family obligations (see Chapters 5 and 6). The second type of solution involved an overhaul of social provision for older and disabled people, with a view to finding ways of reducing social security budgets while maintaining a high standard of care. Economic and demographic pressures may be resulting in convergence of policy objectives in member states but they are also producing conflicts of interests: on the one hand governments are forced to look for ways of containing costs; on the other they are concerned to improve the living standards of older and disabled people. At the time when the Single European Market (SEM) was completed at the end of 1992, more countries were extending rather than reducing coverage, but residential care was not expanding at a rate sufficient to meet demand.

Inequalities are more pronounced in some countries than in others due to differences in the nature and level of social provision. In the absence of detailed and up-to-date information and due to the complexity of pension systems, it is difficult to measure and compare the living standards of older and disabled people across member states, and even more so to draw conclusions about the impact of social policies. National reports to the Community's Observatory on Ageing and Older People suggest that policy may have contributed to the overall rise in the living standards of older people in recent years. The improvement has not, however, benefited all older people equally. In some countries policies have been targeted at the most underprivileged groups, often with noteworthy results. Increases in the pensions supplement in Denmark were targeted at pensioners on the lowest incomes. The Spanish Government also focused on the level of minimum pensions as a means of raising living standards. In Italy due to improved pension provisions since the 1950s, the growth of living standards of older people has been greater than for the population as a whole. The indexing of retirement pensions to wages or prices in France in the 1980s resulted in a marked decrease in the number of older people relying on the minimum pension. Elsewhere the improvement of living standards cannot be directly attributed to social policy for older people but may be 'a "passive" by-product of increases in the scope and coverage of occupational pensions as a result of collective bargaining and pension scheme maturation' (Walker, 1993b, pp. 28–9).

Where the advantages of occupational schemes are not equally distributed amongst different sectors of the population, these 'automatic' improvements may only serve to intensify inequalities amongst older people by widening the differential between those who have recently retired and who are eligible for generous earnings-related pensions and older people of the fourth age who are dependent on a minimum state pension. Attempts to maintain the income levels of former workers have had a different impact from one country to another with regard to age groups. In the early 1990s generational inequalities seemed to be relatively narrow and were becoming narrower still in France and Ireland, while in Belgium, Greece, the Netherlands, Portugal, Spain and the United Kingdom, the generation gap had widened (Walker, 1993b, p. 43).

When measures of poverty are used to assess the impact of pensions on the incomes of older people, four countries – Denmark, Luxembourg, Ireland and Germany – are described as having relatively low poverty rates amongst older people (less than 10 per cent of older people living on or below social assistance). Countries with medium rates (10–30 per cent below social assistance level) of poverty include Belgium, France, the Netherlands and the United Kingdom. The countries of southern Europe all show relatively high rates of poverty amongst older people, although, in the case of Italy, the north has a level equivalent to member states in the middle band, whereas the south has a much higher level (Walker, 1993b, pp. 33–7). The Union's objective of raising living standards for all older people was therefore a long way from being achieved in the early 1990s. Comparisons between member states showed consistently that, for the reasons discussed in this chapter, poverty in old age was increasingly feminised.

The issues raised at European level reflect the problems being encountered by all member states and therefore provide the opportunity to share experiences, learn from one another and look for common solutions. If the objectives of the SEM are to be achieved, some convergence, or at least mutual recognition, of pension schemes and services for older and disabled people is considered necessary to ensure freedom of movement, social and economic cohesion and to prevent unfair competition, social dumping and welfare tourism, but in the longer term the stability of the Union may depend on its success in establishing a balance between its working population and those dependent on the labour force.

Changes in the age structure of the population in member states, better quality health care, lower ages for retirement and higher pensions have led to a reconceptualisation of old age, the formulation of new questions for policy makers and the rethinking of previous assumptions, for example about traditional career patterns, retirement age and the role of families [1.13, p. 39]. Old age and disability have thus been firmly placed on the European policy agenda and are likely to remain there as the dependency ratio shifts more heavily towards older people.

Box 7   Union documents relating to policy for older and disabled people

SECONDARY LEGISLATION

7.1   Council Resolution of 18 February 1982 on the situation and problems of the aged in the European Community (*OJ* C 66/71 15.3.82).

7.2   Council Recommendation of 10 December 1982 on the principles of a Community policy with regard to retirement age (82/857/EEC) (*OJ* L 357/27 18.12.82).

7.3   Resolution of the European Parliament of 10 March 1986 on services for the elderly (*OJ* C 88/17 14.4.86).

7.4   Resolution of the European Parliament of 14 May 1986 on Community measures to improve the situation of old people in the Member States of the Community (*OJ* C 148/61 16.6.86).

7.5   Communication from the Commission on the elderly (COM(90) 80 final, 24 April 1990).

7.6   Commission proposal for a Council Directive on minimum requirements to improve the mobility and the safe transport to work of workers with reduced mobility (COM(90) 588 final, 11 February 1991) (*OJ* C 68/7 16.3.91), amended (COM(91) 539 final) (*OJ* C 15/18 21.1.92).

7.7   Report from the Commission of 18 December 1992 on the application of Council Recommendation of 10 December 1982 on the principle of a Community policy with regard to retirement age (82/857/EEC) (SEC(92) 2288 final).

7.8   Council Resolution of 30 June 1993 on flexible retirement arrangements (*OJ* C 188/1 10.7.93).

OFFICIAL PUBLICATIONS OF THE COMMISSION OF THE EUROPEAN COMMUNITIES (CEC) AND EUROSTAT

7.9   CEC/Economic and Social Consultative Assembly (1986) *Demographic Situation in the Community*, Information Report, CES 602/84 fin.

7.10 CEC (1993) *Internal Market,* vol. 6, *Community Social Policy, Current Status 1 January 1993.*

7.11 CEC (1993) *Social Protection in Europe.*

7.12 CEC (1993) '1993: European Year of Older People and Solidarity between Generations', *Social Europe 1/93.*

7.13 CEC/European Observatory on Ageing and Older People (annual) *Older People in Europe: Social and Economic Policies* (co-ordinated by A. Walker, J. Alber and A-M. Guillemard).

7.14 CEC/Mutual Information System on Social Protection in the Community (1993) *Social Protection in the Member States of the Community: Situation on July 1st 1993 and Evolution.*

7.15 Eurostat (1991) *A Social Portrait of Europe.*

7.16 Eurostat (1993) 'Older People in the European Community: Population and Employment', *Rapid Reports. Population and Social Conditions,* no. 1.

8 Social Exclusion

The emphasis on employment-related rights in the Community's and Union's Treaties and Charter meant that attention was focused on the need to protect workers against major sources of hardship due to incapacity for work as a result of ill health, disability, unemployment, old age and other contingencies. At the time when the Treaty establishing the European Economic Community (EEC) was signed in 1957 [1.2], member states were experiencing a period of economic expansion. Following the German 'continental' model, their welfare regimes were based on the premise that earnings from paid employment would be sufficiently high to enable workers and their families to enjoy a decent standard of living (see Chapter 2). Some provision was made for those who temporarily 'fell through the net' by progressively instituting non-contributory social assistance schemes, but in the postwar boom years the groups considered to be at risk were relatively limited, and unemployment was not seen as a problem area. When the EEC Treaty was signed, many older people, particularly the self-employed, had not accrued the right to generous earnings-related pensions, and not all occupations were subject to a legal age of retirement. In addition, life expectancy was shorter, and the proportion of elderly dependants was therefore relatively small (see Chapter 7). Immigration was sustaining the workforce (see Chapter 9), and the postwar baby boom had resulted in the rapid growth of the younger population who had good prospects for finding employment in a buoyant economy. These attenuating factors did not mean that poverty was non-existent, but rather that it was not a political priority for the EEC founder members.

The centrality of employment, freedom of movement and workers' rights in the Treaty had, to some extent, diverted attention away from the social implications of economic and political union for population groups that were, for one reason or another, excluded from the workforce. It was, however, recognised that industrial restructuring, relocation and centralisation, which were vital components in the Single European Market (SEM), might paradoxically provoke economic dislocation, leading to polarisation, as the prosperous core areas benefited most and the less prosperous peripheral areas degenerated further. Institutional intervention, according to this logic, was neces-

146

sary to offset the effects of market forces and curb the growth of 'new poverty' resulting from changing social and economic structures and rising unemployment. New poverty was recognised as being qualitatively different from the poverty experienced hitherto, since it affected people from a much wider range of socio-economic groups. Whereas in the 1970s most of those in poverty were older people, by the 1990s a more pressing problem was the growing number of people of working age, particularly the long-term unemployed, falling into poverty. Another group found increasingly amongst the poor were single-parent households. Lone parenthood was frequently associated with low incomes and dependence on social assistance for long periods of time. Families with children were over-represented amongst poor people, but poverty was no longer essentially related to large family size. The threat to economic and social cohesion due to the growing proportion of younger people living in poverty also served as a powerful incentive for continuing action at European level.

In this chapter policy to combat social exclusion is examined firstly with reference to the legislative framework and action programmes developed by the Union. Attention is then given to the problems of defining, measuring and comparing poverty in member states and to an assessment of its extent and regional characteristics. Variations in national systems of social assistance and in approaches to policy making for socially excluded people are explored as a means of gaining a better understanding of the ways in which poverty and social exclusion have been conceptualised and dealt with by member states.

THE DEVELOPMENT OF EUROPEAN POLICY ON POVERTY AND SOCIAL EXCLUSION

Concern with poverty and social exclusion at European level developed in parallel with interest in social affairs. Although the legislative route has not been used as a policy instrument to alleviate poverty, for example by formulating directives aimed at imposing minimum income levels, the Structural Funds have provided support for labour market policies in priority regions. Community action programmes to combat social exclusion have been implemented almost continuously since the mid-1970s. In this section the development of European policy for combating social exclusion is tracked through the various overlapping and interconnected measures which have been introduced in an effort to resolve what has been recognised as a common social problem.

The European Structural Funds

The EEC Treaty laid stress on the interests of workers not only in provisions made for employment-related social protection, as illustrated in previous chapters, but also under the terms of the European Social Fund. The ESF was not concerned with socially and economically excluded categories such as older people, lone-parent families or groups living in underprivileged areas. Rather, Article 3 (i) of the Treaty established the fund 'in order to improve employment opportunities for workers and to contribute to the raising of their standard of living'. Article 123 in the section on social policy confirmed that the ESF was intended solely for the working population, stating that: 'it shall have the task of rendering the employment of workers easier and of increasing their geographical and occupational mobility within the Community'. Member states were to be eligible to receive 50 per cent of the expenditures incurred in providing vocational training and resettlement allowances as a means of ensuring productive re-employment of workers following the conversion of an undertaking. Funds were committed to measures aimed at specific population groups as a safety net for designated regions and categories of the population, while also providing opportunities for developing poor areas.

By seeking to relieve the problems of uneven regional development through the ESF, the Community recognised that poverty was structural and could be caused by economic forces over which individuals and local economies have little or no control. The financial support provided was intended to tackle underlying structural problems and was therefore a necessary component for economic integration.

Following the signing of the Single European Act (SEA) in 1986 [1.5], it was agreed that the Structural Funds (European Agricultural Guidance and Guarantee Fund, European Social Fund, European Regional Development Fund) should be doubled in size, that priority areas should be identified and that more rigorous regional development plans should be drawn up. Priority areas were selected for targeted funding: in the case of Greece, Ireland and Portugal, the entire country was designated as an Objective 1, or priority, 'region'; ten regions in Spain were included under Objective 1 and eight in Italy; Northern Ireland fell within this category for the United Kingdom and Corsica in the case of France. Objective 1 regions were eligible to receive a larger proportion of the total cost and of public expenditure on initiatives, with the aim of redistributing resources in relation to need. The long-term unemployed were targeted through training and retraining schemes, the creation of stable jobs and self-employed activities. Long-term unemployed women, migrants and disabled people in general were singled out for special schemes, as were these same categories amongst the young (see Chapters 3 and 6). Provision was made for implementing measures at national, local, regional or sectoral level, with the aim of achieving the best match between the difficulties to be overcome and the requirements of the labour market [8.7].

Despite increases in the size of the budget, by the mid-1990s the Structural Funds were expected to represent not much more than 0.3 per cent of the Union's GDP (Casey, 1993, p.174), a level which was unlikely to make a significant impact on the least favoured regions or prevent the development of what had come to be known as a two-speed Europe. As a proportion of total expenditure from the Structural Funds, the countries with the lowest *per capita* incomes – Greece, Portugal, Ireland, Spain and southern Italy – were the main beneficiaries in the period 1987–92, but the share received by the United Kingdom was also relatively high (Buzelay, 1992, table 3.1, p. 73). The White Paper on European social policy announced that the Structural Funds would have a budget of 141 billion ECU for the period 1994–99, with 40 billion ECU going to the ESF. The Commission was also negotiating Community Support Frameworks (CSF) with member states, setting out strategies for using the Structural Funds through to the end of the century [1.13, pp. 18–20].

Social exclusion in the Single European Market, Community Charter and Maastricht Treaty

The emphasis the SEA placed on economic and social cohesion as a major policy objective focused attention on 'reducing disparities between the levels of development of the various regions and the backwardness of the least favoured regions, including rural areas' (Article 130a). Analysts of the possible effects of the completion of the internal market had concluded that its long-term benefits were likely to be unevenly distributed and that income disparities might even be increased (O'Donnell, 1992, p. 25). Regions with industries that were able to make economies of scale and had the capacity to innovate would stand to draw the greatest benefits from freedom of movement of goods, services and workers.

No direct reference was made to social exclusion or poverty in the Community Charter of the Fundamental Social Rights of Workers

[1.7] (and the Agreement on Social Policy annexed to the Maastricht Treaty [1.6]. A paragraph under point 10 on social protection in the Community Charter made explicit reference to the duty of member states to provide sufficient resources and social assistance to individuals 'who have been unable either to enter or re-enter the labour market and have no means of subsistence', but national governments were again left to make their own arrangements. In not dissimilar terms the section on employment and remuneration in the Charter recommended an equitable wage as the means of maintaining 'a decent standard of living'. In cases where wages might be 'withheld, seized or transferred', it stated that provision should be made so that the worker would 'continue to enjoy the necessary means of subsistence for himself and his family' (point 5).

As in the case of older and disabled people, the least binding forms of secondary legislation have been used to implement measures concerned with poverty (see Appendix 1). One of the most explicit statements of European policy in relation to poverty is to be found in the Council Recommendation, issued four months after the signing of the Maastricht Treaty, 'on common criteria concerning sufficient resources and social assistance in social protection systems' [8.4], which stated that the fight against social exclusion was to be regarded as 'an important part of the social dimension of the internal market' and conducted 'in a spirit of solidarity'. The Recommendation recognised 'the basic right of a person to sufficient resources and social assistance to live in a manner compatible with human dignity' [8.4, section 1A]. The implementation of such a right was to be organised by 'fixing the amount of resources considered sufficient to cover essential needs with regard to respect for human dignity, taking account of living standards and price levels in the Member State concerned, for different types and sizes of household' [8.4, section C 1a]. Although no figure was suggested for the level at which to set such a guaranteed income, the proposal stressed the importance of taking account of the availability of financial resources, national priorities and disparities between national social protection systems. The right to sufficient resources was to be individual and based on need but subject to active availability for work or vocational training or to economic and social integration measures, where appropriate.

In setting the parameters for European social policy through to the year 2000 in its 1994 White Paper, the Commission stressed the need to ensure that the most vulnerable groups in society were not excluded from the benefits of the economic strength associated with a more integrated Europe. The social cohesion of the Union was described as being dependent upon concerted action, designed to stimulate 'a European-wide solidarity' [1.13, p. 37]. Competence to act at European level was founded on Article 2 point 2 of the Agreement on Social Policy annexed to the Maastricht Treaty, which conferred a supportive and complementary role, justifying proposals to take forward the 1992 Recommendation on sufficient resources.

Poverty programmes

By 1974 the impact of the energy crisis on employment and living standards was being felt, and the baby boom had come to an end. The new members that had joined the Community in 1972 – Denmark, Ireland and the United Kingdom – brought with them different welfare traditions which based social protection on universal citizenship rights rather than earnings from employment (see Chapter 2). The nine member states, however, shared a conviction that concerted action was needed to improve national provision for particularly disadvantaged groups (Shanks, 1977, p. 63). Following the Council Resolution of 1974 on a social action programme (see Chapter 1), a proposal for a two-year experimental anti-poverty programme received wide support.

The first poverty programme had to be approved by a unanimous vote of the Council under Article 235 of the EEC Treaty since no provision had been made for this form of action. After a difficult process of negotiation in the context of the oil crisis, with the Germans in particular pressing for retrenchment, Council Decision 75/458/EEC eventually established the programme for the period 1975–80 [8.1]. The Commission undertook to launch twenty-one pilot or action projects, with the aim of achieving a 'balanced range of approaches' across all the Community regions. Each project contained a strong research component, including basic research into the 'dimensions and nature of poverty' (James, 1982, p. 6). Two cross-national studies were also funded for a year on attitudes towards poverty and on research methods for national sample surveys. The second phase of the programme was approved by Council Decision 77/779/EEC in 1977 [8.1] for a three-year period, extending and adding to the pilot projects. The Commission asked for national reports to be drawn up by independent research teams in each member state on the nature, cause and extent of poverty and for an assessment of the policies implemented to combat poverty.

The second European poverty programme was authorised in 1984 for the period 1985–88, with an initial budget of 25 million ECU. Subsequently in 1986, a further 4 million ECU were added to extend the programme to Portugal and Spain when they joined the Community [8.6, p.10]. The Commission was authorised to undertake activities to promote or provide financial assistance for various types of action-research measures, for the collection, dissemination and exchange of knowledge and comparable data on poverty on a regular basis, the co-ordination and assessment of anti-poverty measures and the transfer of innovative approaches between member states. Action was justified by reference to Article 2 of the EEC Treaty which required 'balanced expansion' and 'an increase in stability'. Sixty-five action research projects were selected for support, covering single-parent families, the problems of the long-term unemployed, youth unemployment, second generation migrants, refugees and returning migrants, the homeless and older people. Integrated urban action programmes were funded with the aim of providing a comprehensive approach to the needs of targeted groups of deprived individuals by tackling the underlying problems of the social environment creating the circumstances which define poverty.

In terms of the number of projects selected, Spain and the United Kingdom were by far the greatest beneficiaries from the scheme, raising questions about the extent to which European support was being directed to the regions most in need. The criteria used for evaluating the projects – innovation, participation and cost effectiveness – may well have favoured member states which were already trying out innovatory schemes, where community structures were well developed and where cost effectiveness of services was routinely monitored.

By the end of the 1980s the growing awareness of the multifaceted, relative and changing nature of poverty had made it necessary to adopt a new approach. The number of people experiencing poverty had increased, and new forms of poverty were appearing as a result of changes in economic and social structures. Within the framework of the action programme implementing the provisions of the Community Charter, Council Decision 89/457/EEC established 'a medium-term Community action programme concerning the economic and social integration of the economically and socially less privileged groups in society' [8.2]. An additional reason for the decision was the need to take preventive measures against any short-term negative effects of the completion of the internal market by the end of 1992 for the social groups most at risk. The 'Poverty 3' programme for the period 1989–94 was to provide corrective measures for groups already marginalised, with the purpose of ensuring greater economic and social cohesion, an important theme in the SEA and the Maastricht Treaty. The Commission decided to focus on three keywords: partnership, active participation and a multidimensional strategy. By partnership and participation it was referring to collaboration between government bodies, associations and the individuals concerned, since past experience had shown that integrated actions were most effective. The multidimensional strategy underlined the complexity of situations of social exclusion and the processes involved. An attempt was to be made to formulate policies which adopted a global approach to the problem of social exclusion. The funding devoted to the programme was 55 million ECU, which represented an increase over the amount allocated to previous programmes but remained a very small budget when compared, for example, with the average level of expenditure of social security departments in the wealthier member states.

In line with developments in other areas of social policy, the Commission sought to give its action against poverty a more formal structure. A Council Resolution of 29 September 1989 established an Observatory on National Policies to Combat Social Exclusion [8.3]. The Observatory was set up to promote policy analysis, to stimulate the exchange of information and experience and to report back annually to the Commission. Like the Observatories for family policies, older people and employment, its aim has been to develop a common understanding of the policy framework and to monitor and analyse trends in member states. In recognition of the importance of the voluntary sector's contribution in combating poverty, Directorate General V also initiated and funded a European Anti-Poverty Network of non-governmental organisations, which was set up in 1990 to coordinate efforts across member states and to act as a poverty lobby.

To ensure continuity of the poverty programmes, in 1993 the Commission presented a proposal for a new medium-term action programme to combat exclusion and promote solidarity for the period 1994–99 [8.5]. The new programme took account of the fact that social exclusion was continuing to increase and spread due to changes in economic, social and demographic structures. A total budget of 121 million ECU for five and a half years was proposed for the programme, double the amount for Poverty 3, confirming the Union's commitment to intensifying its effort in this area. Previous programmes had shown that sustained targeted action over several years could produce positive results. National policies against social exclusion had demonstrated that welfare systems needed modernising. The Commission called for greater co-operation between different agencies in the public and private sectors. While upholding its view that individual member states were responsible for combating social exclusion, the Commission presented its role as contributing to the development and transfer of methods and expertise, identifying good practice and setting up and maintaining networks for sharing experience and deepening understanding of the problem. Model actions were to be used at local, national or regional level, transnational networks of projects were to be developed, information was to be collected and comparative studies were to be carried out as a means of furthering the understanding of social exclusion and finding ways of controlling it.

Active labour market policies

As in the areas of education and training and equality of opportunity between men and women, action programmes have served as an important policy instrument in combating social exclusion. In addition to providing targeted resources through the Structural Funds to help regions undergoing economic restructuring, during the 1980s the Commission responded to the growing problem of long-term unemployment by launching a number of active labour market initiatives, including establishing an Employment Observatory, documentation systems on employment and a series of action programmes, supported by the ESF (see Chapters 3 and 9). The Observatory conducts annual surveys on employment trends, published as *Employment in Europe*. The Network of Employment Co-ordinators (Nec) produces research reports on different themes relating to unemployment. Reports are also published by the European System of Documentation on Employment (Sysdem) and the Mutual Information System on Employment Policies (Misep) on the measures adopted in member states.

The Commission's action programmes have targeted specific groups and issues: the Research Action and Evaluation programme (Ergo) was, for example, intended to raise awareness of the problems faced by the long-term unemployed and evaluate the actions taken; the Local Employment Development Action (Leda) was designed to promote local employment initiatives; the Support Programme for Employment Creation (Spec) aimed to provide technical and financial support for innovative regional or local employment creation projects.

The active approach to labour market policy was reinforced in the 1994 White Paper on European social policy where the Commission described three priority themes for the ESF: access to and quality of initial training and education through the implementation of the Youthstart scheme, designed to promote the labour market integration of young people, particularly those with no basic qualifications or training; increasing competitiveness and the prevention of unemployment through a systematic approach to training; the improvement of employment opportunities for the long-term unemployed [1.13, pp. 18–19]. Two new programmes were launched (Employment and Adapt), aimed specifically at disadvantaged groups such as the young unemployed, disabled people, the socially excluded and women, or those at risk due to industrial or technological change.

By the mid-1990s the Union had acquired considerable experience in generating research and action into the problems of poverty and social exclusion [8.11]. Funds had been earmarked to support its projects and formalised institutional structures were in place for implementing and monitoring them. The Commission's programmes had developed in parallel with and were complementary to the Structural Funds since they targeted categories of poor people by cutting across regional divisions. While these different forms of intervention do not constitute a coherent European policy, and social exclusion clearly remains an area where the Union is intent on observing the subsidiarity principle, they are evidence of both the persistence of the problem and the awareness in member states of the need for greater co-ordination of policies at national and European levels to achieve more concerted action in the search for longer term solutions.

DEFINING AND MEASURING POVERTY AND SOCIAL EXCLUSION

The poverty programmes developed since the early 1970s have become more comprehensive and ambitious, and the coverage of the Structural Funds has been extended as the problems to be tackled have changed, and new forms of social exclusion have emerged, particularly among the long-term unemployed. In spite of the accumulation of a vast body of information, the Union continues to be faced with the fundamental question of how to define and measure poverty so that data that are comparable both over time and across different member states can be collated and used to track the development of the problem and monitor progress in resolving it. In this section some of the materials assembled over the years are considered as a basis for comparing the situation in different member states.

Defining poverty, exclusion and marginalisation

The Commission's aim in asking member states to provide national reports on levels of poverty and policies to combat exclusion has been to monitor and compare the situation and develop its own action programmes. A definition was therefore needed which could be operationalised in different national contexts. The Commission chose initially to define poverty in terms of income. Any individual with a disposable income falling below a specified level could be considered to be living in poverty. In the first poverty programme the line was drawn at less than 50 per cent of the national average disposable *per capita* income in the relevant member state. Definitions of poverty as determined by an income poverty line are, however, problematic for both practical and ideological reasons. In practice, low income is a very crude measure of poverty, particularly from a comparative perspective: for example, services in kind such as social housing and health care, which are unevenly distributed across member states, may affect the level of expenditure in cash; and within and between countries, households vary considerably in their ability to manage their budget. Ideological factors are important because the level at which a poverty line is set can be interpreted as 'a highly political act', raising issues such as the level of social security benefits, definitions of low wages and minimum wage levels, eligibility for assistance with education or housing costs (Brown, 1986, p. 49).

Poverty is not only relative, it is also cumulative: people on low incomes generally also experience poor housing, educational facilities, transport and communications. Poverty can therefore be defined more broadly in terms of individuals and groups whose resources are so far below the average that they are excluded from the living conditions and amenities which are widely available in the society concerned (Townsend, 1979, p. 31). The concept of exclusion was present in the first poverty programme. Article 1 of the Council Decision setting up the programme in 1975 provided a definition of 'persons beset by poverty' as 'individuals or families whose resources are so small as to exclude them from the minimum acceptable way of life of the Member State in which they live'. Resources were defined as 'goods, cash income, plus services from public and private sources [8.1, p. 34].

The evaluation made of the first poverty programme pointed to a number of inadequacies in the Council's definition (Room, 1982, pp. 159–61); the focus on individuals and families tended to obscure wider societal processes and structures; while the Council recognised that the 'minimum acceptable way of life' would differ from one member state to another, important variations were also found within societies; the focus on resources concealed the way in which poor people were excluded from social participation and also the need for structural changes in society.

While the definition used in the second poverty programme was close to that of the first, it was extended, as in Peter Townsend's definition, to take account of other resources. The poor were defined as 'persons, families and groups of persons whose resources (material, cultural and social) are so limited as to exclude them from the minimum acceptable way of life in the Member States in which they live' [8.6, p. 11]. By not being confined to income poverty, this definition had the advantage that it introduced the concept of social exclusion, thereby recognising that poverty brings with it a sense of powerlessness and marginalisation, or exclusion, and engenders dependence. It did not resolve the question of how to determine what might be considered as a 'minimum acceptable way of life' or how to apply such a minimum across Europe.

The Observatory on National Policies to Combat Social Exclusion has defined social exclusion in relation to social rights with reference, for example, to the right to employment, housing and health care, asking questions about the effectiveness of national policies in ensuring access to such rights and the barriers which exclude people from them. In its second annual report it goes on to study the evidence that 'where citizens are unable to secure their social rights, they will tend to suffer processes of generalised and persisting disadvantage and their social and occupational participation will be undermined' [8.8, p. 17].

Although the manifestations of relative poverty have probably not changed significantly – the standard of living and access to resources for the poor is by definition well below the average for the population as a whole – the nature and determinants of poverty have undergone substantial change since the mid-1970s. The term 'new poverty' was created to record the way in which poverty had extended to a much broader cross-section of the population, spanning different age groups, social and economic categories, ethnic groups and geographical areas and threatening people who had previously been in stable employment and well paid jobs with periods of sporadic and recurrent poverty.

The terms 'polarisation', 'dualisation' and 'marginalisation' were also introduced into the vocabulary of poverty analysts to describe the growing rift between those who are able to take advantage of the social and economic systems and those who are excluded from them; between those in work covered by generous social insurance and the unemployed, between urban and rural populations, between core and periphery, between the able bodied and those with handicaps, between men and women, and so forth. Categories of individuals can thus be identified who are living on the margins of society and require special help: the long-term unemployed, the young unemployed, older people, single-parent families, migrants and refugees, the underprivileged in rural and urban areas.

Measuring poverty and social exclusion

Although the first national reports on poverty in member states were drawn up using a common framework and an agreed method for calculating poverty lines, the quality of the comparative data was very uneven. Some countries had a long tradition of research on poverty, for example researchers in the United Kingdom had been studying poverty for over 150 years, as testified by authoritative accounts such as those of Rowntree (1901) and Townsend (1979). Others had only begun to carry out research in this area in the late 1960s. While some member states had available regular data series on topics such as expenditure, earnings, social security provision, education and housing, others had given low priority to collecting and analysing data on indicators of poverty levels. The information which could be assembled therefore rarely lent itself to reliable comparisons across countries.

Using the Commission's definition of a poverty line – those persons whose disposable income is less than half of the average equivalent *per capita* income in their country – the final report of the first poverty programme estimated that in the mid-1970s the number of poor in the nine member states was about 30 million. When the three new southern European member states – Greece, Portugal and Spain – were included, the level of poverty across the Community rose to 38 million [8.6, p. 5]. By the late 1980s according to the same definition about 52 million people, or more than 15 per cent of total population, were considered to be living at or below the 50 per cent poverty threshold [8.5, p. 82]. If the poor are defined as the population suffering from material, cultural and social deprivations, which is even more difficult to measure, a much larger proportion of Europe's population would be identified.

The proportion of the population living in poverty, according to the 50 per cent poverty line for *per capita* disposable income, varies from one member state to another: figures for the late 1980s show that rates were particularly high in Portugal, followed by Italy, Greece, Ireland

and Spain. France and the United Kingdom recorded relatively high rates, with Denmark and the Netherlands showing the lowest rates and Belgium, Luxembourg and Germany below the average [8.5, p. 82]. Figures for relative income poverty reflect inequalities in earnings but do not say anything about the extent of homelessness or the inadequacy of access to social services and benefits in kind. When, in the mid-1980s, poverty was assessed on the basis of expenditure, both for households and for individuals, measured in terms of a poverty threshold of 50 per cent of the equivalent mean national expenditure of adults, Portugal showed by far the highest rates for both households and individuals; the countries of southern Europe, Ireland and the United Kingdom were found to have the largest proportions of households and individuals in poverty [8.13, table 6.28]. In relation to population size, again using the expenditure measure, Belgium, Denmark, Germany and the Netherlands accounted for a small percentage of poor people in the Union, whereas Portugal, followed by Spain and the United Kingdom, had a disproportionately large share [8.13, table 6.30].

When findings such as these are produced and compared, some national governments have objected to the basis on which they are drawn up. Their statistical validity can also be questioned. A rigorous comparison of levels of poverty in France and the United Kingdom, using different definitions, which take account of household size, the number of older people and housing costs, have, for example, revealed up to 100 per cent variation between the two countries depending on the measures used (Gardiner, 1992, p. 28).

Estimates of the number of beneficiaries of social assistance, another means of calculating poverty levels, are equally unreliable and problematic for comparative purposes since the criteria for gaining access to social assistance and the level of benefits differ from one country to another, as shown below. Take-up rates may vary too in accordance with social attitudes, the stigma attached to means-tested welfare and the reliability of data: for example, in the United Kingdom 80 per cent of those eligible to claim social assistance do so, compared with 50 per cent in Germany (Lødemel, 1992, p. 16). In 1990–91 take-up of the *revenu minimum d'insertion* (RMI) in France and the social assistance pension in Spain was said to be 100 per cent, whereas only a third of those eligible to receive family income support in Ireland were found to be claiming benefit [8.8, fig. 2].

In order to circumvent problems of non-comparability, the Commission has been trying to establish a common definition of poverty, according to a European base line of living (EBL), or the capacity to satisfy a body of needs, either by income from earnings or by other means. Attempts are also being made to collect data using a battery of indicators: what the population regards as a minimum income; what individuals consider as an absolute minimum for them; the degree of deprivation in terms of actual consumption and participation in social life; the number of people living on an income below a certain percentage of average *per capita* income; and the number of persons at or below the social assistance level used in each country.

More effective measures of poverty and social exclusion and the establishment of the necessary data collecting apparatus would enable member states to assess the dimension of the problem and possibly to monitor the success of policies to combat poverty, but measurement of the manifestations of poverty does not contribute substantially to identifying or eliminating its causes. Nor can international information gathering be a substitute for national policies and action aimed at solving what are often underlying structural problems.

NATIONAL RESPONSES TO SOCIAL EXCLUSION

Although changing economic conditions had intensified the need for greater solidarity between member states by the 1990s, no legally binding rights and obligations had been generated at European level, leaving national governments to introduce provisions appropriate to their own needs. The growing recognition by the Union that poverty is a result of the inadequacy of cultural and social as well as material resources may help to explain why official documents emphasise the subsidiarity principle in formulating measures to combat social exclusion. The Council Recommendation 'on common criteria concerning sufficient resources and social assistance in social protection systems' [8.4] expected member states to institute their own schemes to provide the necessary financial aid to bring resources up to a minimum level, but in accordance with national conditions.

By the early 1990s all member states already had unemployment insurance systems, which were being stretched by rising unemployment rates. The proportion of unemployed people in the Union stood at 9.5 per cent, with particularly high levels in Ireland and Spain, especially amongst the under-twenty-fives, a group also showing very high rates in Italy and Portugal [8.14, tables 3.21–30]. Most member states had instituted guaranteed income maintenance schemes for individuals not entitled to insurance benefits. Just as different national models of retirement and invalidity pension schemes or health services can be identified in member states due to differences in their welfare traditions, diversity is also found in arrangements for income maintenance during unemployment or other contingencies. The extent to which social assistance is needed to supplement the resources of older, disabled and unemployed people, lone mothers and other socially excluded groups, and its effectiveness in doing so vary from one member state to another. In order to assess the relative importance of insurance benefits and social assistance within different welfare regimes, in this section the distinction is again made between the continental model of corporatist welfare which was dominant amongst the EEC founder member states, the more universalistic model common to the countries that joined the Community in the early 1970s and the less developed southern European welfare system in the three countries that became members in the 1980s.

Unemployment benefits and social assistance in continental welfare states

The corporatist welfare regimes, which were generally derived from the Bismarckian employment-related social insurance model of social protection, were more concerned with protecting and compensating workers through the insurance principle than with providing national minimum standards for all citizens. As in the other EEC founder member states, unemployment benefits in Germany (*Arbeitslosengeld*) are earnings related, thereby reinforcing the conceptual link with work (Clasen, 1992). Claimants who have exhausted their rights move on to a form of income security (*Arbeitslosenhilfe*) which, while being means tested and paid for from general taxation, is again income related. In the early 1990s it was of unlimited duration as long as no suitable job was available [8.9, pp. 160–1; 8.12, table XI].

In France earnings-related unemployment benefits were of limited duration and were followed by a flat-rate payment for a further six months. In Luxembourg benefits were based on former earnings up to a ceiling for 365 days. They were closely tied to availability for work and efforts made to find employment. Employment-related benefits for the unemployed in Belgium were of unlimited duration but degressive, varying according to individual and local conditions and subject to maximum and minimum levels. Young graduates could receive a low flat-rate waiting benefit, and those in part-time education were entitled to a bridging benefit. Unemployed people in the Netherlands were eligible to receive an income based on previous earnings for a varying length of time determined by their employment record and age, with a follow-on benefit at the level of the minimum wage. Italy is an example of a country that followed the continental approach as far as contributory social insurance was concerned, but where, in the early 1990s, coverage was still limited, at a low level and variable from one sector of employment to another. The wage compensation fund (Cassa Integrazione Guadagni), however, guaranteed an income to workers who were partially or temporarily unemployed.

Unemployment insurance schemes offered rates ranging from 80 per cent of gross earnings in Luxembourg to 20 per cent of average earnings in the last three months in Italy. The duration of benefits varied from a minimum of four months for earnings-related benefits in France to indefinite in Belgium.

For job-seekers and the young employed who may not be eligible for any form of employment-related benefits and for those who have exhausted all other rights and whose parents or partners are unable to support them, the only resort may be social assistance [8.12, table XII]. All the EEC founder member states provide entitlement to social assistance on the basis of nationality and residence. In Germany, in the early 1990s, social assistance (*Sozialhilfe*) benefits were flat rate, based on a standard which is set and administered at regional level, with additions for children, rent and heating and including cover for health insurance. Belgium, Luxembourg and the Netherlands all operated minimum subsistence schemes of unlimited duration. In Belgium means-tested minimum subsistence (*minimum de moyens d'existence* or *Minimex*) was guaranteed for all Belgian residents and could take the form of social services or cash benefits at the discretion of the relevant administrative authorities. Luxembourg guaranteed a minimum income (*revenu minimum garanti*) for an unlimited period of time. At local level, social assistance payments were made either in cash or in the form of support enabling the beneficiaries to carry out useful work or to help them find employment. In the Netherlands social assistance (*sociale bijstand*) was means tested and designed to provide subsistence at a level which was a set percentage of the minimum net national wage, with adjustments for family circumstances. In Italy social assistance provided a minimum income (*minimo vitale*) for a limited period of time, and public provision was supplemented by private and voluntary welfare.

In the late 1980s income maintenance in France was adapted to target particular groups. The unemployment benefit scheme, RMI, which was introduced in 1988, was operated on the principle that benefits should be paid only to individuals aged over twenty-five (or under twenty-five with a child) who committed themselves to re-entering the labour market by agreeing to follow counselling, training or re-entry schemes. The RMI was a differential benefit, paid for three months, renewable for up to one year and intended to raise income from all sources to a minimum level, determined and financed nationally, although the scheme was administered locally.

Unemployment benefits and social assistance in Nordic and Anglo-Saxon welfare states

As in the continental welfare states, unemployment benefits in Denmark were related to former earnings. In the early 1990s they were calculated on the basis of 90 per cent of the gross wage up to a ceiling, the highest level in the Union, for up to 2.5 years and with a possible extension up to seven years. Individuals not eligible for unemployment insurance benefits received social assistance (*social bistand*), which was provided irrespective of nationality, age and occupation and of the reasons for the need. The level was determined by the state which paid out a basic means-tested benefit with a supplement for housing. Caring for children and for physically or mentally handicapped persons gave entitlement to additional allowances.

The United Kingdom was the only member state in the early 1990s where the qualifying conditions for unemployment insurance included a requirement for a weekly earnings limit and where benefits were paid solely at a flat rate with no reference to former earnings. The job-seekers' allowance was proposed in 1994 to replace unemployment benefits, with the aim of easing the return to work and helping beneficiaries escape from the poverty trap. Social assistance had been conceived as an integral part of social security in the United Kingdom. In 1988 it was reorganised into two separate schemes providing a guaranteed minimum income: family credit was paid to families with low income from work; income support was a benefit for families and individuals with no income from work for an unlimited period. Since the level of income available from family credit was higher than from income support, the system was also intended to act as an incentive for work.

The unemployment benefits and social assistance systems in Ireland shared some features in common with the United Kingdom. Both offered a low flat-rate unemployment benefit which was payable for a limited period. But in Ireland beneficiaries were also eligible to receive an earnings-related payment and, after they had exhausted their rights, moved on to means-tested unemployment assistance. The supplementary welfare allowance provided support for the long-term unemployed and other disadvantaged groups by ensuring a basic weekly income for an unlimited period, which could be supplemented by discretionary payments to meet exceptional circumstances.

It has been argued that in countries where the social insurance principle was not originally adopted as the basis for social protection, as in Denmark and the United Kingdom, reforms of social assistance have gone in two different directions: in the United Kingdom emphasis has been on creating a rights oriented scheme to meet the needs of the large number of individuals and groups excluded from occupational insurance schemes; in the Scandinavian countries, on the other hand, state funded social insurance has been extended in such a way that social assistance has been limited to only a very small section of the very poorest groups in society (Lødemel, 1992, p. 16).

Unemployment benefits and social assistance in rudimentary welfare states

The social security systems developed in the southern European countries that joined the Community in the 1980s have largely followed the continental employment-related insurance model of social protection with emphasis on entitlements derived from employment, but large sectors of the population were still not covered by social insurance by the early 1990s, and the distinction between insurance and assistance was not always clearly made.

Provision for unemployment in all three countries included contributory and assistance benefits. Greece, Portugal and Spain provided short-term earnings-related benefits which varied depending on the length of employment. Non-contributory unemployment assistance was paid for short periods in Portugal and Spain at a standard level subject to a qualifying period and a means test.

Although Spain had a minimum income (*ingreso mínimo de inserción* or *renta mínima*), it was not uniformly applied. Social assistance was also the responsibility of the regions which meant that provision was subject to variations for political and financial reasons. Neither Greece nor Portugal had a general guaranteed minimum income, but their social assistance systems comprised a number of programmes targeted at particular social groups in need, based on a means test and a low level of benefits. The safety net was provided by the family rather than the state and through discretionary regional and local support.

The rates paid by unemployment assistance and social assistance schemes vary substantially from one member state to another in a relationship which seems to be inversely proportional to need. In the early 1990s, some of the countries with the highest *per capita* incomes – Belgium, Denmark, Luxembourg and the Netherlands – were found to provide the highest levels of minimum income at about 50 per cent of net average earnings. Greece, Portugal and Spain, which encompassed some of the poorest regions in the Union and therefore some of the largest pockets of need, were together with Italy the only member states where a single person aged forty with no entitlement to employment benefits, yet available for work, would be without a minimum income [8.10, p. 62].

CONCERTED ACTION AGAINST POVERTY

Even if agreement could be reached on how to define and measure poverty and social exclusion across member states, it does not follow that the same solution could or should be adopted throughout the Union to deal with poverty as a social problem. In some contexts the optimal policy choice may be to concentrate resources on raising the incomes of the poorest of the poor, whereas in other cases the preference may be to spread resources more thinly in order to reduce the hardship of a larger number of individuals and households, or governments may choose to target job creation and training programmes to prevent long-term unemployment.

The Union seems to have favoured a mixed approach. By supporting projects which targeted specific groups at risk in the poverty programmes and through the selective distribution of the Structural Funds, the aim was to concentrate resources on some of the most problematic categories. The Council Recommendation 'on common criteria concerning sufficient resources and social assistance in social protection systems' [8.4] aimed to combat exclusion by encouraging the improvement of existing national provisions. The Council stressed the importance of integrating persons excluded from the labour market and the need for solidarity with the most deprived individuals and groups across the Union. It stopped short, however, of making the Recommendation into a directive which would have given it legal force, and the text reiterated the principles of subsidiarity and sovereignty of member states in the area of social protection.

Even if all member states were to institute a guaranteed minimum income, the prospect of reaching agreement on the level at which such a minimum might be set is unlikely to be resolved in the foreseeable future, and it would not necessarily eliminate poverty. Although considerable progress has been made since the time of the first poverty programme in 1975 in defining and measuring poverty, the difficulty remains of how to determine a level of 'sufficient resources' for each member state in such a way as to dissuade both welfare tourism and social dumping (see Chapters 1 and 2) and to ensure take-up by those most in need. The entry in the 1980s of new member states with less developed social protection systems and low *per capita* income made this issue more pressing.

Despite the considerable problems in moving towards a common social policy on poverty and social exclusion, by the early 1990s the Union had made some progress. Member states had undoubtedly reached a greater understanding of the problems of poverty and recognised that the economic dislocation which was expected to follow the completion of the internal market could have important social consequences for peripheral regions in the Union. This realisation brought a renewed commitment to the task of developing measures to combat poverty and social exclusion, placing the issue firmly on the Commission's social agenda. Proposals in the 1994 White Paper on European social policy confirmed the shift away from support in the form of unemployment assistance benefits towards more active labour market measures with the object of maintaining incentives for job-seekers [1.13, p. 38].

Box 8   Union documents relating to social exclusion

SECONDARY LEGISLATION

8.1   Council Decision 75/458/EEC of 22 July 1975 concerning a programme of pilot schemes and studies to combat poverty (*OJ* L 199/34 30.7.75), amended by Council Decision 77/779/EEC of 12 December 1977 (*OJ* L 322/28, 17.12.77).

8.2   Council Decision 89/457/EEC of 18 July 1989 establishing a medium-term Community action programme concerning the economic and social integration of the economically and socially less privileged groups in society (*OJ* L 224/10 2.8.89).

8.3 Council Resolution of 29 September 1989 on combating social exclusion (*OJ* C 277/1 31.10.89).

8.4 Council Recommendation of 24 June 1992 on common criteria concerning sufficient resources and social assistance in social protection systems (92/441/EEC) (*OJ* C 245/46 26.8.92).

8.5 Commission proposal for a medium-term action programme to combat exclusion and promote solidarity (1994–1999) (COM(93) 435 final, 22 September 1993).

OFFICIAL PUBLICATIONS OF THE COMMISSION OF THE EUROPEAN COMMUNITIES (CEC) AND EUROSTAT

8.6 CEC (1989) 'The Fight against Poverty', *Social Europe Supplement 2/89*.

8.7 CEC (1991) 'The European Social Fund', *Social Europe 2/91*.

8.8 CEC/Observatory on National Policies to Combat Social Exclusion (1991) *Second Annual Report of the European Community Observatory on National Policies to Combat Social Exclusion* (co-ordinated by G. Room).

8.9 CEC (1992) *Employment in Europe 1992*.

8.10 CEC (1993) *Social Protection in Europe*.

8.11 CEC (1993) 'Towards a Europe of Solidarity: Combating Social Exclusion', *Social Europe Supplement 4/93*.

8.12 CEC/Mutual Information System on Social Protection in the Community (1993) *Social Protection in the Member States of the Community: Situation on July 1st 1993 and Evolution*.

8.13 Eurostat (1991) *A Social Portrait of Europe*.

8.14 Eurostat (1993) *Basic Statistics of the Community. Comparison with the Principal Partners of the Community*, 30th edn.

9 Social Policy and Mobility

While the Treaty establishing the European Economic Community (EEC) [1.2] was not intended to provide a fully developed framework for social policy across member states, a major reason for promoting the social dimension and for seeking to harmonise national social protection systems was to remove obstacles to intra-European mobility. The Treaty firmly endorsed the policy aim of creating the necessary conditions so that persons, services and capital could move freely between member states. This continued to be a primary objective as membership of the Community was extended in the 1970s and 1980s. The Single European Act (SEA) [1.5], the Community Charter of the Fundamental Social Rights of Workers [1.7] and the Maastricht Treaty [1.6] reaffirmed that employment, adaptability, training and mobility were to be keywords for the Single European Market (SEM) and the European Union (EU).

Most economists would argue that mobility of labour is determined by a whole range of factors operating at the level of the socio-economic environment. If mobility is to be encouraged, incentives are therefore needed through company law, taxation, wage systems and employment law, supported by qualifications, education and training and transferable social protection rights. Either directly or indirectly, the Community's and Union's Treaties and Charter have addressed all these issues. Little attention has, however, been paid in official documents to social and cultural factors which may also impede mobility.

This chapter begins by analysing the principle of freedom of movement as embodied in the Union's primary and secondary legislation. An attempt is then made to assess the impact of European legislation on intra-European migratory flows and the implications of the lifting of formal barriers to mobility, following ratification of the Maastricht Treaty. Informal obstacles to mobility, such as cultural and linguistic differences and family commitments and obligations, are also examined as factors which may explain why only relatively small numbers of European nationals have become mobile since the Community was formed. At the same time as the Union was formulating policies to promote freedom of movement between member states, it was limiting immigration flows from non-European countries. To conclude the chapter, the issue of immigration from outside the Union is discussed with reference to European social policy and the concept of 'Fortress Europe'.

EUROPEAN LEGISLATION ON FREEDOM OF MOVEMENT

The EEC was premised on the assumption that the free movement of labour was necessary if the common market was to become a reality. The Community's and Union's Treaties and Charter have all reiterated this objective, and binding legislation has been implemented to ensure that formal obstacles to mobility are removed. In this section the development of the Union's legislative framework is examined and its underlying assumptions are reviewed.

Freedom of movement in the EEC Treaty

In the early years of the EEC, migration within Europe was mainly of unskilled workers from the southern region of the Community moving north. In combination with non-EEC immigrants, many of whom came from Greece, Portugal and Spain, this mobility was a response to the needs of the labour market for low paid manual workers. Intra-European migration served a double purpose: for the host countries it answered the demand for manpower at a time of economic expansion and labour shortage; for the provider countries it offered job opportunities for unskilled workers from areas of high unemployment. Italy, as the only EEC founder member with a persistent unemployment problem, had an interest in ensuring that unemployed workers within the Community were given preference over recruits from elsewhere (Collins, 1975, p. 99).

Articles 48–51 of the EEC Treaty contained the main clauses establishing the right to freedom of movement of workers. Article 48 reiterated the principle of non-discrimination set out in Article 7: all discrimination based on nationality was prohibited with regard to 'employment, remuneration and other conditions of work and employment'; it confirmed the right of workers to accept an offer of employment in another member state, to take up employment under the same conditions as nationals and to remain in the territory of another member state after having been employed there, with the exception of public service employment.

The measures required to ensure freedom of movement of workers were contained in Article 49, which covered close co-operation between employment services, the elimination of administrative procedures and practices and of qualifying periods previously concluded between member states and machinery to facilitate a balance between supply and demand in the employment market. Article 50 made specific reference to the need to encourage the exchange of young workers, while Article 51, which was subject to unanimous voting, focused on the measures required in the field of social security, covering arrangements for aggregation of all periods taken into account under the laws of the countries concerned 'for the purpose of acquiring and retaining the right to benefit and of calculating the amount of benefit' as well as 'payment of benefits to persons resident in the territories of Member States'. The aim of implementing common measures for the social security of migrant workers was reiterated in Article 121 under the section on social provisions.

In the years immediately following the signing of the EEC Treaty, action with regard to freedom of movement was primarily concerned with administrative procedures, the easing of restrictions on mobility (work permits, visas, labour and residence permits) and the transfer of wages and social security rights. By the mid-1960s, awareness was growing that more positive action was needed to ensure non-nationals from other member states and their families were integrated into the host community. Policies were therefore formulated to improve proficiency in the relevant language and provide assistance with housing and schooling for the children of long-term migrants. Early EEC legislation, such as Regulations Nos. 3–4 [9.1], Regulation (EEC) No. 1612/68 [9.2] and Directive 68/360/EEC [9.3], set out the conditions for freedom of movement for workers within the Community and for 'the abolition of restrictions on movement and residence within the Community for workers of member states and their families'. This binding legislation (see Appendix 1) was intended to abolish discrimination on the basis of nationality. Member states were to recognise the fundamental right of workers and their families to choose where they wished to work and reside. Equality of treatment in gaining access to work, housing and social protection was to be ensured, as was the social integration of migrant workers.

The EEC Treaty laid down the principle that workers should be suitably equipped to conduct their business in another member state and that the conditions of employment should be at least as good as those in the country they were leaving. The social security rights they had accrued should be transferable. The co-ordination and application regulations, (EEC) No. 1408/71 [9.4] and (EEC) No. 574/72 [9.5], provided for equal treatment in matters of social security, the nomination of one competent state in order to resolve conflicts of law, the aggregation (and proratisation) of periods of insurance or employment records and the exportability of social security benefits.

Freedom of movement from the Single European Act to the Maastricht Treaty and beyond

The Single European Act (SEA) of 1986 and the Maastricht Treaty of 1992 expressly excluded the use of qualified majority voting for matters relating to free movement of persons (Article 100a of the SEA) or the conditions of third-country nationals (Article 100c of the Maastricht Treaty), signalling that mobility was to continue to be an area where all member states must reach agreement (see Chapter 1). In the Community Charter the continuing priority attributed to the free movement of workers was indicated by its position at the beginning of the document. The right of workers to freedom of movement throughout the Community was reiterated. Equal treatment was confirmed with regard to 'access to employment, working conditions and social protection in the host country', implying: 'harmonisation of conditions of residence in all Member States, particularly those concerning family reunification; elimination of obstacles arising from the non-recognition of diplomas or equivalent occupational qualifications; improvement of the living and working conditions of frontier workers' (points 1–3). The initiatives put forward by the Commission to implement the Charter included actions to protect posted workers [9.12], to co-ordinate supplementary social security schemes for transfrontier workers [9.11] and to ensure the rights of workers in frontier regions [9.10].

The Maastricht Treaty marked an important stage in the development of European policy on freedom of movement. A new Article 8 was inserted establishing the principle of 'citizenship of the union'. In addition to freedom of movement within the territory of member states, citizens of the Union were to have the right to vote and stand as candidates at municipal elections and at elections for the European Parliament under the same conditions as nationals.

By the mid-1990s European policy on freedom of movement had confirmed the principle that member states should ensure workers can move freely from one country to another without prejudicing their right to employment and to employment-related benefits. To facilitate the movement of labour, information would be supplied on job availability in other countries, professional qualifications and experience would be recognised, social security entitlements would be transferable from one state to another, and every effort would be made to ensure the social and economic integration of migrant workers in the host country. Intra-European mobility was, however, no longer being advocated as an end in itself. The Union's social priority through to the year 2000 was to reduce unemployment, and freedom of movement was subordinated to the aim of creating jobs through economic growth and competitiveness [1.13, pp. 27–30].

THE IMPACT OF UNION POLICY ON MOBILITY

It is difficult to assess the extent to which the movement of workers between member states has been encouraged by European social policy rather than economic and demographic factors and national policies. The impact of Community policy, whether social or economic, in the first twenty-five years of the postwar period is thought to have been limited (Collins, 1975, p. 114). In practice the labour shortage was such that the preference which was to be given to EEC nationals probably had little effect in encouraging mobility. Despite the lack of evidence of increased mobility due to the provisions of the EEC Treaty, the need to promote freedom of movement was used constantly as a justification for policy developments in areas such as education and training, the improvement of living and working conditions and social protection (see Chapters 3 and 4). In this section the possible implications of the completion of the SEM on the movement of labour are considered, together with an analysis of attempts to measure intra-European mobility.

The impact of the Single European Market on migratory flows

The completion of the internal market, following the signing of the SEA, was expected to provide an incentive for accelerating existing trends, such as the flow of Portuguese workers to France. Because of the changing nature of the labour market in the Community, by the end of the 1980s the demand for unskilled workers had, however, fallen to a low level and was expected to remain so as further automation was introduced. The assumption that 1993 would bring an increase in Mediterranean migration (Greeks, Portuguese and Spaniards) to the north was also offset to some extent by the displacement of the industrial core through the withdrawal of manufacturing to peripheral areas outside the Union with lower labour costs. Some growth was recorded in non-labour migration, due to student mobility (see Chapter 3) and to the attraction for pensioners and private income migrants of warmer climates in the Union's sun belt.

Demographic factors were also expected to have an impact on migratory movements. In the late 1980s, due to the ageing of the population throughout Europe (see Chapter 7), a gradual fall was predicted in the number of young people entering working life, provoking skill shortages in most member states, particularly in high technology industries with rapid staff turnover. In the short term, the problem was expected to be offset to some extent by the increase in the number of migrant women becoming economically active. In the longer term, however, non-European migrants or previously inactive women were not thought likely to compensate for the shortfall in the labour supply. Another possible implication of an ageing workforce was that upward pressures would be exerted on labour costs, leading to the reduction of geographical and occupational mobility, since it is the young and unattached, and often low paid, workers who tend to be the most mobile (Ardittis, 1990).

Much of what was being said and written in the late 1980s was premised on the assumption that skill shortages would continue to be a major factor influencing labour markets (Lindley, 1991). As these shortages lead to greater staff turnover and increased competition among employers for professional workers and managers with high levels of qualification, future migration between member states was expected to affect mainly highly qualified workers in multinational companies [9.14, p. 153], encouraging the brain drain ('brain migration' for Ardittis, 1990, p. 465). Much of the movement in this area was, however, likely to be short stay resettlement.

Even before 1 January 1993 when the internal market was to come into force, predictions about increasing levels of intra-European mobility of labour were being revised downwards, except in so far as border areas were concerned, and it seemed increasingly unlikely that migration would be a cohesive force (Pickup, 1990, p. 106).

Measurements of intra-European mobility

Until the mid-1980s little information about intra-European migration was available. The Community Labour Force Survey (LFS) has since monitored migratory flows between member states on an annual basis by asking a small non-representative population sample where they were living one year previously. Data from this source are of limited value since they do not record short-term mobility and rely on individual recall. Nor do they show how many intra-European migrants are living in another country having taken up its nationality and citizenship. They do, however, give some indication of trends over a period of years.

Before the Union began monitoring intra-European mobility using the LFS, one means of assessing movement was by counting the number of labour permits issued. During the ten years between 1958 and 1968 when labour permits were issued for Community nationals, the proportion taken by Italy, the country which had insisted on the need for freedom of movement for labour and stood to gain most from it, actually decreased. By the beginning of the 1970s probably about 1 million Community nationals and 2.5 million non-EEC migrants were working in other member states, and about 2 million EEC nationals were estimated to be living in a member state other than their own (Collins, 1975, pp. 114–5).

During the 1980s annual mobility was on average equivalent to less than 0.1 per cent of Community population. By the mid-1980s fewer than 2 million Community nationals were working on a more or less permanent basis in another member state. When family members were counted, foreign residents were estimated to number 12.5 million, including nearly 5.5 million Community nationals [9.14, p. 153]. The entry of Greece, Portugal and Spain, who were in the past major suppliers of non-European workers, into the Community in the 1980s did not coincide with a major increase in internal migratory flows; intra-European mobility may even have decreased by comparison with the level reached in the early 1970s.

By the 1990s about 1.4 per cent of the Union's citizens lived in another member state [9.20, fig. 1]. Luxembourg was a special case with almost a third of its working population composed of nationals from elsewhere in the Union. Although the proportion of nationals of working age from another member state reached 5 per cent in Belgium, in no other country did it exceed 3 per cent. In Portugal and Spain the figure was well below 1 per cent. Germany was the country which received the largest number of European migrants: most Danish and Greek workers moving to another country went to Germany. The United Kingdom, together with Germany, received about 70 per cent of people moving between member states. France accounted for another 15 per cent. Belgium, Denmark, Greece, Ireland, the Netherlands and Spain were all net losers in terms of flows of migrants. Although Greece, Ireland, the Netherlands, Portugal and Spain all tended to lose job-seekers, only 60 per cent of total mobility was explained by people moving in search of jobs [9.16, pp. 108–13].

More men were mobile than women in the early 1990s, and female migrants were more likely to be unemployed. Most male other Community nationals were employed in industry (almost two-thirds, which was higher than the proportion for nationals and non-European immigrants). For women the proportions were very similar to those for nationals and non-European immigrants, with the services accounting for over 70 per cent of employment [9.19, table 4.36).

Amongst the managerial and professional grades, the brain migration categories, expatriates accounted for about 0.02 per cent of employees within member states. The United Kingdom tended to be a net exporter of managerial and professional people, although only a small proportion of this mobile population were relocating in the Community. In the ten-year period between 1976 and 1986 analysis of the flows of managerial and professional workers between the United Kingdom and the rest of.the Community showed that the number leaving the United Kingdom for other member states had increased threefold, whereas the inflow had increased only marginally (Council for Industry and Higher Education and Institute of Manpower Studies, 1989, p. 5).

At the end of the 1980s cross-border migration was less important within the Community than between member states and Switzerland. The Federal Republic of Germany was a net importer of frontier workers, with the largest single movement of intra-European frontier workers being from France to Germany. Major flows were reported from Belgium, France and Germany into Luxembourg, between Belgium and the Netherlands, Belgium and France and from the Netherlands to Germany. Most frontier mobility was from lower to higher wage countries and by men rather than women [9.14, p. 155].

Whatever the measures used and the categories considered, the striking feature is the relatively low level of labour movement within the Union, particularly since some of the flow may be explained by nationals returning to their country of origin after spending a period in another member state [9.16, pp. 112–13]. In sum, the impact of efforts by the Community to ensure priority for European workers is minimal when compared with the scale of immigration and emigration among member states before the EEC was established.

OVERCOMING OBSTACLES TO INTRA-EUROPEAN MIGRATION

Despite the removal of administrative barriers, attempts to harmonise social protection systems and to implement directives on the mutual recognition of qualifications (see Chapter 3), intra-European mobility has not increased at the rate which might have been expected if the main obstacles to freedom of movement were legal restrictions. Cases can be quoted where unequal treatment has undoubtedly resulted from inadequate adaptation of national laws and practices to Union legislation, the narrow interpretation of regulations concerning pension rights, the recognition of qualifications and skills and social security benefits, insufficient information exchange between states over job vacancies and applications, restrictions on employment in the public service, and also housing availability. Analysis of migratory patterns suggests, however, that regulations may be only one of a number of variables influencing decisions about labour mobility: personal choice may be affected by individual factors such as health, income and qualifications, and also by the social and relational context, including the working environment and household circumstances; opportunities for mobility may be determined by the structure of labour markets as well as formal regulations (Pickup, 1990, pp. 5, 24).

Although the SEM rules theoretically removed the formal constraints on employment in other member states, many practical barriers may remain for reasons which have little to do with legal restrictions on mobility and establishment. In this section a range of institutional, social and cultural obstacles to mobility are considered, which cumulatively may help to explain why the completion of the internal market may not accelerate migration flows to the extent which might have been expected by policy makers.

Transferability of rights

Under the terms of European legislation, nationals from the Union who take up employment in another member state can expect to be covered by the social security system of the country in which they are pursuing their activity and to be eligible to receive the same benefits in kind under sickness, maternity and unemployment insurance. Insurance rights acquired in another member state are not lost but can be aggregated. In some cases, such as old age and invalidity pensions, it may be possible to draw benefits in two or more countries at the same time. Entitlements to rights conditional on qualifying periods may also be maintained and carried over to another member state to satisfy its qualifying conditions.

Unemployment benefit cannot normally be exported, nor can pensions which are not covered by European law, for example war pensions or public service retirement pensions. Assistance benefits – minimum subsistence, guaranteed income for older people – are provided in the host country on the same basis as for nationals. Since all member states have a residence condition for social assistance, benefits are not exportable, and in some cases the provision may be lower in the host country (see Chapter 8).

Considerable attention has been devoted to descriptions of the rights of migrant workers and to measures designed to facilitate the exercise of an occupation in another member state (Séché, 1988). The problem of how to deal with occupational pension schemes, which provide very different coverage across member states, was placed on the agenda in the early 1990s. The Commission clearly saw supplementary pension schemes as an important obstacle to mobility and a difficult question to deal with since the Communication issued on the subject in 1992 [9.11] was intended to start a discussion without at that stage presenting a proposal for legislation.

Education, training and recruitment

The enforcement of agreements over the mutual recognition of diplomas and qualifications has undoubtedly removed a serious formal obstacle to intra-European mobility (see Chapter 3), but cases are quoted of the non-recognition of formal education or on-the-job training acquired abroad and of migrants being denied access to certain activities despite regulations (Ardittis, 1990, p. 466).

The removal of formal barriers through the mutual recognition of qualifications has not eliminated important differences in approaches to education and training and their relationship with the labour market (see Chapter 3). Nor have attempts to encourage mobility amongst students led to a more uniform product from national educational systems. Differentiation in the structure of internal labour markets may result from disparities in national systems of vocational education and training, in particular between countries with well developed apprenticeship training schemes for skill acquisition and those where vocational training is less highly valued.

National practices followed traditionally in recruitment and training are also important in understanding the likelihood of acceptance and integration of workers who are the products of different educational systems (see Chapter 3). Doubts continue to be expressed about the acceptability of nationals from elsewhere in the Union because of differences in the approach to the assessment of competence, skills and abilities (Rajan, 1990, p. 111; Rainbird, 1993, p. 195). These differences in formal and informal practices may serve as exclusionary mechanisms making it difficult for outsiders to enter labour markets in other countries. When combined with imbalances in the demand and supply of specialists, they seem likely to continue to have an impact on the transferability of labour.

Job information and access to employment

Lack of information about jobs is also quoted in surveys as a reason for limited intra-European mobility. In this area Community action did not gather momentum until the end of the 1980s. In 1989 the Commission established a European System for the International Clearing of Vacancies and Applications for Employment (Sedoc) to enable the matching and clearance of jobs. The procedures were revised in 1992, and in 1994 a computerised system for exchanging job vacancies came into operation under the European Employment Services Project (Eures), in conjunction with the Commission and public employment services in member states. The aim of the project was to provide detailed information on job vacancies and job applications as well as general information on living and working conditions and labour markets to assist both individuals looking for work and employers wanting to recruit elsewhere in the Union. A network of appropriately trained Euroadvisers are linked by an electronic mail system and are expected to provide job-seekers with the guarantee of a standard of service at least the equivalent of what they would obtain if they were in the member state to which they were trying to move.

– Obtaining information about vacancies is, however, only the first stage in a job search. The many complications of pursuing an application and contemplating relocation are likely to deter large numbers of job-seekers from embarking on the process (Mc Cartney and Porter, 1993).

Public sector employment

Despite the general agreement over arrangements to facilitate and encourage freedom of movement amongst employees and self-employed workers, Article 48 of the EEC Treaty explicitly excluded public servants from the freedom of movement clause. This restriction was intended to safeguard the general interests of the state and does not therefore apply to all public sector employment. Posts in the judiciary, police, armed forces and diplomatic service and also as architects and supervisors in public administration may be reserved for nationals, whereas access to professional employment, as nurses for example, is not restricted.

Some member states – Belgium, France, Italy and Luxembourg – have invoked the nationality clause as a means of preventing nationals from other countries from entering public sector employment. In Denmark, Greece, Ireland, the Netherlands, Portugal and the United Kingdom 10 per cent of public sector jobs are not accessible to non-nationals (Gastines and Sylvestre, 1992, p. 201). While programmes like Lingua were intended to encourage the mobility of teachers, by providing in-service opportunities for practising teachers to spend periods abroad, barriers to their freedom of movement remained in some member states where they were classified as civil servants and were not therefore considered to be covered by mobility rules. The fact that civil servants have access to more generous social security arrangements, as in Germany or France, as well as a guarantee of employment, may also help to explain why governments have been reluctant to make public sector jobs available to non-nationals in cases where national interest is not paramount.

Language and culture

Ultimately the reluctance of employers to recruit senior staff from other member states or for well qualified labour to move between countries, except in the case of multinational firms, may be explained by cultural differences and knowledge of foreign languages.

Programmes such as Lingua may have some impact, but the size of the language problem continues to be daunting (see Chapter 3). Although qualified skilled workers may be able to exercise their occupation without being fluent in the language, proficiency is essential for professional practice by the highly qualified. English was the most widespread foreign language learnt in schools in the Union in the early 1990s, accounting for more than 50 per cent of language learning in all regions other than the French-speaking area of Belgium [9.19, table 3.9]. French was the next most widely learnt language, while Italian, Dutch, Portuguese, Greek and Danish accounted for less than one per cent of language courses across the Union. Individuals from other member states seeking employment in the United Kingdom are therefore likely to have a linguistic advantage over English native speakers contemplating migrating to other parts of Europe.

Language policy is an area where the Union can do little more than make recommendations about what would be desirable and launch programmes to encourage language acquisition. Within member states which are multilingual, such as Belgium, language is already a contentious issue, and Brussels, Luxembourg and Strasbourg are prime examples of the difficulties of reaching agreement about official languages, a problem exacerbated by the arrival of new member states and internal power struggles.

Lack of proficiency in the relevant language is often combined with an insufficient understanding of other national cultures. Cultural differences are a source of major problems not only for participants in international meetings and business undertakings who need to understand the assumptions, expectations and cues provided in other national contexts, but also for migrants wanting to settle in another member state. Understanding time-keeping or what is acceptable behaviour in terms of employment practices or social interchange, to give only a few examples, may affect the ability of migrants to adapt to living in countries which, as members of a political and economic union, might be expected to share cultural norms.

Personal and family factors

Workers, particularly in dual career couples, may be constrained by personal and family factors which the completion of the SEA in itself could probably do little to change. Reasons frequently put forward by well qualified workers for not being mobile are their concern about their children's education or about finding employment for a spouse. Despite legislation on equal treatment, the social and economic position of women and attitudes towards female economic activity and provision of support for families may, for instance, vary from one member state to another (see Chapters 5 and 6), and this may help to explain reluctance to move to another country. The much higher cost of living in some member states and problems of finding suitable accommodation in what are often very different market conditions may also reduce the attractiveness, feasibility and financial viability of moving within the Union.

As with internal mobility, many of the factors determining the stability of the labour force are also likely to explain low intra-European mobility rates. The male population aged thirty-five to fifty-five is more stable than the female and younger population; individuals occupying full-time long-term well paid jobs in large firms and requiring a high level of skills and qualifications are more stable; owner occupation of housing, which increases with age, reduces geographical mobility. The occupational groups which would be most attractive to employers in another member states may therefore be the least likely to want to exercise their right to become geographically mobile.

UNION POLICY AND NON-EUROPEAN IMMIGRATION

In its 1992 report on the employment situation in the Community, the Commission revised some of the earlier predictions about the impact of demographic trends on labour markets, suggesting that the slowing down in population growth and the consequent ageing of the population of member states would not in fact lead to a decline in the size of the labour force, due to the increasing participation of women in paid employment, particularly in the southern European countries, Greece, Portugal and Spain [9.15, p. 10]. The contribution of women to the labour force is, however, qualitatively different from that of men (see Chapter 6), and it seems unlikely that their growing participation rates will provide a direct substitute for any decrease in the number of male workers. Female economic activity rates are already very high in Portugal, and much of the increase for women in most member states has been in temporary and part-time work. Migratory pressures might be expected to come rather from neighbouring countries to the south of the Union (North Africa and the Middle East) and to the east from Central and Eastern Europe.

In this section the possible implications of the Union's policies for non-European immigrants are examined in the context of growing incentives for intra-European mobility as a result of the completion of the SEM. Attention is given to questions concerning nationality, citizenship and social protection rights and to the prospects of the European Union contributing to an underclass of non-European migrants.

Policies on non-European immigration

Freedom of movement, as provided for in the EEC Treaty, was not intended to apply to non-EEC nationals. While the freedom of movement clause in the Treaty outlawed discrimination based on nationality (Article 48 paragraph 2), it said nothing about racial discrimination against non-EEC nationals.

The issue of non-European migration was placed on the social agenda in 1976 when Council Regulation (EEC) No. 311/76 was adopted 'on the compilation of statistics on foreign workers' [9.6], at the same time as an action programme for migrant workers and their families [9.7]. From the mid-1980s the need was accepted for a Community policy on immigration. A Council Resolution 'on guidelines for a Community policy on migration' [9.8] was followed in 1986 by a Declaration 'against racism and xenophobia' from the European Parliament, Council and Commission [9.9], which recognised immigration and the associated issues of racism and xenophobia as problems which the Community should address. The Declaration outlawed all forms of discrimination and expressions of racism, calling on member states to adopt measures to protect the identity and dignity of all members of society regardless of race, religion, nationality or ethnic group, to prevent or eliminate discrimination and raise awareness of the dangers of racism and xenophobia.

While the rights to freedom of movement were being actively developed at European level for migrants within the Community, individual member states were tightening controls over non-European immigration and extending visa requirements, lending a social justification to the description of the Community as 'Fortress Europe'. Analysis of the demographic situation showed that by the mid-1980s, following decisions taken in 1973/74 by the main host countries, immigration into the Community had been halted [9.17, p. 6], although residual immigration was continuing through reunification of families, the arrival of political refugees and illegal entry.

In the absence of Community jurisdiction for third-country nationals, member states continued to pursue their own immigration policies. Martin Baldwin-Edwards (1991) has identified four national policy regimes in Europe: he describes Belgium, France, Germany, Luxembourg and the Netherlands as conforming to the Continental or Schengen model; the United Kingdom is said to have shifted away from its former liberal policy to strict control and a redefinition of citizenship; Denmark exemplifies the Scandinavian model; and Greece,

Italy, Portugal and Spain, as well as Ireland, represent the semi-peripheral or Mediterranean regime.

The Continental or Schengen immigration regime is characterised by a move towards stricter control over immigration in the traditional labour importing industrialised countries, a position which the United Kingdom also adopted, while Denmark, in common with other Nordic states, continued to pursue more liberal policies. The semi-peripheral countries have in common their emigratory histories and have not therefore developed infrastructures for absorbing immigrants, although Portugal, Italy and Spain have all introduced visa controls.

By the early 1990s member states were beginning to approach a common position over third-country migrants. The Maastricht Treaty gave the Council the power, acting unanimously (with provision subsequently for qualified majority voting), to 'determine the third countries whose nationals must be in possession of a visa when crossing the external borders of the Member States' (Article 100c). Provision was made for extending these powers to asylum and immigration policy and to policy regarding nationals of third countries, covering conditions of entry and residence, family reunion and employment and efforts to combat unauthorised immigration (Article K.1). At the same time the Commission was working to strengthen co-operation with third countries and to ensure the integration of legal immigrants resident in the Union. It was also looking for ways of easing migratory pressure by improving the economic position of developing countries [9.13]; for example in the Lomé Convention between the Community and sixty-nine African, Caribbean and Pacific countries. Other programmes have been established for the Mediterranean countries and for Central and Eastern Europe. The Commission has set up information networks on immigration from third countries (Rimet) and for local authorities on ethnic minorities (Elaine). In addition, it funds projects submitted by non-governmental organisations to promote the integration of migrants. The 1994 White Paper on European social policy demonstrated that the Union was concerned to develop a policy on third-country nationals and asylum-seekers through measures to ensure their social and economic integration [1.13, pp. 29–30].

While the Council seemed unsure about its competence in the area of migration, as indicated by the decision to leave a number of issues concerning immigration in abeyance in the Maastricht Treaty, two agreements were being negotiated by member states independently. The Schengen Agreement on asylum and visas was signed in 1985, initially by the EEC founder members except for Italy, and had been ratified by all member states except Denmark, Ireland and the United Kingdom by the time it was due for implementation in 1994. The intention of the signatories was to harmonise frontier controls and procedures over asylum-seekers. Since questions of drug traffic and terrorism were also on the agenda, the expectation was that the group would favour tight restrictions and would do little to protect the rights of legal refugees and immigrants (Rex, 1992, p. 116). The Dublin Convention on the right of asylum was signed in 1990 by all member states. One of its objectives, as in the Schengen Agreement, was to ensure that an application for asylum could not be submitted in several member states at the same time. Both agreements raised important issues concerning national sovereignty since they implied that a decision reached in one member state should be accepted without renegotiation in another

As approaches to immigration vary historically across the Union, this is not an area where concerted action is easy to achieve. France, Germany and the United Kingdom have, for example, all been major importers of non-European immigrants, but each has developed its own ideology and approach. France, which became a country of immigration in the mid-nineteenth century, sought to assimilate its immigrants and therefore made it relatively easy to obtain French nationality. Since French policy left little room for cultural diversity, the major tensions in French society tended to be ethnic and cultural rather than racial (Rex, 1992, pp. 110, 114). The United Kingdom pursued a policy of encouraging and absorbing immigration from its colonies, particularly after the Second World War, and demonstrated its intention to create a multicultural society, for example by setting up a Commission for Racial Equality in 1976. Germany developed a combination of what John Rex (1992, p.111) has called 'the ethnic nationalist and the guest-worker ideologies', whereby its foreign workers have been considered as temporary guest workers who would return home in due course and did not therefore need to be assimilated. At the same time it adopted a liberal policy towards asylum-seekers, especially with respect to ethnic Germans (*Aussiedler*), at least until 1991 when a bill was drawn up to end automatic right of entry.

Whatever their immigration policy regimes, all member states have moved towards quota systems. Since the mid-1970s, borders have progressively been closed, particularly to unskilled workers. In 1987 Belgium, Denmark, Germany and the United Kingdom introduced legislation to impose fines on airlines carrying passengers without the necessary papers. Countries such as France and Germany have tried to reverse the flow of immigrants by providing incentives to encourage immigrants to return home, sometimes in the form of forced repatriation for unemployed immigrant workers.

Measurements of migratory flows from non-European member states

Precise estimates of the number of non-European migrants are difficult to obtain since many immigrants are not legally registered, and foreign born residents who have been naturalised in a member state are no longer recognised as non-European. Official figures suggest that, in the early 1990s, non-European citizens outnumbered citizens from member states residing in the Union, accounting for about 2.8 per cent of the Union's population [9.20, fig. 1). Germany and France had the highest percentage of non-European citizens, with 43 and 24 per cent of the total respectively, followed by the United Kingdom with 11 per cent; the proportion in Greece, Ireland, Portugal and Spain was very small [9.20, fig. 5).

European and national policies on immigration affected the nature of non-European migration in the 1980s: family reunification became a dominant source of immigration, and the number of asylum-seekers rose, particularly towards the end of the decade following German unification. Illegal immigration into southern Europe, especially from North Africa, increased, however, largely due to demographic pressures in the countries supplying immigrants and to the inadequate control of some of the Union's external borders.

Nationality and citizenship

Under the terms of the Maastricht Treaty nationality and citizenship rules remained within the competence of member states, but they are subject to any bilateral international agreements that may have been concluded. Just as it is difficult to measure the extent of intra-European mobility because many migrants become citizens of the country in which they take up residence, variations in ways of attributing nationality and citizenship make it difficult to compare the size of non-European migrant populations in member states. In cases where nationality has been attributed on the basis of the place of birth (*jus soli*), as in Belgium, France, Greece, Italy, Luxembourg, the Netherlands, Spain and the United Kingdom, the number of individuals described as 'foreigners' may be much smaller than in countries where it has been attributed on the basis of descent (*jus sanguinis*) or parental nationality, as in Denmark, Germany, Ireland and Portugal. In both cases the state has normally had discretionary power to grant citizenship by naturalisation and can therefore control the process. When *jus sanguinis* applies and naturalisation has been difficult to achieve, second and third generation 'migrants' may still not have obtained nationality of the country where they were born. The number of years of residence required before naturalisation becomes possible has also varied: from five in France, Ireland, Italy, the Netherlands and the United Kingdom to ten in Germany, Luxembourg and Spain (Baldwin-Edwards, 1991, table 8). Germany has imposed strict requirements concerning language, attitude and employment before granting naturalisation, whereas the Netherlands have been much more liberal. The United Kingdom has given officials making decisions great discretion; in the early 1990s it had six categories of nationality, but only one that conferred the right to reside in the country. Nationality did not therefore necessarily coincide with citizenship.

Differences in nationality laws mean that, depending upon the place of birth and the country to which they or their parents migrate, the children of immigrants may or may not be able to acquire another nationality and the citizenship rights that it confers.

FREEDOM OF MOVEMENT IN A MULTISPEED EUROPE

Paradoxically, despite the implementation of the SEM, by the early 1990s European policy on migrant workers seemed to be shifting away from incentives to encourage movement to areas of higher labour demand. Instead, it was directed at building up regional and local economies in areas with job shortages [9.16, p. 108]. Non-European immigration was strictly controlled at the level of individual member states, but the Union had shown its reluctance or inability to formulate policies based on a common agreement over the citizenship rights of third-country nationals.

Social protection rights, which had been a major issue for intra-European mobility, were being used by some member states as an exclusionary mechanism limiting access to benefits and services for non-European nationals. It has been argued that a passport conferring citizenship of a country in the Union is a valued possession for immigrants from Third World countries because it brings with it 'relatively generous safeguards of existence', explaining why 'states have been so reluctant to grant it' (De Swaan, 1990, p. 19). Rather than serving as an attraction for migrants, social welfare benefits may have become a source of discrimination, thereby further reinforcing the division, already highlighted in previous chapters, between workers who have earned eligibility to social protection and the rights conferred by their nationality, residential and employment status as citizens of the Union and those who are excluded and discriminated against, either directly or indirectly, because of an accident of birth and strict rules on naturalisation.

Access to social protection and citizenship rights has been shown throughout this book to vary from one member state to another and for different categories of migrants. Whereas attempts to encourage mutual recognition of social protection systems have led to transferability of rights for European nationals from one member state to another, these rights have become more difficult to obtain for non-European nationals in some countries than in others. By the early 1990s the right to a basic minimum income was not, for example, subject to any nationality requirements in Denmark and Luxembourg; in France, Ireland and the Netherlands it was dependent on having a residence permit or being legally resident; Belgium, Germany and Italy imposed some restrictions; in the United Kingdom non-European nationals were eligible to receive benefits if their government had a bilateral agreement with reciprocity clauses; Greece and Portugal had no general scheme and Spain was non-specific [9.18, table XII]. In many cases non-European nationals could be less favourably treated than European nationals if they wanted to export benefits: pensions could not, for example, be claimed from France by non-nationals outside the country; the United Kingdom allowed such claims to be made for contributory but not for non-contributory pensions. Since most benefits were conferred or became advantageous only after long terms of residence, non-European migrants without transferable contributions were likely to be excluded from cumulative contributory insurance rights such as income-related pensions, paid sick leave or maternity benefits. Citizenship was required to gain not only political rights but also access to public employment and freedom of movement within the Union. All non-European nationals entering a member state were required to obtain prior authorisation and a residence permit, which could be subject to the holder having the offer of employment. Residence permits could be withdrawn for public order offences or for claiming social assistance.

The elaborate legislative machinery put in place to ensure freedom of movement of labour has been relatively effective in achieving its stated goals of removing formal obstacles to mobility for citizens of the Union, even if intra-European movement has remained limited. Provision for the free movement of workers may, however, have produced an unintended outcome by contributing to the development of a two or possibly three-speed Europe since it restricted access for non-European nationals to many of the social rights guaranteed for workers in member states. In its 1994 White Paper on European social policy the Commission demonstrated its awareness of the problems associated with the integration of non-European migrants and its intention to act [1.13, pp. 26–30]. According to the Commission, the principle of free movement implied that all legally resident third-country nationals should enjoy the right to live and work in the EU country of their choice: they should be given priority for job vacancies after EU nationals and third-country nationals residing in the relevant member state, and their entitlement to social protection should be ensured when they are moving within the Union.

Box 9   Union documents relating to social policy and mobility

SECONDARY LEGISLATION

9.1   Regulations Nos. 3–4 on social security for migrants (*Journal Officiel*, No. 30, 1958).

9.2   Council Regulation (EEC) No. 1612/68 of 15 October 1968 on freedom of movement for workers within the Community (*OJ* L 257/2 19.10.68).

9.3   Council Directive 68/360/EEC of 15 October 1968 on the abolition of restrictions on movement and residence within the Community for workers of member states and their families (*OJ* L 257/13 18.10.68).

9.4   Council Regulation (EEC) No. 1408/71 of 14 June 1971 on the application of social security schemes to employed persons, to self-employed persons and to members of their families moving within the Community (*OJ* L 149/2 5.7.71), amended (EEC) No. 1248/92 (*OJ* L 136/7 19.5.92), consolidated version (*OJ* C 325/1 10.12.92).

9.5 Council Regulation (EEC) No. 574/72 of 21 March 1972 laying down the procedures for implementing Regulation (EEC) No. 1408/71 (*OJ* L 74/1 27.3.72), consolidated version (*OJ* C 325/96 10.12.92).

9.6 Council Regulation (EEC) No. 311/76 of 9 February 1976 on the compilation of statistics on foreign workers (*OJ* L 39/1 14.2.76).

9.7 Council Resolution of 9 February 1976 on an action programme for migrant workers and members of their families (*OJ* C 34/2 14.2.76).

9.8 Council Resolution of 16 July 1985 on guidelines for a Community policy on migration (*OJ* C 186/3 26.7.85).

9.9 European Parliament, Council, Commission Declaration against racism and xenophobia (*OJ* C 158/1 25.6.86).

9.10 Commission Communication on the living and working conditions of Community residents in frontier regions, with special reference to frontier workers (COM(90) 561 final, 27 November 1990).

9.11 Commission Communication of 22 July 1991 on supplementary social security schemes (SEC(91) 1332 final) (*OJ* C 223/13 31.8.92).

9.12 Commission proposal for a Council Directive concerning the posting of workers in the framework of the provision of services (COM(91) 230 final, 13 May 1992) (*OJ* C 150/119 15.6.92).

9.13 Commission Background Report on immigration (ISEC/B26/93, 29 September 1993) (London: CEC).

OFFICIAL PUBLICATIONS OF THE COMMISSION OF THE EUROPEAN COMMUNITIES (CEC) AND EUROSTAT

9.14 CEC (1989) *Employment in Europe 1989.*

9.15 CEC (1992) *Employment in Europe 1992.*

9.16 CEC (1993) *Employment in Europe 1993.*

9.17 CEC/Economic and Social Consultative Assembly (1986) *Demographic Situation in the Community*, Information Report, CES 602/84 fin.

9.18 CEC/Mutual Information System on Social Protection in the Community (1993) *Social Protection in the Member States of the Community: Situation on July 1st 1993 and Evolution.*

9.19 Eurostat (1991) *A Social Portrait of Europe.*

9.20 Eurostat (1993) 'Population by Citizenship in the EC –
1.1.1991', *Rapid Reports. Population and Social Conditions,*
no. 6.

10 Assessing European Social Policy

/After serving for three years as Director General for Social Affairs at the Commission in the 1970s, Michael Shanks could still ask: 'does the European Community have a role to play in the social field . . . over and above that of its member-States? If so, what is it? If not', he wondered, 'what is the degree of social diversity . . . which the European Community can tolerate and survive?' (Shanks, 1977, p. 9). The next two decades brought many signs that the Community was actively developing a social dimension. A spate of social action programmes were initiated in the 1970s, followed in the 1980s by strong statements in support of a social space from the President of the Commission, Jacques Delors, culminating in the signing of the Community Charter of the Fundamental Social Rights of Workers in 1989 [1.7]. The Maastricht Treaty of 1992 on European Union [1.6] extended the sections of the original EEC Treaty [1.2] on social policy to cover education, vocational training and youth, culture and public health (Articles 118–29) and amended the section on economic and social cohesion (Articles 130a-e), which had been introduced in the Single European Act (SEA) in 1986 [1.5]. An Agreement on Social Policy was annexed to the Treaty. Then in 1994, following a lengthy process of consultation, the Commission published a wide-ranging White Paper [1.13] setting the scene for European social policy through to the year 2000.

(Whether this growing interest in the social dimension of the internal market and the apparent extension of Union competence in social affairs are sufficient to justify calling its actions in the social area a 'social policy' is a matter for on-going debate. Despite the use of the heading 'Social Policy' in the EEC Treaty, there was no clear consensus in the 1950s about the need for social intervention, the form it might take and the instruments which might be used to carry it out (see Chapter 1). The EEC had been established as a European Economic Community, and its objectives were therefore defined in economic terms, implying that any harmonisation of social policies between member states could be justified only in so far as it was likely to support and strengthen economic policies) Reference was made in the 1957 EEC

Treaty to harmonisation of social protection systems on the grounds that disparities in provision might impede freedom of movement and distort competition (see Chapter 2). Despite the subsequent name change to the European Communities under the 1967 Merger Treaty [1.4], the focus of attention in the European Council remained resolutely on economic concerns and on the rights of mobile workers. Categories of the population who were not full-time members of the indigenous labour force or undergoing training or retraining for employment were totally neglected under the terms of the original Treaty.

From the early 1970s awareness was growing, however, that economic developments were resulting in regional inequalities. 'Social' intervention was called for at European level as a means of redressing the balance. At the same time the differences in approaches to social protection amongst the founder members were exacerbated as new countries joined the Community in the 1970s (see Chapter 2). The social problems with which the Community was beginning to grapple were brought to the forefront by the energy crises of the mid-1970s and then further intensified as the less economically and socially developed states of southern Europe became members in the early 1980s, making the prospects of harmonising social systems seem ever more remote and unrealistic.

The social action programmes of the 1970s had heightened awareness of the problems of poverty and the needs of disabled people, marginalised and socially excluded groups who had not benefited from the postwar economic boom and whose interests had been neglected in the drive for efficiency, increased productive capacity and competitiveness. The late 1970s and early 1980s saw a burgeoning of new action programmes and legislation to promote equal opportunities between men and women, followed by the creation of a series of national observatories and networks responsible for collecting and co-ordinating information about trends and for monitoring the situation, so that policy makers would be in a stronger position to recommend appropriate action.

The Community Charter of the Fundamental Social Rights of Workers, the social chapter in the Maastricht Treaty and the White Paper on European social policy might therefore appear as the logical outcome of many years of monitoring and negotiation, affording the Union an opportunity to make a clear statement on its social policy aims and objectives and to raise the social dimension to a more elevated status. Despite the assertion in its preamble that, in the context of the internal market, 'the same importance must be attached to the social aspects as to the economic aspects', which were to 'be developed in a balanced manner', the Charter itself did not turn out to be a strong policy document capable of demonstrating the commitment of member states to social affairs on a par with their support for economic cohesion. Rather, it highlighted persistent differences between member states in policy-making objectives and styles.

The solemn declaration on the Fundamental Social Rights of Workers, even though much diluted in its final stages, was adopted by only eleven member states. Three years later, after considerable debate in national parliaments and referenda in Denmark, France and Ireland, the Maastricht Treaty was signed, but only after the chapter on social policy had been removed from the main body of the text on the insistence of the United Kingdom. The United Kingdom's opt-out, the emphasis in the Charter and Treaty on the principle of subsidiarity and the need for unanimous voting on the subject of social protection, whereas other social areas such as health and safety required only qualified majority voting, meant that initiatives from the Commission on social affairs could still be easily blocked or rendered ineffectual. Doubts about the ability of member states to agree over social policies had been confirmed; the competence of the Union to take policy decisions had been called into question, and member states had demonstrated that they were not prepared to forgo national sover-eignty in the interests of greater European social solidarity.

But does this failure to reach agreement over the social chapter necessarily signify that the Union had not developed a capability in the area of social policy or that its initiatives had not influenced national policy making? Does the Union, perhaps in spite of itself, have a social policy of its own, which is not simply an aggregate of the social policies of its member states, enabling it to respond to needs which cannot be satisfied at the national level? In this concluding chapter, an attempt is made to answer these two complex and interrelated questions with reference to the materials and policy areas discussed throughout the book, before going on to speculate about the future of social policy in the European Union in the light of the proposals outlined in the 1994 White Paper.

THE PARAMETERS OF A EUROPEAN SOCIAL POLICY

Opinions on whether or not the Union has progressively established a coherent social policy of its own depend to a large extent upon definitions. If a broad definition of social policy is used, it would probably be difficult to deny that the Community has developed a social policy competence, although, as argued below, doubts could still be expressed about its coherence and autonomy. Social policy broadly defined, following Richard Titmuss (1974, pp. 23–32), might be described in terms of the principles governing actions directed towards achieving specified ends, through the provision of welfare, minimum standards of income and some measure of progressive redistribution in command over resources, in such a way as to shape the development of society. In seeking to ground social policy more firmly in social theory, Ramesh Mishra (1977) also needed a broad definition. Accordingly he defined social policy as 'those social arrangements, patterns and mechanisms that are typically concerned with the distribution of resources in accordance with some criterion of need' (Mishra, 1977, p. xi).

The parameters identified in these two general definitions, and generally adopted in the social policy literature, can be used in retracing the themes which recur throughout the book. Firstly, in delimiting the scope of a European social policy, evidence is reviewed in support of the claim that the Single European Market (SEM) gives equal importance to the social and economic dimensions. The theme of redistribution is considered both in this context and with reference to the citizenship versus worker's rights debate in the provision of welfare and income maintenance. Social policy arrangements, patterns and mechanisms of distribution are then examined in the context of the shift away from the aim of harmonising social protection systems towards a convergence strategy. Disparity between national social protection systems is considered as an obstacle to convergence and is illustrated with reference to the models of welfare provision which can be identified in different policy areas.

Equalising the economic and social dimensions

In the early years of the EEC, a complementary relationship existed between economic and social policy objectives, but the dominant partner was undoubtedly the economic dimension. Although the social aspects of the Community were gaining salience in the mid-1980s, the equal importance that was being advocated for the social dimension of the internal market, as indicated in the preamble to the Community Charter, was not substantiated by other statements in the same text which spoke of top priority being given to employment development and creation in the SEM; the social consensus was to be seen as strengthening the competitiveness of undertakings and the creation of employment. Social policy was, in sum, to be a pre-requisite and a support for economic integration, or even a facilitator, rather than an equal partner, an essential condition for ensuring sustained economic development.

Later paragraphs more explicitly outlined the action necessary to counter the possible adverse spill-over effects for the social area of the completion of the internal market. Measures would be needed, according to the preamble, to ensure that the SEM resulted in improvements in the social field for workers, especially in the areas which had long before been identified in the EEC Treaty: freedom of movement, living and working conditions, health and safety at work, social protection, education and training. More innovative recommendations were made on the subjects of equal treatment and social exclusion. Member states were enjoined to combat all discrimination on grounds not only of sex, as in the EEC Treaty and directives of the 1970s and 1980s, but also with reference to colour, race, opinions and beliefs. The fight against social exclusion, which had been pursued since the 1970s through social action programmes, was to be continued 'in a spirit of solidarity'. The Charter itself did not develop these themes or reproduce the emotive language of the preamble. The declaration was couched in bland and imprecise turns of phrase, which the Agreement on Social Policy annexed to the Maastricht Treaty did nothing to remedy. The relationship between the economic and social dimensions, as revealed in the Community's and Union's Treaties and Charter, has been aptly summarised in terms of 'the trade-off between equity and efficiency' (Gold and Mayes, 1993, p. 35).

The genesis of the social dimension of the SEA and European Union can perhaps best be understood within the context of the debate in the 1980s about the impact of economic dislocation resulting from the completion of the internal market on regions in the less developed areas of the Union. The social dimension, according to this interpretation, was a response to the growing concern amongst member states over the regional imbalance that would stem from the free play of the market and ultimately be to the detriment of the whole Union. Intervention through social policy at European level was therefore justified as a means of redressing the balance, assisting labour mobility and maintaining the supply of social benefits and services on grounds of efficiency.

Another economic argument used in support of social policies was that disparities between social protection systems would result in social dumping if nations with higher labour costs sought to move production to countries where labour was cheaper. This argument was losing some of its force in the early 1990s in a situation where national governments in all member states were looking for ways of containing the cost of social spending and reducing unemployment because of their negative effects on productivity and competitiveness in non-European markets. Any relocation of industry on the basis of social costs was therefore more likely to be in Third World countries where labour was still relatively cheap and workers enjoyed little or no social protection.

The equity argument is also part of the debate over the relative importance of the social and economic dimensions of the internal market and contributes to an understanding of the Union's social policy objectives. Intervention at European level was advocated on the grounds that, by giving free rein to market forces, the SEM would produce a two-speed Europe with some regions falling behind. Although the Commission has always had social funds to allocate to priority regions in order to offset the harmful effects of economic dislocation, they have represented only a very small proportion of the Union's budget (see Chapter 8). Spending on the poverty programmes and other social actions has done little to raise the overall social expenditure to a level which might have an enduring and truly redistributive impact on social problem areas and underprivileged population groups.

The relative lack of concern (and of competence) on the part of the Community with redistribution and direct reduction of disadvantage distinguishes it from social policy commitments in member states (Gold and Mayes, 1993, p. 28), suggesting that the social dimension may be destined to continue to play a subordinate role in the European Union. A cynical view of the reason why social aspects were built into the economic integration package is that the intention was 'to ease the transition into the internal market by reassuring workers that there will be a social dimension; and to assist the casualties of the process of economic restructuring which is at the heart of the whole integration project' (Kleinman and Piachaud, 1993, p.10). This view finds some support in the opening remarks to the 1994 White Paper where reference was made to the vital part to be played by social policy at European level in underpinning the process of change. Solidarity was juxtaposed to competitiveness as shared values, and high social standards were presented as a 'key element in the competitive formula' [1.13, pp. 1–2].

The citizenship versus workers' rights debate

The priority which has constantly, and understandably, been given to economic objectives has gone hand in hand with an emphasis on workers' rather than citizenship rights. If social policy is by definition universally applicable and redistributive, then the focus on workers could be seen as creating a serious deficit in coverage.

Even though the preamble to the Community Charter and the action programmes for implementing it suggest that intervention at European level was intended to go beyond the needs of workers, at the last minute, largely for pragmatic reasons, the term 'workers' was substituted in the Charter for 'citizens'. Every section of the Charter makes reference to workers, working life or employment: freedom of movement applies to workers (points 1–3); a decent standard of living is to be achieved for workers through equitable wages from employment (point 5); improvements are sought in working conditions for all workers (points 7–9); freedom of association applies to workers (points 11–14); vocational training is to be provided for every worker throughout working life (point 15); equal treatment for men and women applies in the realm of employment (point 16); information, consultation and participation are intended for the working population (points 17–18); provision for health protection and safety is at the workplace (point 19); protection of children and adolescents is intended to ensure that they are properly prepared for work and that young workers are provided with suitable working conditions (points 20–3); workers are to be guaranteed sufficient resources in retirement (points 24–5); and disabled persons are to be assisted in their social and professional integration (point 26).

The emphasis on workers can be explained by two main reasons. Firstly, the social protection systems in most member states were derived from the employment insurance-related model characteristic of continental Europe rather than being based on universal access as of right, such as applied generally in Denmark or in the national health services of the United Kingdom and Italy (see Chapters 2 and 4). Social protection rights were therefore conceptualised by most member states with reference to employment and labour markets. Secondly, the EEC had been established as an economic community, where the justification for any interest in human and social rights was a consequence of the need to ensure the free movement of labour as an important component in factor mobility. The objectives of creating the conditions for economic restructuring in the context of the SEM similarly gave priority to workers' rights in the context of freedom of movement (see Chapter 9).

The aims of the Maastricht Treaty were broader. It was intended 'to promote economic and social progress which is balanced and sustainable . . . through the strengthening of economic and social cohesion', and also 'to strengthen the protection of the rights and interests of the nationals of its Members States through the introduction of a citizenship of the Union' (Article B). Member states undertook to 'respect fundamental rights, as guaranteed by the European Convention for the Protection of Human Rights and Fundamental Freedoms' (Article F). The rights of 'citizens of the Union', as set out in the Treaty, concerned political representation. Social rights did not figure as such in the body of the Treaty, although two new social policy areas which made no reference to workers were introduced: in a section on culture (Title IX Article 128) the signatories to the Treaty asserted their intention to encourage the 'flowering of cultures' while respecting national and regional cultural diversity; under the heading 'Public Health' (Title X Article 129) high levels of human health protection and co-ordination of health policies were to be promoted.

The Agreement on Social Policy, however, focused even more resolutely on workers as, for example, in Article 2 point 1, which referred to the 'integration of persons excluded from the labour market' but said nothing about minimum levels of social protection for non-workers. In the early 1990s it was estimated that between a quarter and a third of the population of working age in member states were temporarily or permanently excluded from the labour market (Abrahamson, 1992, p. 11). Women are particularly likely to be marginalised by the employment model of welfare (see Chapter 6). Since they are more often than men in low paid precarious forms of employment, many women not only lack the benefits of a reasonable and secure income from paid work, but they are also denied access to good pensions, sickness benefits and other payments that accrue from long-term employment. Additionally, the caring role (for children, older and disabled people), which is most often performed by women, is known to affect their eligibility for employment-related benefits (Chapter 7). Although the theme of equal treatment was present in the EEC Treaty and was reiterated in both the Community Charter and the Maastricht Treaty, the emphasis was again on labour market opportunities and treatment at work. The Community Charter did attempt to take some account of the status of women as mothers by proposing that help should be given to both men and women to enable them to reconcile family and employment responsibilities (point 16), but the topic was only obliquely alluded to in the Maastricht Treaty (Article 6), suggesting that even the eleven signatories had difficulty in supporting a principle which might result in a broadening of the scope of the Union's action to the rights of non-workers.

Another category whose interests were neglected, despite the reference in the preamble to the Charter, was the heterogeneous group of non-European immigrants (see Chapter 9). Although freedom of movement of workers was an essential pre-requisite for the efficient functioning of the internal market, for the purposes of the Community's and Union's Treaties migrant workers were understood to be European nationals. Since the 1970s all member states have been closing their doors to immigrants from third countries. While paying lip service to integration policies, they have been tightening up their nationality laws, justifying the description of a Fortress Europe, where non-European migrants have become an underclass, the lowest of the low, often deprived of citizenship rights. The Maastricht Treaty demonstrated that member states had reached agreement over provision for visa require-ments for third-country nationals (Article 100c), but that they were reluctant to commit themselves to a common policy on asylum-seekers and immigration, although they did, nonetheless, make provision for co-operation in this area at a later stage (Article K.1).

The White Paper attempted to present a more broadly based European social policy, concerned not only with working conditions but also with people's lives when they are not at work. Although top priority was still to be given to job creation, growth and competitive-ness, the Commission's stated aim was 'to develop and improve standards for *all* the Members of the Union' [1.13, p. 5], by which it meant workers as well as older and disabled people and their carers, young people, the long-term unemployed and third-country nationals.

From harmonisation to convergence strategy

The issue of how member states should deal with individuals and groups that do not fall directly within the terms of reference of the Community's and Union's Treaties and Charter highlights the problems of trying to eliminate national differences in the provision of social protection. Although the term harmonisation, which first appeared in Article 117 of the EEC Treaty, was not removed either by the SEA or the Maastricht Treaty, it was clear from the Council

Recommendation 'on the convergence of social protection objectives and policies' [2.1] that harmonisation had been recognised to be a wholly unrealistic aim that did not have the support of member states. When the EEC was established economic arguments had been used to justify the need to align social protection systems (approximation was introduced in Article 100 and was retained in Article 100a of the SEA) in order to remove obstacles to labour mobility and to prevent distortion of competition in a situation where labour costs were much higher in some countries than in others. As Denmark, Ireland and the United Kingdom joined the Community in the 1970s, and then the southern European countries in the 1980s, the case for establishing a level playing field was even stronger, but disparities between social protection systems had become greater, making harmonisation even more difficult to achieve both in practical and ideological terms (see Chapter 2). The debate about the social dimension in the late 1980s and early 1990s took place in a context where harmonisation of systems was no longer considered appropriate. Even the concept of convergence' was being approached with caution. Although it was not used explicitly in the Community Charter, subsidiarity had become a key concept by the time the Maastricht Treaty was signed in 1992 (Article 3b) and was reaffirmed in the 1994 White Paper, which referred to 'a positive and active conception of subsidiarity' as the key to a co-operative partnership between the Union, member states, social partners and European citizens [1.13, p. 4].

The desire to protect national interests was clearly articulated in both the Charter and the social chapter. In the Charter social protection rights and provision for elderly persons were to be considered 'According to the arrangements applying in each country' (introduction to points 10, 24 and 25). Implementation of the Charter was to be the 'responsibility of the Member States, in accordance with the national practices' (point 27). In the Maastricht Treaty measures to be implemented under the Agreement on Social Policy were to 'take account of the diverse forms of national practices' (Article 1). In the Council Recommendation 'on convergence of social policy objectives and policies', because of the diversity of national systems, member states were left 'to determine how their social protection schemes should be framed and the arrangements for financing and organizing them' [2.1, p. 50].

Article 118 of the EEC Treaty had introduced another concept which was not far removed from the position eventually reached in the 1990s: close co-operation in the social field. Although the title of the 1992

Recommendation focused on convergence, co-operation might have been a more accurate description of the Council's intentions. The 'convergence strategy' being promoted was aimed at setting 'common objectives able to guide Member States' policies in order to permit the co-existence of different national systems and to enable them to progress in harmony with one another towards the fundamental objectives of the Community' [2.1, p 50], an aim confirmed by the 1994 White Paper. In this context convergence would be *de facto*, and Community action was justified on the grounds that comparable trends were leading to common economic and demographic problems – ageing of the population, changing family situations, the persistence of high levels of unemployment and the spread of poverty – which required common, or at least co-ordinated, solutions in order to reduce any disparities impeding freedom of movement.

Another form of spontaneous convergence was thought to be occurring due to the difficulties being experienced by all member states, primarily as a result of economic recession and demographic ageing, in meeting the rising cost of social policy provisions. In their search for ways of curbing state spending all member states were reviewing their welfare systems (see Chapters 4, 5, 7 and 8). Universal benefits and services paid for from taxation were being called into question in Denmark. Health care was being off-loaded from the state to the private sector in Italy and the United Kingdom. Child benefits were being targeted at low income families in Spain. In France the burden of labour costs was being reduced by progressively replacing employer contributions to family allowances by a tax on all incomes, and by exemptions from social insurance contributions for firms taking on unemployed workers. The duration of unemployment benefits was being reduced, and the conditions for claiming pensions and social assistance were being revised in several member states.

Rather than the upwards convergence towards a high standard of provision, which was being sought in the 1980s, the likelihood in the 1990s was that member states might converge towards the form of provision that had developed in the United Kingdom, whereby social protection costs were kept low by paying flat-rate subsistence level benefits (Walker and Simpson, 1993, p. 112). The prospect of further convergence towards the employment insurance-related model of welfare, with the dualisation and polarisation it was expected to engender, was equally disconcerting (Abrahamson, 1992, p. 10). The 1992 Council Recommendation on convergence was non-committal on the question of the model towards which systems might converge: while it referred to the need to ensure maximum efficiency and effectiveness and to guarantee a minimum means of subsistence enabling people at risk to maintain their standard of living in a reasonable manner, these objectives were to be achieved either through flat-rate benefits or benefits calculated in relation to earnings, leaving member states to make their own choices.

The 1994 White Paper emphasised the need for minimum standards of social protection which would not over-stretch the economically weaker member states but would not prevent the more developed ones from implementing higher standards [1.13, p. 5]. In the absence of any clear guidance in official documents, several policy analysts have attempted to define specific objectives towards which national systems might be converging. In order to ensure as high a level of provision as possible, some have supported the idea of operating a 'European social snake' or a 'European social policy band' (Berghman, 1990, pp. 13–14; Pieters, 1991, p. 188; Leibfried, 1992, pp. 109–10), modelled on the European Monetary System (EMS), with the objective of reducing divergence and encouraging upward convergence. These proposals included mechanisms for monitoring both the level of social protection in each member state and the average European level: the convergence of social security systems, based on a European average of social protection, would be combined with the maintenance and, if possible, raising of levels of social protection in all member states.

National arrangements for welfare provision

The emphasis on workers in the Community's and Union's Treaties and the Charter can be seen both as a reflection of the economic forces driving the internal market and as an indication of the continuing influence of the employment-related model of welfare that was dominant amongst the social protection systems of the founder members. In its revisions to the EEC Treaty and in statements on social policy, as illustrated above, the Commission has been careful to affirm its recognition of national differences in social protection arrangements and to state that any moves towards convergence, however desirable, should respect national systems. These provisions are an acknowledgement that the Commission has learnt from experience that it cannot override national sensitivities and interests. One of the reasons why the first Danish referendum on the Maastricht Treaty did not gain support was that the Danes feared European union would result in a reduction of their high level of social protection. The

United Kingdom invoked the opposite argument, claiming that labour costs would increase due to the need to raise the level of social protection. The responses received to the Green Paper on European social policy in 1993–94 confirmed the lack of consensus between member states over the need for further legislation on labour standards at European level [1.13, p. 23].

In the absence of a clearly defined role for the Union as a social state in its own right, as argued below, the representation of social policy which emerges from Commission documents remains largely a reflection of strong national policies. The EEC Treaty included social policy as an answer to the insistence by the French that they should not be put at a competitive disadvantage by their relatively high labour costs. Article 119 on equal pay for men and women was introduced to accommodate provision in the French constitution, and the free movement of labour was intended to help Italy relieve its unemployment problem (see Chapters 1, 6 and 9). The mark of the French social policy-making style under the Mitterrand presidency can be found in the Community Charter and the Agreement on Social Policy in the emphasis on social dialogue between the social partners and the representation and collective defence of the interests of workers.

Numerous differences can still be easily identified between member states not only in social protection arrangements but also in the policy-making process. Consequently it is difficult to talk of a common social policy for the Union such as might be formed from the sum of its parts. The different social policy styles of member states can be loosely grouped with reference to the three waves of membership of the Union: the continental model of the founder members, although Italy with its national health service shared some characteristics of the Nordic and Anglo-Saxon members that joined in the second wave of membership in the 1970s, and the less developed forms of welfare represented by the southern European states that became members in the 1980s, although their social protection systems were largely dependent on employment-related insurance (see Chapter 2 and Appendix 2).

The distinction between the continental and Nordic/Anglo-Saxon models, as referred to here, focuses essentially on the underlying conceptual difference between welfare systems which depend on employment-related insurance benefits and those which offer universalist services on a flat-rate basis funded primarily from taxation. This classification can be readily applied in areas such as pensions for older people, and is helpful in understanding arrangements for income maintenance (see Chapters 7 and 8). Provision for older people in member states may be made according to several different models: through policies ensuring income security, so that retirement is a logical extension of working life, as operated mainly in the continental welfare states; or by providing basic security as in the Nordic and Anglo-Saxon countries, bordering on residual state welfare in the United Kingdom; and what may be described as rudimentary or formative welfare in the southern European countries, where provision is basic and coverage fragmentary. Similar distinctions can be found in the provision made by member states for unemployment benefits where the link with previous earnings remains strong in the continental welfare states, particularly in Germany. The difference between national arrangements is less clear cut in the case of social assistance. The level of benefits varies considerably from one country to another for different categories of beneficiaries, with no general scheme at all in Greece and Portugal. Emphasis on reintegration into the labour market is more explicit in some countries, for example France, than in others.

The provision of health services reflects the distinction between countries that rely on the insurance model as compared with the welfare model of social protection: the insurance principle is the basis of the systems in Belgium, France, Germany, Luxembourg and the Netherlands, whereas the Nordic and Anglo-Saxon countries, as well as the southern European member states and Italy, relied on publicly funded health services. Within these broad categories, differences can be found in access to treatment, arrangements for payment and the cost of providing services (Chapter 4).

National policies for the welfare of women tend to cut across the distinction between the employment-related insurance model and the universal citizenship rights model: some member states stressed the dependence of women on the male breadwinner, namely Germany, Ireland, the Netherlands and the United Kingdom, while in others women were well protected as mothers, as in Italy, or they have acquired rights both as mothers and as workers, as in Denmark and France (see Chapter 6).

Analysis of national approaches to family policy tends to highlight distinctions between countries which, at one end of the spectrum, have adopted a relatively coherent, autonomous and explicit policy stance, such as France, Belgium and Luxembourg, from those at the other end of the spectrum which tend to pursue more implicit family policies, playing down the interventionist role of the state, namely the United Kingdom, Ireland and the Mediterranean countries (see Chapter 5).

Yet other models emerge from an analysis of the relationship between education, training and labour markets: whereas Belgium, Denmark, France and the Netherlands have training-led school-based systems, Germany relies heavily on industrial apprenticeship training, and the United Kingdom is sometimes described as a laggard in the field of training and operates an educational system characterised by early specialisation and low participation rates in higher education (see Chapter 3).

Policy on non-European immigration also points to a dominant continental model, but within it a distinction can be made between a very strict attitude in Germany towards acquisition of nationality, an emphasis in France on assimilation and a multicultural approach in the Netherlands, similar to that found in the more liberal regimes of the United Kingdom (at least in the past) and Denmark. The Mediterranean or semi-peripheral member states have tended to be countries of emigration rather than immigration (see Chapter 9).

Faced with such diversity and competing models of welfare, either the Union could have adopted policies in line with the dominant and majority continental welfare model, but at the risk of alienating member states which would feel their interests were being ignored, or it could have tried to identify a level of provision, possibly a lowest common denominator, around which systems could be aligned. Here the risk, as mentioned above, was that some of the wealthier countries would not wish to forgo their higher levels of provision, while some of the poorer member states might have difficulty in meeting even a low level of provision. The issue was raised again by proposals for further enlargement of the Union in the 1990s. Amongst the states which had applied to take up membership of the Union in 1995, Austria was close to the continental model of welfare, while Finland and Sweden represented the Nordic model, thus slightly shifting the balance away from the dominance of the earnings-related systems. Another alternative, which was not necessarily incompatible with either of the other two possibilities, was for the Union to become a social policy actor in its own right.

THE UNION AS A SOCIAL POLICY ACTOR

When individual member states were developing their own more comprehensive social security systems, mostly in the first half of the twentieth century in the case of northern Europe, they did not start from a clean slate. France affords a good example of a country which was unable to overcome fundamental ideological divisions and vested interests in trying to conceive a unified social security system in 1945 (Laroque, 1985). Regional disparities have also made comprehensive social welfare provision elusive, not only in federal states such as Germany (the two Germanys present a special case) but also in Italy, where harmonisation of social protection has yet to be achieved at national level. With examples such as these in their midst, it is difficult to understand the optimism of the founder members in expecting harmonisation of social systems to occur automatically as a result of the functioning of the common market or even with support from procedures for approximation, as provided for in Article 117 of the EEC Treaty. It is not altogether clear why harmonisation or approximation of national policies was considered to be the best solution to the issues raised by the common market.

The need to make provision for migrant workers, the main motivation for including harmonisation of social policy in the Treaty, could have been answered by establishing the Union as a social state in its own right (Leibfried, 1992, p. 97). The 'thirteenth state', a solution suggested by Danny Pieters (1991, pp. 186–8), would have involved superimposing an additional European scheme on top of existing national arrangements. To be effective, it is argued that such a scheme would need to cover all risks and be at least as attractive as national social security systems and as advantageous as the system offering the most favourable arrangements. Benefits could be funded by employers' and employees' contributions and subsidised by the Union. In the longer term such a 'federal social security system' might be extended to other categories of workers or to whole member states. In the absence of a supranational or federal social protection system, the Union does provide social security entitlements for its own employees, but no single programme covers all European citizens for any one risk, whether it be health, disability, old age, unemployment, poverty or family responsibilities, leaving unanswered the question whether the Union has its own social policy.

In the 1970s Shanks described 'the role the Commission has been able to play in the social policy field in recent years as a catalyst, an educator and influencer, a co-ordinator of research, a data-bank and a standard-setter' (Shanks, 1977, p. 84). He was prepared to judge the Commission's effectiveness in the social policy area on its success in this role, defending his view that: 'It [social policy] is . . . about a common approach to problem-solving, about pooling of ideas and efforts to overcome defects in the quality of life, about a gradual coming together in the search for a European society which will better meet the needs of all its citizens' (Shanks, 1977, p. 85). From a reading of the Community's and Union's Treaties and Charter, with their focus on workers and their lack of precision over boundaries and recommended levels of provision, it is tempting to draw the conclusion that the European Union of the 1990s had not moved on from Shanks's conception of social policy. Almost twenty years later another Commissioner for Social Affairs, Pádraig Flynn, used very similar terms to describe the Commission's role as 'a clearing house for information and catalyst for action' (Flynn, 1993, p. 3).

The Union has been said to lack 'any coherent, consistent or comprehensive social philosophy or policy' (Kleinman and Piachaud, 1993, p. 3), and doubts have been expressed about its ability to redistribute resources (Gold and Mayes, 1993, p. 36). The Union's social policy may not encompass all disadvantaged groups, its resources may be limited and its objectives may not always be coherent, but the same can be said of most national social policies. It can be argued, for example, that France has one of most coherent and comprehensive family policies amongst member states, but it is not difficult to find inconsistencies in objectives or provisions (see Chapter 5). Denmark is credited with making the most generous social protection provision on a universal citizenship basis, yet the Danes have also had to cut back on services and look for alternative means of funding benefits (see Chapter 7), and they have been forced to admit that the equality goal has not been achieved (Carlsen and Larsen, 1993). The United Kingdom has shifted away from tax-funded flat-rate universal coverage to a system which depends increasingly on targeted means-tested benefits, occupational insurance schemes and privatisation of services (see Chapter 2).

In the social policy context comprehensiveness and coherence are relative concepts, but the Treaties and Charter provide only a limited view of the social policy competence of the Union. Scrutiny of the social action programmes of the 1970s and 1980s, the 1990 action programme to implement the principles of the Community Charter [1.9], the *acquis communautaire* in the area of social affairs and the Green and White Papers on European social policy shows that the Commission has not been negligent. As demonstrated throughout this book, the Union's institutions have intervened actively in the areas of education and training, health, living and working conditions, social protection, equal pay and treatment of workers, the protection of children, older and disabled people and in regional development, and they have also shown their interest in resolving the problem of social exclusion. The instruments used have involved legislation, action programmes, financial incentives as well as direct provision of resources under the Structural Funds.

The Commission has moved forward social action by promoting its own programmes in the areas of vocational training, disabled people, unemployment, poverty and equal opportunities for women. It has established the means for monitoring social developments through its observatories on social exclusion, older people, family policies and employment, its networks on childcare, women in the labour market, education, vocational training, local employment, job vacancies and employment policies and social protection systems. It has set up specialised institutions such as the European Centre for the Development of Vocational Training (Cedefop), the European Foundation for the Improvement of Living and Working Conditions and the European Agency for Health and Safety at Work. Its capacity for data collection and analysis and for evaluation of its own programmes has become prodigious.

While national governments have been fighting to defend their interests, the Commission has brought forward proposals for legislation, collected information, monitored trends, initiated research and action programmes, supported and evaluated projects. While member states were agonising over the wording of the Charter and social chapter, proposals were being drafted for Council recommendations which went beyond the terms of the Charter and Agreement on Social Policy eventually adopted by only eleven of the twelve member states.

Together some of the documents issued by the Commission offer a more comprehensive and coherent statement of the Union's social policy than in the much more widely publicised formal texts. The 1974 social action programme [1.8], the Recommendations 'on the convergence of social protection objectives and policies' [2.1] and 'on common criteria concerning sufficient resources and social assistance in social protection systems' [8.4] and the White Paper on European social policy [1.13] provide a succinct summary of the Union's social policy thinking. In the 1990s the areas in which common objectives and policies were identified as part of the convergence strategy covered sickness, maternity, unemployment, incapacity for work, older people and families. Reference was made to the principles of equal treatment and fairness, but no precise targets were set for standards of provision: the level of resources to be achieved was to be 'compatible with human dignity' [2.1, p. 47], enabling beneficiaries to 'maintain their standard of living in a reasonable manner' [2.1 p. 50]; health care was to be provided for legal residents, regardless of income; social and economic integration was to be afforded to those able to work; guaranteed income maintenance was to be ensured for the non-working population; and family benefits were to be targeted at the most disadvantaged families and those with the greatest child-related costs; women wanting to return to the labour market were to be given assistance, and obstacles were to be removed for parents seeking to combine family and professional responsibilities. In addition the White Paper focused attention on the Union's competence in the areas of education and training, active labour market policy, working conditions, health and safety at work and public health, social security for migrant workers, the integration of migrants, equality of opportunity between women and men, as well as the role of European social policy in international co-operation with countries outside the Union.

The Commission is not, of course, the only social policy actor in the Union. With the institution of direct elections in 1979 and the extension of its powers under the SEA in 1986, increasingly the European Parliament, with its many committees and lobbies, has been able to influence social affairs. Jacques Delors' overtures to the social partners, through the Val Duchesse talks and the social dialogue, strengthened the involvement of management and labour in the Union's social dimension.

Commissioners, and to a certain extent also members of the European Parliament, are expected to act independently of national interests for the greater good of the Union as a whole. The Commission's role, like that of any national civil service, is constrained by the bodies which take policy decisions. Despite the modification in the consultative procedure put into effect by the SEA, strengthening the role of the European Parliament and introducing voting by qualified majority in the Council, it is still the Council of Ministers that has the ultimate power of decision. The Council is the body which represents and upholds national interests and can effectively block proposals for new legislation. The impact of the Union's power structure and *modus operandi* in the area of social policy has been to dilute or block many of the measures which might have resulted in a more coherent and autonomous social policy. Even though the Agreement on Social Policy annexed to the Maastricht Treaty was signed by only eleven of the twelve member states, it still required unanimous voting by the Council on proposals concerning social security and social protection of workers (Article 3), suggesting that several countries were resisting further encroachment into national social space. While the Maastricht Treaty marked 'a new stage in the process of creating an ever closer union among the people of Europe', decisions were to be 'taken as closely as possible to the citizen' (Article A), in accordance with the principle of subsidiarity (Article 3b). The power of any one nation to block social legislation in order to protect its own interests was retained. National policies and interests, especially those of the more powerful countries, have clearly restricted the Union's ability to develop its own social policy.

Even when measures are agreed at European level, compliance is not guaranteed by national governments, and it may take several years before cases brought before the European Court of Justice (ECJ) can be resolved, as exemplified by the time taken for all member states to implement legislation on equal opportunities (see Chapter 6). Some countries have much better records on compliance than others. Of the legislation applicable to employment and social policy at the end of 1993, Portugal and the United Kingdom had notified measures by that date for 92 per cent of the relevant directives, compared with only 57 per cent in Italy and 59 per cent in Luxembourg [1.13, table 1]. It is significant that the Union's least binding instruments – decisions, recommendations and opinions – have been used increasingly in preference to regulations, resolutions and directives, which are more difficult to steer through the consultative process and to monitor (see Appendix 1). Health and safety of workers provides a good example of a topic over which agreement has been more easily reached and where qualified majority voting has enabled binding legislation to be enacted in record time, as demonstrated by Framework Directive 89/391/EEC [4.1], which passed through all the stages of the consultation process in under sixteen months (see Chapter 4).

On the basis of comparisons with national systems, it could be argued that the Commission has developed the potential and the administrative instruments necessary for formulating and implementing a relatively coherent and comprehensive social policy. It has, however, been thwarted in its efforts by its limited financial base in this area, the great variety of disparate systems it has had to contend with and the numerous attempts to undermine its actions, generally for political reasons. The Commission would seem to have gathered together the necessary ingredients for a European social policy but has been held back by other political actors from creating an autonomous system. The decision to include the principle of subsidiarity in the Maastricht Treaty can be interpreted as confirmation that an overarching social policy was still not to be given an official seal of approval.

THE FUTURE OF EUROPEAN SOCIAL POLICY

The White Paper on European social policy published in July 1994 was the outcome of a long process of consultation with social actors and social partners over the role of the social dimension of the Union through to the end of the century. It therefore provides an indication of thinking at European and national level and amongst interest groups on the Union's competence in social affairs and the directions that policy might take in the late 1990s.

As shown throughout this book, after almost forty years of action at European level, resulting in a proliferation of legislative texts, few areas of social life remain untouched by official regulations, directives, decisions, recommendations, resolutions, communications or memoranda. Negotiations over the Community Charter of the Fundamental Social Rights of Workers and the social chapter of the Maastricht Treaty had demonstrated that the United Kingdom was not alone in its concern about the pervasiveness of the Union's powers, as confirmed by the national debates surrounding ratification. The White Paper did not, however, signal that the Commission would be reducing the scope of its action. Rather, it announced its intention to look for new areas to explore and develop: for example homeworking and teleworking and the individualisation of rights and contributions were placed on the agenda. The Commission confirmed that emphasis in secondary legislation would be on the need to respect national social protection systems and to observe the principle of subsidiarity. The Commission would intervene only when an issue could best be dealt with at Union level, as for example in responding to the problem of social exclusion which called for overall mobilisation of efforts and the combination of both economic and social measures. The consultation process over the White Paper was in itself an indication of the Commission's intention to ensure awareness of the added value of its actions and the transparency of its initiatives. The reciprocal relationship between member states and the Union was to be founded on the Union's respect for the choices made by member states in return for their respect for Union-wide objectives and standards.

The White Paper set out ambitious aims for social policy as it sought to meet the challenges the Union was facing due to growth in the numbers of poor and unemployed, the possible emergence of an underclass and increasing pressure on social services. By the end of the century the primary goal was a significant reduction in the numbers of unemployed, while promoting competitiveness and social progress, which was in turn presented as being dependent on economic prosperity. Productivity gains were to be the basis for reconciling high social standards with the capacity to compete in global markets. Efficiency, investment in new technologies and human resources were needed to ensure economic growth. The policy response was therefore to initiate programmes to support the creation of jobs through training, flexibility and a wider concept of work, while preserving the basis of social protection through a process of adaptation, rationalisation and simplification, with member states learning from one another's experience.

The Commission was to continue to play a co-ordinating, monitoring and evaluative role, supporting and complementing the activities of member states. It intended to use its information sources to feed into legislation and action programmes, assisting member states in defining quantitative targets, where appropriate, and proposing the most suitable form of legislation compatible with the aims to be achieved. Emphasis was to be on consolidating the *acquis communautaire*, while initiating discussions with the social partners about new proposals. In the area of labour standards, the term used to describe the social protection of workers, and labour markets (particularly with reference to freedom of movement), in the immediate future the Commission was planning to consolidate and implement existing legislation with the aim of ensuring that competition would not be distorted by non-transposition of Union law at national level.

Rather than proposing binding legislation, in several areas the Commission planned to adopt codes of good practice: against racial discrimination, on equal pay, training and vertical desegregation of women's jobs and for disabled workers. Social and economic integration were to continue to be major themes for the remainder of the decade. Here the Commission proposed to define common objectives and guidelines rather than making detailed provisions or setting down uniform solutions. The White Paper suggested that targeted help should be given to categories of individuals or neighbourhoods, as in the urban initiative agreed in 1994. While continuing to establish a framework of basic minimum standards of provision, the Commission announced that it would be seeking ways of shifting from assistance to employment generation; older people were also to be encouraged to make an active and creative contribution to society.

Where progress was being blocked by lack of agreement, the Commission announced that it would be prepared to bring forward proposals under Article 118a of the Maastricht Treaty which enables the Council to adopt directives under the co-operation procedure (see Appendix 1). The Commission also proposed revising the Union's Treaties to take account of an important omission of competence in combating discrimination on the grounds of race, religion, age and disability, where it felt the value added of specific Union-level actions could be demonstrated.

When the White Paper was published in 1994 European social policy was said to be at a watershed: much had been achieved but much remained to be done. The Commission recognised that the Union had adopted a strong body of legislation ensuring high labour standards but that the fundamental social rights of citizens had still be to secured as a constitutional element of the European Union. As more countries become member states and the earlier members seek to renegotiate their positions, the last few years of the twentieth century might be expected to show whether consensus can be reached over this objective so as to enable the Union to develop a more coherent and comprehensive common social policy.

Appendix 1
The European Social Policy-Making Process

POLICY-MAKING INSTITUTIONS

The **Council of Ministers**, generally meeting in Brussels, is the 'government' of Europe, which takes decisions on laws to be applied throughout the Union. The Council consists of a minister from each member state, chosen according to the subject under discussion, and is therefore a body representing national interests. The Council's main work is to deliberate on proposals from the Commission and to decide on policy. The heads of government of all member states meet twice a year as the European Council to take major decisions on policy directions. The presidency of the Council rotates between member states every six months, providing an opportunity for heads of national governments to set the agenda and leave their mark on policy. The Council is supported by a Committee of Permanent Representatives (COREPER) to which it may refer proposals from the Commission for detailed negotiations. Under qualified majority voting the largest member states – France, Germany, Italy and the United Kingdom – each have a block of ten votes; Spain has eight; Belgium, Greece, the Netherlands and Portugal have five; Denmark and Ireland have three; and Luxembourg has two. In the enlarged Union, Austria and Sweden have been allocated four votes and Finland three.

The degree of coercion exercised by the Council depends upon the perceived importance of the achievement of a particular objective at European level and the extent to which agreement can be reached between member states. Where social affairs are seen to be central to achieving the goals of economic and social cohesion, more pressure will be exerted than in cases where the benefits for the Union as a whole are less obvious.

The **Commission** is the formal initiator and implementer of European legislation. Although commissioners are political appointments, the Commission acts as the Community's 'civil service', independently of national interests, to advise the Council of Ministers, initiate legislation by making proposals for European law, monitor compliance with the treaties and administer common policies. Commissioners are appointed by member states. The United Kingdom, France, Italy, Germany and Spain each have two members, and the other countries one each. They operate through twenty-eight directorates general, which prepare proposals and working documents for consideration by the Council of Ministers and for opinions from Parliament and the Economic and Social Committee.

The Directorate-General for Employment, Industrial Relations and Social Affairs, DG V, is the main directorate dealing with social policy, covering: industrial relations and social dialogue; employment and labour market; social security, social protection and living conditions; the European Social Fund; and health and safety. The Commission has established a number of observatories and networks in the social area composed of government officials and independent experts, with general responsibility for monitoring, describing and analysing social measures and social policies. Their main purpose is to improve mutual understanding by encouraging the flow of information and by fostering international networks. The information gathered is used by the Commission in formulating its proposals. The observatories and networks produce regular consolidated reports, newsletters and bulletins on activities and developments across the Union which are published under the Commission's imprint by the Office for Official Publications of the European Communities.

The Commission also disseminates information on social affairs to a wider audience through its own publications. Under the title *Social Europe*, three times a year the Commission's Coordination and Information Policy Unit publishes a review of current European social affairs aimed at a non-specialist readership. The *Social Europe Supplements* deal with specific topics in more depth. In 1993 DG V produced the first annual report on *Social Protection in Europe* and, as required by the Maastricht Treaty, in 1994 it began preparing reports on the demographic situation in Europe.

The **European Court of Justice**, which sits in Luxembourg, is the Union's legal voice and the guardian of its treaties and implementing legislation. The ECJ consists of thirteen judges appointed by the governments of member states for six-year terms of office. It has two main tasks: ensuring that legal instruments adopted by the Council of Ministers, the Commission or national governments are compatible with European law; interpreting European law to make sure that it is applied in a uniform way.

European law is an autonomous legal system with its own institutions which have sovereign rights and are independent of the legal systems of member states. The Union's legal sources are written (treaties, secondary legislation) or unwritten (general legal principles or judicial precedent). European law takes precedence over national law on the grounds that the Union could not function if member states disregarded its legislation. Consequently, any provision of national law which is not compatible with European law is inapplicable. Member states may not adopt or maintain measures which are likely to jeopardise the functioning of the treaties. Nor can national courts go against the ECJ's interpretation. If the ECJ finds that a treaty has been infringed, the member state concerned is obliged to take the necessary measures to comply with its ruling. Member states can also bring cases against one another, and the ECJ has become the final Court of Appeal for European citizens.

In the social policy area, the ECJ therefore plays an important role in ensuring that European legislation is implemented and in constituting a body of case law to interpret European law.

The **European Parliament** has been described as the 'democratic conscience' of the Union (Thomson, 1989, p. 213). Since 1979 it has been a directly elected body. Elections are held every five years for the 567 members (in 1994), with the number from each country depending broadly on population size. Members tend to form political rather than national blocks and to work more closely with the Commission than with the Council. The Parliament, which meets in Strasbourg, has budgetary and supervisory powers. By declining to take up a position on a Commission proposal it can prevent implementation by the Council of Ministers. Although the European Parliament cannot initiate bills, it can choose to debate an issue and require the Commission to answer its questions. For example point 30 of the Community Charter stipulated that reports on the application of the Charter had to be considered by the European Parliament.

The Single European Act gave the European Parliament the power of veto over agreements made between the Union and other countries and introduced a new co-operation procedure, allowing the Parliament a second reading stage in the legislative process, thereby enabling it to play a more effective role in forming social policy. By developing a good working relationship with the Parliament in areas such as health and safety at work, the Commission has been able to expedite the legislative process.

Most of the detailed work of the European Parliament is handled by eighteen specialised committees, which report back and make recommendations. Social policy is served by several committees: Youth, Culture, Education, Information and Sport; Social Affairs and Employment, which oversees the Social Fund; Environment, Public Health and Consumer Protection; and Women's Rights.

The **Economic and Social Committee** comprises 189 members who are representatives of employers, workers and other interest groups, covering agriculture, consumers, small firms, the professions, the scientific world, family organisations, environmental protection and transport. The function of the ESC is to produce opinions on Community issues referred to it by the Council or the Commission or taken up by the Committee on its own initiative. The ESC must be consulted on draft legislation concerned with social policy, including the ESF, freedom of movement for workers, right of establishment and vocational training. It has the right to advise on its own initiative in all areas of Community interest. Of its nine sections two deal specifically with social affairs: social, family, educational and cultural affairs; protection of the environment, public health and consumer affairs.

The **Committee of the Regions** was established under Article 198a of the Maastricht Treaty. It has advisory status, its constitution is the same as that of the ESC and its terms of reference are very similar, except that its main remit is to issue opinions where it considers that specific regional interests are involved.

PRIMARY LEGISLATION

Primary European law is based in international acts (treaties establishing the Communities, treaties or agreements amending or adapting the former): the three founding treaties, revising treaties and the Merger Treaty of 1965, the Single European Act of 1986 and the Treaty on European Union of 1992 (see Box 1).

SECONDARY LEGISLATION

Secondary European law is based on acts passed to ensure the application of the treaties establishing the Communities.

Regulations are binding and have direct legal force in member states. Where necessary they may supersede national legislation. In the social area very few new regulations have been introduced by the Council since the 1970s, with the notable exception of arrangements for free movement of workers and for the activities of the Structural Funds.

Directives lay down an objective to be achieved and are legally binding, but individual states are free to select the most suitable form of implementation in their own legal systems. By following the spirit of directives, member states are expected to bring national legislation into line with European law, which may leave relatively little room for manoeuvre. Directives have been widely used by the Council in the areas of equal treatment (see Chapter 6) and health and safety at work (see Chapter 4).

Decisions provide the means for implementing treaties or regulations. They are addressed to a specific government, firm or individual and are binding on the parties concerned. In the social area they have been used by the Council to establish action programmes, for example to combat social exclusion (see Chapter 8).

Recommendations, resolutions or **opinions** are purely advisory and have no mandatory authority. Examples of Council recommendations can be found in the areas of social protection and equal treatment. Resolutions have been drafted on older people (see Chapter 7). Opinions are produced by the ESC.

A **communication** or **memorandum** may be issued by the Commission in the preparatory stages of legislative proposals to solicit views of interested parties and to signify initial thinking as in the case of the 1993 Green Paper on European social policy.

PUBLICATION OF LEGISLATION

Published texts of European secondary legislation appear in the 'L' series of the *Official Journal of the European Communities (OJ)*, produced by the Office for Official Publications of the European Communities. They indicate the institutional origin of the act, the form, act number, year of enactment, institutional treaty basis and the date the act was passed. For example, the Council Directive of 9 February 1976 'on the implementation of the principle of equal treatment for men and women as regards access to employment, vocational training and promotion and working conditions' was presented as 76/207/EEC and recorded in the *Official Journal* L 39/ 40 14.2.76, beginning on page 40. Information and notices, which do not have the force of law, are published in the C series: for example the Council Resolution announcing the social action programme in 1974.

After drafting a communication or memorandum the Commission subsequently issues COM documents which become published documents when placed on the agenda for a meeting of the Commission. COM documents may be proposals for legislation, broad policy documents or reports on the implementation of policy. When accepted a document is presented as a COM document final, as illustrated by the case of the action programme submitted by the Commission to the Council on 29 November 1989 to implement the Community Charter, identified as COM(89) 568 final. COM documents may also be published in the C series of the *Official Journal*.

Appendix 2
The Structure of Welfare in Member States

A full account of administrative arrangements of social security systems in member states is given by Danny Pieters (1990). The reports on *Social Protection in the Member States of the Community*, produced for the Commission by the Mutual Information System on Social Protection in the Community (Missoc), present a detailed annual update of levels of provision and the conditions under which benefits are paid. The general principles underlying different welfare systems are examined in Chapter 2, and the features of national policies are developed in subsequent chapters with reference to specific policy areas.

CONTINENTAL WELFARE STATES (THE EEC FOUNDER MEMBERS)

Belgium (10 million inhabitants)

Belgian social security law covers social insurance and social assistance. Four schemes apply to wage earners, civil servants and public service workers, self-employed workers and a residual category for the non-economically active. They are organised on an occupational basis, with some categories of workers having their own schemes for all risks, for example miners and merchant seamen. Administrative responsibility lies with semi-public agencies and public institutions of social security, which have administrative autonomy. As in Germany and France, employers bear the largest proportion of the funding, the rest being shared almost equally between employees and the state, which subsidises all insurance funds except industrial injuries and accidents. By the early 1990s Belgium occupied an intermediate position for its spending on social protection, which had declined steadily over the previous decade.

France (57 million inhabitants)

The French have maintained several statutory social security schemes, including a general scheme for all employees in industry and the service sector, except civil servants, and different occupational schemes, each covering specific contingencies. Three separately administered self-governing funds, under state supervision, cover sickness, family allowances/benefits and old age pensions. Unemployment, which does not fall within the general social security scheme, is jointly administered by representatives of employers and employees. Friendly societies (*sociétés mutuelles*) offer more generous benefits to their members, for example to enable them to be reimbursed at a higher rate for medical expenses. Social assistance, which is organised at local level, is mainly covered by the *revenu minimum d'insertion* (RMI), a scheme introduced in 1990 for re-integrating certain categories of the poor into the workforce. Other schemes provide for disabled and older people and lone parents. More than 50 per cent of income for social spending is derived from employer contributions, the highest proportion amongst the six founder members. Employees contribute less than a quarter, and the state only a small proportion, the lowest level in the Union. Until the early 1990s employers alone contributed to family allowances and benefits. Since 1991 the state has levied an additional contribution of over 1 per cent on all sources of income (*contribution sociale généralisée*) to supplement income from insurance. Spending on social protection increased in France during the 1980s, placing it amongst the member states with the highest levels of expenditure under this budgetary head in relation to Gross Domestic Product (GDP).

Germany (80 million inhabitants since unification)

Social security in Germany is governed only indirectly by law according to the principle of the social state (*Sozialstaatsprinzip*). The German social security system distinguishes between three branches: social insurance, social compensation and assistance. The compensation fund was originally established for war victims and was later extended to compensate victims of criminal violence or negligence. Social insurance has developed over the years to cover health, accidents, pensions and unemployment. In 1995 a new compulsory care insurance (*Pflegerversicherung*) was introduced for the nursing of older or disabled people. The legal framework of the German system is derived from case law and legal doctrine as established in Articles 20 and 28 of the constitution. Social rights are also written into the constitutions of the German *Länder*. The social insurance funds are self-governing, although they are closely supervised by the state. With the exception of child benefits, which are paid for from taxation, and social assistance, which is financed by local government and the *Länder*, social protection is funded primarily by contributions from employers and employees, particularly the former, with state subsidies amounting to almost a quarter of income. Germany was one of the few member states which reduced spending on social protection during the 1980s, bringing it close to the European average.

Italy (57 million inhabitants)

Unlike the other founder members, the Italians have a system of social protection which is a combination of employment-based insurance and universal provision, but where corporatism and patronage continue to play an important role. Centralised decision making combines with fragmented implementation, and the division between north and south produces stark differences in provision. In addition to social insurance schemes, covering the standard contingencies and administered by boards of governors, where employers are by law in the majority, social assistance and social services are provided by local authorities. The Italian social protection system bears some similarity to the Nordic/ Anglo-Saxon model in that health care has been provided by a national health service as a constitutional right. Social spending is funded from wage-related contributions, as in France, with employers bearing more than 50 per cent of the cost, the third highest proportion in the Union. Employees contribute only a very small proportion of the total. Italy was the only one of the original EEC members where, despite an increase over the previous decade, spending on social protection as a proportion of GDP was below the European average in the early 1990s.

Luxembourg (under 400 000 inhabitants)

Luxembourg's social security system had been strongly influenced by German law and was therefore established on an occupational basis. Social insurance schemes distinguish between sickness and maternity, old age and industrial injuries and occupational diseases. Separate institutional arrangements are made for family allowances, which are funded by a combination of contributions and taxation, and for unemployment benefits, which are funded by a special tax. Social assistance and a National Solidarity Fund are part of the broader concept of social security. As in France, friendly societies offer enhanced benefits to their members. Central government is closely involved in managing the social insurance scheme and subsidises or contributes to the different funds at a level above that found in the other continental welfare states. Unlike these other countries, the state contributes more than either employers or employees, with the latter covering less than a fifth of the cost.

The Netherlands (15 million inhabitants)

The Dutch social protection system is organised into four main social security schemes: employee social insurance covering everyone in employment for loss of wages; a general insurance scheme covering all residents for old age, death, invalidity, maternity and medical care; supplementary social services, including social assistance, financed entirely from general taxation; special schemes for civil servants. Private non-compulsory occupational pension insurance schemes are also available. The employee insurance scheme is administered by industrial councils composed of representatives of employees and employers, who are also represented in the Social Insurance Bank which administers benefits. Unlike the other founding member states, employees are the main contributors to social protection, bearing almost a third of the cost, the highest proportion for employees in the Union. Employers in the Netherlands contribute a smaller proportion than in other countries in this grouping. As in Germany, family allowances are entirely funded by public means. Throughout the 1980s and into the 1990s the Netherlands remained in first place in the Union for the level of spending on social protection.

NORDIC AND ANGLO-SAXON WELFARE STATES (EC MEMBERS IN 1972)

Denmark (5 million inhabitants)

Social protection in Denmark is provided on a universal basis, with flat-rate benefits. The Danish system does not clearly distinguish between social benefits and services. Both social insurance and social assistance are funded from general taxation and managed at local level. Industrial injuries remain under the control of private insurance companies, and unemployment insurance funds are managed by trade unions. Social security spending is borne almost solely by the state and local government, who together contribute 80 per cent of the cost, the highest level in the Union. Employers and employees consequently make only a very small contribution to the total. In the early 1990s Denmark was well above the European average for spending on social protection and in second place overall.

Ireland (3.5 million inhabitants)

Three categories of schemes can be distinguished in Ireland: social insurance, social assistance and a residual category of income maintenance schemes for child benefits and supplements to families on low income from employment. As in the United Kingdom, medical care falls outside the concept of social insurance, but entitlement to free services is on the basis of income. The Irish constitution recognises fundamental rules for social policy, which serve as guidelines for parliament. The administration of social security is entirely controlled by the state, with social assistance being managed at regional level. Social assistance and residual payments are covered by central and local government. Apart from industrial accidents and occupational diseases, which are funded solely by employers, social insurance is financed primarily by the state, although at a lower level than in Denmark or the United Kingdom. Family benefits are funded from taxation. Employers' contributions to social protection are amongst the lowest in the Union, and those of employees are lower than in most other member states. In the early 1990s Ireland was amongst the countries with the lowest level of spending on social protection in relation to GDP.

The United Kingdom (58 million inhabitants)

Despite its Beveridgian origins, by the 1990s the British social security system encompassed contributory benefits, based on the insurance principle, universal non-contributory benefits for certain contingencies and means-tested benefits in the form of income support and family credit. Both the benefit system, which includes social assistance, and health care are administered by central government, with responsibilities delegated to regional and local level, but representatives of employers and employees have very little involvement. Contributory benefits are covered almost entirely from employer and employee contributions. Child benefit is completely funded from taxation. Medical care is provided for the whole population through the National Health Service, which is almost entirely state funded. As in Denmark, the state is the main contributor to social protection, but at roughly half the Danish level, with employers contributing less than a quarter and employees under 15 per cent. In the early 1990s the United Kingdom, like Italy, devoted less than a quarter of its GDP to spending on social protection.

SOUTHERN EUROPEAN WELFARE STATES (EC MEMBERS IN THE 1980s)

Greece (10 million inhabitants)

The state in Greece has a constitutional duty to provide social protection for its citizens, but legal doctrine and case law leave a large area of discretion. The scope of social insurance cover varies considerably from one area to another, since it encompasses five major schemes and more than 300 non-standardised organisations, many of them covering specific occupational groups, such as employees in the banking sector or the press, each with its own administrative structures, which may be public or private. Cover varies considerably from one scheme to another. Social assistance is relatively unimportant and under-developed compared with most other member states. Although there is no general provision, a number of schemes target specific categories of individuals who fall through the social insurance net. Funding for social protection is primarily from employers and employees, with the state contributing at a very low level comparable to that in France but, throughout the 1980s, Greece had one of the lowest levels of spending on social protection in the Union.

Portugal (10 million inhabitants)

Social security in Portugal is a relatively new concept originating in the constitution of 1976 and covering both contributory and non-contributory schemes. Under the constitution central government has responsibility for organising, co-ordinating and subsidising a unified and decentralised social security system, but non-profit private institutions can be established under the control of the state. Health care is provided on a universal basis free of charge and administered by a national health service. Since the 1970s an attempt has been made to integrate social security schemes, so that the system has become more unified and decentralised, while maintaining the principle of autonomy and with participation from employers, employees and beneficiaries. Employers bear the major share of the cost of social protection. The contribution from employees represents a fifth of the total and that of the state nearer a third. Central government does not participate at all in the contributory schemes, whereas the non-contributory scheme is entirely funded by the state. Spending on social insurance in relation to GDP was well below the European average in the early 1990s.

Spain (39 million inhabitants)

Spanish social insurance is a combination of general and special occupational and categorial schemes. Although reference is made to social security in the 1978 constitution, its articles do not have legal status. Under the constitution the state has exclusive control over social security but can delegate administration of the schemes to autonomous communities, a process which is gradually being extended to all areas of social security, except for the administration of resources. Employers and employees are represented on the administrative boards. Health care and minimum pensions are universal and non-contributory. As in France and Italy, funding for social protection is primarily provided by employers, who, with over 50 per cent of the total, contribute a higher proportion than in any other member state. The contribution of employees is below the European average, while that of the state is close to the average. Expenditure on social protection rose during the 1980s, but Spain remained amongst the countries with lower levels of spending in relation to GDP.

Bibliography

Abrahamson, P. (1992) 'Welfare Pluralism: Towards a New Consensus for a European Social Policy?', *Cross-National Research Papers*, 2 (6), pp. 5–22.

Alber, J. (1993) 'Health and Social Services', in A. Walker, J. Alber and A-M. Guillemard, *Older People in Europe: Social and Economic Policies. The 1993 Report of the European Observatory* (Brussels: Commission of the European Communities), pp. 100–33.

Ardittis, S. (1990) 'Labour Migration and the Single European Market: a Synthetic and Prospective Note', *International Sociology*, 5 (4), pp. 461–74.

Baldwin, S. (1991) 'Statistiques communautaires sur la population et les ménages: harmonisation et standardisation', in 'Actes du colloque, Beyond National Statistics: Household and Family Patterns in Comparative Perspective', *INSÉÉ Méthodes*, no. 8, pp. 111–16.

Baldwin-Edwards, M. (1991) 'Immigration after 1992', *Policy and Politics*, 19 (3), pp. 199–211.

Barrère-Maurisson, M-A. and Marchand, O. (1990) 'Structures familiales et marchés du travail dans les pays développés. Une nette opposition entre le Nord et le Sud', *Économie et statistique*, no. 235, pp. 19–30.

Beretta, D. (rapporteur) (1989) *Social Aspects of the Internal Market. European Social Area* (Brussels: European Communities/Economic and Social Committee).

Berghman, J. (1990) 'The Implications of 1992 for Social Policy: a Selective Critique of Social Insurance Protection', *Cross-National Research Papers*, 2 (1), pp. 9–17.

Berthod-Wurmser, M. (ed.) (1994) *La santé en Europe* (Paris: La Documentation Française, Collection Vivre en Europe).

Bimbi, F. (1993) 'Gender, "Gift Relationship" and Welfare State Cultures in Italy', in J. Lewis (ed.), *Women and Social Policies in Europe: Work, Family and the State* (Aldershot: Edward Elgar), pp. 138–69.

Bourdelais, P. (1993) *Le nouvel âge de la vieillesse. Histoire du vieillissement de la population* (Paris: Éditions Odile Jacob).

Bradshaw, J., Ditch, J., Holmes, H. and Whiteford, P. (1993a) 'A Comparative Study of Child Support in Fifteen Countries', *Journal of European Social Policy*, 3 (4), pp. 255–71.

Bradshaw, J., Ditch, J., Holmes, H. and Whiteford, P. (1993b) *Support for Children: a Comparison of Arrangements in Fifteen Countries*, Department of Social Security Research Report no. 21 (London: HMSO).

Brown, J. (1986) 'Cross-National and Inter-Country Research into Poverty: the Case of the First European Poverty Programme', *Cross-national Research Papers*, 1 (2), pp. 41–51.

Buckley, M. and Anderson, M. (1988) 'Introduction: Problems, Policies and Politics', in M. Buckley and M. Anderson (eds), *Women, Equality and Europe* (London: Macmillan), pp. 1–19.

227

Buzelay, A. (1992) 'Restructuring European Industry and Redistributing Regional Incomes: Prerequisites for Community Cohesion', in A. Hannequart (ed.), *Economic and Social Cohesion in Europe: a New Objective for Integration* (London/New York: Routledge), pp. 65–74.

Byre, A. (1988) 'Applying Community Standards on Equality', in M. Buckley and M. Anderson (eds), *Women, Equality and Europe* (London: Macmillan), pp. 20–32.

Carlsen, S. (1993) 'Men's Utilization of Paternity Leave and Parental Leave Schemes', in S. Carlsen and J. Elm Larsen (eds), *The Equality Dilemma: Reconciling Working Life and Family Life, Viewed in an Equality Perspective. The Danish Example* (Copenhagen: Danish Equal Status Council), pp. 79–90.

Carlsen, S. and Elm Larsen, J. (eds) (1993) *The Equality Dilemma: Reconciling Working Life and Family Life, Viewed in an Equality Perspective. The Danish Example* (Copenhagen: Danish Equal Status Council).

Casey, B. (1993) 'Employment Promotion', in M. Gold (ed.), *The Social Dimension: Employment Policy in the European Community* (London: Macmillan), pp. 172–83.

Chassard, Y. (1992) 'The Convergence of Social Protection Objectives and Policies: a New Approach', *Social Europe Supplement 5/92*, pp. 13–20.

Chisholm, L. (1992) 'A Crazy Quilt: Education, Training and Social Change in Europe', in J. Bailey (ed.), *Social Europe* (London/New York: Longman), pp. 123–46.

Clasen, J. (1992) 'Unemployment Insurance in two Countries: a Comparative Analysis of Great Britain and West Germany in the 1980s, *Journal of European Social Policy*, 2 (4), pp. 279–300.

Clasen, J. and Freeman, R. (eds) (1994) *Social Policy in Germany* (London: Harvester Wheatsheaf).

Collins, D. (1975) *The European Communities. The Social Policy of the First Phase*, vol. 2 *The European Economic Community 1958–72* (London: Martin Robertson).

Council for Industry and Higher Education and Institute of Manpower Studies (1989) *How Many Graduates in the Twenty-First Century? A Summary of the Report* (Brighton: IMS).

Council of Europe (1988) *The European Social Charter and its Protocol* (Strasbourg: Council of Europe).

Cox, S. (1993) 'Equal Opportunities', in M. Gold (ed.), *The Social Dimension: Employment Policy in the European Community* (London: Macmillan), pp. 41–63.

Crawley, C. (1990) 'The European Parliament Committee on Women's Rights', *Cross-National Research Papers*, 2 (3), pp. 7–9.

De Swaan, A. (1990) 'Perspectives for Transnational Social Policy: Preliminary Notes', *Cross-National Research Papers*, 2 (2), pp. 7–22.

Debizet, J. (1990) 'La scolarité après 16 ans', *Données sociales 1990* (Paris: INSÉÉ), pp. 330–5.

Delors, J. (1985) 'Preface', in J. Vandamme (ed.), *New Dimensions in European Social Policy* (London: Croom Helm), pp. ix–xx.

Drake, K. (1994) 'Policy Integration and Co-operation: a Persistent Challenge', in L. McFarland and M. Vickers (eds), *Vocational Education and Training for Youth: Towards Coherent Policy Practice* (Paris: OECD), pp. 143–68.

Esping-Andersen, G. (1990) *The Three Worlds of Welfare Capitalism* (Cambridge: Polity).

European Institute of Social Security (1988) 'The Role of Social Security in the Context of the Completion of the Internal Market by 1992', unpublished report for the Commission of the European Communities, V/1653/EN–88 (Louvain: European Institute of Social Security).

Fagnani, J. (1992) 'Les Françaises font-elles des prouesses ? Fécondité, travail professionnel et politiques familiales en France et en Allemagne de l'ouest, *Recherches et prévisions*, no. 28, pp. 23–38.

Flora, P. and Alber, J. (1981) 'Modernization, Democratization, and the Development of Welfare States in Western Europe', in P. Flora and A.J. Heidenheimer (eds), *The Development of Welfare States in Europe and America* (New Brunswick/London: Transaction), pp. 37–80.

Flynn, P. (1993) 'Preface', in 'Towards a Europe of Solidarity: Combating Social Exclusion', *Social Europe Supplement 4/93*, pp. 3–4.

Gardiner, K. (1992) 'Measuring Poverty: Comparing Low Incomes in France and the United Kingdom', *Cross-National Research Papers*, 2 (7), pp. 25–35.

Gastines, B. de and Sylvestre, J-M. (1992) *Le guide SVP de l'Europe* (Paris: Éditions SVP).

Gillion, C. (1991) 'Ageing Populations: Spreading the Costs', *Journal of European Social Policy*, 1 (2), pp. 107–28.

Ginn, J. and Arber, S. (1992) 'Towards Women's Independence: Pension Systems in Three Contrasting European Welfare States', *Journal of European Social Policy*, 2 (4), pp. 255–77.

Glendinning, C. and McLaughlin, E. (1993) *Paying for Care: Lessons from Europe*, Social Security Advisory Committee, Research Paper 5 (London: HMSO).

Gold, M. and Mayes, D. (1993) 'Rethinking a Social Policy for Europe', in R. Simpson and R. Walker (eds), *Europe: for Richer or Poorer?* (London: CPAG), pp. 25–38.

Guillemard, A-M. (1993) 'Older Workers and the Labour Market', in A. Walker, J. Alber and A-M. Guillemard, *Older People in Europe: Social and Economic Policies. The 1993 Report of the European Observatory* (Brussels: Commission of the European Communities), pp. 68–99.

Hannequart, A. (1992) 'Economic and Social Cohesion and the Structural Funds: an Introduction', in A. Hannequart (ed.), *Economic and Social Cohesion in Europe: a New Objective for Integration* (London/New York: Routledge), pp. 1–18.

Hantrais, L. (1990) *Managing Professional and Family Life: a Comparative Study of British and French Women* (Aldershot/Vermont: Dartmouth).

Hantrais, L. (1993) 'Women, Work and Welfare in France', in J. Lewis (ed.), *Women and Social Policies in Europe: Work, Family and the State* (Aldershot: Edward Elgar), pp. 116–37.

Haut Conseil de la Population et de la Famille (1987) *Vie professionnelle et vie familiale, de nouveaux équilibres à construire* (Paris: La Documentation Française).

Heclo, H. (1981) 'Toward a New Welfare State?', in P. Flora and A.J. Heidenheimer (eds), *The Development of Welfare States in Europe and America* (New Brunswick/London: Transaction), pp. 383–406.

Higgins, J. (1981) *States of Welfare: Comparative Analysis in Social Policy* (Oxford: Basil Blackwell and Martin Robertson).

Holloway, J. (1981) *Social Policy Harmonisation in the European Community* (Farnborough: Gower).

James, E. (1982) 'From Paris to ESCAP', in J. Dennett, E. James, G. Room and P. Watson, *Europe against Poverty: the European Poverty Programme 1975–80* (London: Bedford Square Press/NCVO), pp. 3–13.

James, P. (1993) 'Occupational Health and Safety', in M. Gold (ed.), *The Social Dimension: Employment Policy in the European Community* (London: Macmillan), pp. 135–52.

Jani-Le Bris, H. (1993) *Family Care of Dependent Older People in the European Community* (Luxembourg: Office for Official Publications of the European Communities).

Jones, H. (1990) 'New European Challenges for Education - the Impact of 1992', IBM Annual Lecture 1990, London, 11 July.

Kamerman, S. B. and Kahn, A. K. (eds) (1978) *Family Policy: Government and Families in Fourteen Countries* (New York: Columbia University Press).

Kempeneers, M. and Lelièvre, E. (1991) 'Employment and Family within the Twelve', *Eurobarometer 34*.

Kiernan, L. and Estaugh, V. (1993) 'Cohabitation. Extra-marital Childbearing and Social Policy', *Occasional Paper 17* (London: Family Policy Studies Centre).

Kleinman, M. and Piachaud, D. (1993) 'European Social Policy: Conceptions and Choices', *Journal of European Social Policy*, 3 (1), pp. 1–19.

Knapp, M., Montserrat, J. and Fenyo, A. (1990) 'Inter-Sectoral and International Contracting-Out of Long-term Care: Evidence on Comparative Costs and Efficiency from Britain and Spain', *Cross-National Research Papers*, 2 (2), pp. 46–73.

Land, H. and Parker, R. (1978) 'United Kingdom', in S. B. Kamerman and A. K. Kahn (eds), *Family Policy: Government and Families in Fourteen Countries* (New York: Columbia University Press), pp. 331–66.

Laroque, P. (1985) 'Quarante ans de sécurité sociale', *Revue française des affaires sociales*, vol. 39, special issue, pp. 7–35.

Lefaucheur, N. (1991) 'Les familles dites monoparentales', in F. de Singly (ed.), *La famille: l'état des savoirs* (Paris: Éditions la Découverte), pp. 67–74.

Leibfried, S. (1992) 'Europe's Could-be Social State: Social Policy in European Integration after 1992', in W. J. Adams (ed.), *Singular Europe: Economy and Polity in the European Community after 1992* (Ann Arbor: University of Michigan Press), 97–118.

Leibfried, S. and Pierson, P. (1992) 'Prospects for Social Europe', *Politics and Society*, 20 (3), pp. 333–66.

Lesemann, F. and Martin, C. (1993) 'La part des familles. Les conditions d'une comparaison internationale', in F. Lesemann and C. Martin (eds), *Les personnes âgées. Dépendance, soins et solidarités familiales. Comparaisons internationales* (Paris: La Documentation Française), pp. 197–205.

Lewis, J. (1992) 'Gender and the Development of Welfare Regimes', *Journal of European Social Policy*, 2 (3), pp. 159–73.

Lewis, J. (ed.) (1993) *Women and Social Policies in Europe: Work, Family and the State* (Aldershot: Edward Elgar).

Lindley, R. (1991) 'Interactions in the Markets for Education, Training and Labour: a European Perspective on Intermediate Skills', in P. Ryan (ed.), *International Comparisons of Vocational Education and Training for Intermediate Skills* (London/New York: Falmer), 185–206.

Lødemel, I. (1992) 'The Poor and the Poorest in European Income Maintenance', *Cross-National Research Papers*, 2 (7), pp. 13–23.

Lohkamp-Himmighofen, M. (1993) 'Ansätze für Förderung der Vereinbarkeit von Familie und Beruf', in E. Neubauer, C. Dienel and M. Lohkamp-Himmighofen (eds), *Zwölf Wege der Familienpolitik in der Europäischen Gemeinschaft. Eigenständige Systeme und vergleichbare Qualitäten?*, vol. 1 (Bonn: Bundesministerium für Familie und Senioren), pp. 313–67.

Luckhaus, L. (1990) 'The Social Security Directive: its Impact on Part-time and Unpaid Work', *Cross-National Research Papers*, 2 (3), pp. 11–19.

Mc Cartney, P. and Porter, S. (1993) *Meeting the European Challenge* (Derry: Guildhall).

Meehan, E. (1993) 'Women's Rights in the European Community', in J. Lewis (ed.), *Women and Social Policies in Europe: Work, Family and the State* (Aldershot: Edward Elgar), 194–205.

Merle, V. and Bertrand, O. (1993) 'Comparabilité et reconnaissance des qualifications en Europe. Instruments et enjeux', *Formation emploi*, no. 43, July-September, pp. 41–56.

Meulders-Klein, M-T. (1993) 'The Status of the Father in European Legislation', in Ministry of Social Affairs, Denmark, and the European Commission, Report from the Conference *Fathers in Families of Tomorrow* (Copenhagen: Ministry of Social Affairs), pp. 107–50.

Mishra, R. (1977) *Society and Social Policy: Theoretical Perspectives on Welfare* (London: Macmillan).

Neubauer, E. (1993) 'Familienpolitische Ansätze zum Ausgleich der Aufwendungen für Kinder', in E. Neubauer, C. Dienel and M. Lohkamp-Himmighofen (eds), *Zwölf Wege der Familienpolitik in der Europäischen Gemeinschaft. Eigenständige Systeme und vergleichbare Qualitäten?*, vol. 1 (Bonn: Bundesministerium für Familie und Senioren), pp. 267–312.

Neubauer, E., Dienel, C. and Lohkamp-Himmighofen, M. (eds) (1993) *Zwölf Wege der Familienpolitik in der Europäischen Gemeinschaft. Eigenständige Systeme und vergleichbare Qualitäten?*, vol. 1 (Bonn: Bundesministerium für Familie und Senioren).

O'Donnell, R. (1992) 'Policy Requirements for Regional Balance in Economic and Monetary Union', in A. Hannequart (ed.), *Economic and Social Cohesion in Europe: a New Objective for Integration* (London/New York: Routledge), pp. 21–52.

OECD (1991) *Labour Force Statistics, 1969–89* (Paris: OECD).

OECD (1993) *Education at a Glance: OECD Indicators* (Paris: OECD).

Ostner, I. (1993) 'Slow Motion: Women, Work and the Family in Germany', in J. Lewis (ed.), *Women and Social Policies in Europe: Work, Family and the State* (Aldershot: Edward Elgar), pp. 92–115.

Petersen, H. (1993) 'Law and Order in Family Life and Working Life', in S. Carlsen and J. Elm Larsen (eds), *The Equality Dilemma: Reconciling Working Life and Family Life, Viewed in an Equality Perspective. The Danish Example* (Copenhagen: Danish Equal Status Council), pp. 41–52.

Pickup, L. (1990) *Mobility and Social Cohesion in the European Community - a Forward Look* (Luxembourg: Office of the Official Publications of the European Communities).

Pieters, D. (ed.) (1990) *Introduction into the Social Security Law of the Member States of the European Community* (Brussels/Antwerp: Bruylant/Maklu).

Pieters, D. (1991) 'Will "1992" Lead to the Co-ordination and Harmonization of Social Security?', in D. Pieters (ed.), *Social Security in Europe: Miscellanea of the Erasmus-Programme Social Security in the E.C.* (Brussels/Antwerp: Bruylant/Maklu), pp. 177–90.

Quintin, O. (1988) 'The Policies of the European Communities with Special Reference to the Labour Market', in M. Buckley and M. Anderson (eds), *Women, Equality and Europe* (London: Macmillan), pp. 71–7.

Quintin, O. (1992) 'The Convergence of Social Protection Objectives and Policies: a Contribution to Solidarity in Europe', *Social Europe 5/92*, pp. 9–12.

Rainbird, H. (1993) 'Vocational Education and Training', in M. Gold (ed.), *The Social Dimension: Employment Policy in the European Community* (London: Macmillan), pp. 184–202.

Rajan, A. (1990) *1992: a Zero Sum Game. Business Know-how and Training Challenges in an Integrated Europe* (London: The Industrial Society).

Rex, J. (1992) 'Race and Ethnicity in Europe', in J. Bailey (ed.), *Social Europe* (London/New York: Longman), pp. 106–20.

Richard, I. (1985) 'Community Action on Economic and Social Relance', in J. Vandamme (ed.), *New Dimensions in European Social Policy* (London: Croom Helm), pp. 199–205.

Roll, J. (1992) *Lone Parent Families in the European Community: a Report to the European Commission* (London: European Family and Social Policy Unit).

Room, G. (1982) 'The Definition and Measurement of Poverty', in J. Dennett, E. James, G. Room and P. Watson, *Europe against Poverty: the European Poverty Programme 1975–80* (London: Bedford Square Press/NCVO), pp. 155–62.

Room, G. (1994) 'European Social Policy: Competition, Conflict and Integration', in R. Page and J. Baldock (eds), *Social Policy Review 6* (Canterbury: Social Policy Association), pp. 17–35.

Rowntree, B. S. (1901) *Poverty: a Study of Town Life*, 1st edn (London: Thomas Nelson).

Ryan, P. (1991) 'Introduction: Comparative Research on Vocational Education and Training', in P. Ryan (ed.), *International Comparisons of Vocational Education and Training for Intermediate Skills* (London/New York: Falmer), pp. 1–20.

Schultheis, F. (1990) 'Familles d'Europe sans frontières: un enjeu social par dessus le marché', Conference Proceedings, *Familles d'Europe sans frontières*, 4–5 December 1989 (Paris: Institut de l'Enfance et de la Famille), pp. 73–80.

Séché, J-C. (1988) *A Guide to Working in a Europe without Frontiers* (Luxembourg: Office for Official Publications of the European Communities).

Shanks, M. (1977) *European Social Policy, Today and Tomorrow* (Oxford/New York: Pergamon).

Siim, B. (1993) 'The Gendered Scandinavian Welfare States: the Interplay between Women's Roles as Mothers, Workers and Citizens in Denmark', in J. Lewis (ed.), *Women and Social Policies in Europe: Work, Family and the State* (Aldershot: Edward Elgar), pp. 25–48.

Soisson, J-P. (1990) 'Observations on the Community Charter of Basic Social Rights for Workers', *Social Europe 1/90*, pp. 10–13.

Spicker, P. (1991) 'The Principle of Subsidiarity and the Social Policy of the European Community', *Journal of European Social Policy*, 1 (1), pp. 3–14.

Springer, B. (1992) *The Social Dimension of 1992: Europe Faces a New EC* (New York/London: Praeger).

Steindorff, C. and Heering, C. (1993) 'Familienpolitik und Recht im Europäischen Integrationsprozeß', in E. Neubauer, C. Dienel and M. Lohkamp-Himmighofen (eds), *Zwölf Wege der Familienpolitik in der Europäischen Gemeinschaft. Eigenständige Systeme und vergleichbare Qualitäten?*, vol. 1 (Bonn: Bundesministerium für Familie und Senioren), pp. 131–59.

Taylor-Gooby, P. (1991a) *Social Change, Social Welfare and Social Science* (London/New York: Harvester Wheatsheaf).

Taylor-Gooby, P. (1991b) 'Welfare State Regimes and Welfare Citizenship', *Journal of European Social Policy*, 1 (2), pp. 93–105.

Teague, P. (1989) *The European Community: the Social Dimension. Labour Market Policies for 1992* (London: Kogan Page in association with Cranfield School of Management).

Teague, P. and McClelland, D. (1991) 'Towards "Social Europe"? Industrial Relations after 1992', *Cross-National Research Papers*, 2 (5), pp. 8–22.

Thomson, I. (1989) *The Documentation of the European Communities: a Guide* (London: Mansell).

Tilly, L.A. and Scott, J.W. (1987) *Women, Work and Family*, new edn (London: Methuen).

Titmuss, R.M. (1974) *Social Policy: an Introduction* (edited by B. Abel-Smith and K. Titmuss) (London: George Allen & Unwin).

Townsend, P. (1979) *Poverty in the United Kingdom: a Survey of Household Resources and Standards of Living* (Berkeley and Los Angeles: University of California Press).

Ungerson, C. (ed.) (1990) *Gender and Caring. Work and Welfare in Britain and Scandinavia* (London: Harvester Wheatsheaf).

United Nations (1993) *Statistical Yearbook - 1990/91* (New York: United Nations)

Vale, A. (1991) 'The European Women's Lobby', *Social Europe 3/91*, pp. 107–9.

Venturini, P. (1989) *1992: the European Social Dimension* (Luxembourg: Office for Official Publications of the European Communities).

Walker, A. (1993a) 'Introduction', in A. Walker, J. Alber and A-M. Guillemard, *Older People in Europe: Social and Economic Policies. The 1993 Report of the European Observatory* (Brussels: Commission of the European Communities), pp. 7–17.

Walker, A. (1993b) 'Living Standards and Way of Life', in A. Walker, J. Alber and A-M. Guillemard, *Older People in Europe: Social and Economic Policies. The 1993 Report of the European Observatory* (Brussels: Commission of the European Communities), pp. 18–67.

Walker, R. and Simpson, R. (1993) 'Conclusion: whose Europe?', in R. Simpson and R. Walker (eds), *Europe: for Richer or Poorer?* (London: CPAG), pp. 105–18.

Wicks, M. (1991) 'United Kingdom: the Family to the Fore', in W. Dumon (co-ordinator), *National Family Policies in EC-countries in 1990*, V/2293/91 (Brussels: Commission of the European Communities), pp. 48–50.

Index

Abrahamson, Peter   36, 198, 201
acquis communautaire   14, 207, 212
action programmes   191–2, 195, 197,
   208, 212, 218
   for education   40–2
   for employment   154–5
   for equal opportunities   103,
      108–10
   implementing the Community
      Charter   11–12, 197
   for living and working
      conditions   64–7
   for migrant workers   [9.7], 182
   for older and disabled
      people   127–9
   against poverty   147, 154, 196
   see also social action programme
Adapt   155
Advisory Committee on Safety,
   Hygiene and Health Protection
   at Work   61
age   32, 163, 181, 213
   see also retirement age, working
      age
ageing, of population   17, 56, 124,
   129–33, 139, 173, 181, 201
aggregation
   of entitlements   125, 170–1
   of rights   176–7
Agreement on Social Policy   [1.6]
   and equal opportunities   81, 105
   and harmonisation   25
   and living and working
      conditions   67
   and the social dimension   12–13
   Article 1   25, 200
   Article 2   12, 25, 68, 151, 198

Article 3   13, 26
Article 5   25
Article 6   25, 105
Article 7   82
AIDS   75
   Europe against AIDS   67
Alber, Jens   131, 140
alcohol   131
alcohol abuse   75
allowances   *see* family allowances
Anglo-Saxon countries   19, 28, 204
   see also models of welfare
apprenticeship(s)   54, 177–8, 205
approximation   7, 19–21, 23, 25–6,
   61, 63, 68, 76, 106, 200, 206
Ardittis, Solon   173, 177
asylum   183–4
asylum-seekers   183–5, 199
atypical work   66, 70
Austria
   family policy   92
   voting rights   214
   welfare models   205

Baldwin-Edwards, Martin   182
Belgium
   ageing, older and disabled
      people   132–4, 143
   education and training
      arrangements   52–4, 205
   EEC membership   1
   equality legislation and equal
      opportunities   110, 114,
      116–18
   family policy   90–1, 93, 95, 97–8,
      204
   family structure   84–6

235

Belgium (*cont.*)
  health and safety at work   69
  migration   174–5, 179–80, 184–5,
    187
  public health   74, 75
  social exclusion   159, 161, 165
  social protection system   29, 32,
    35, 204
  social spending   31, 220
  voting rights   214
  working conditions   70–1
benefit(s)   22, 79, 97, 106, 125, 127,
    161, 195, 203, 204, 206
  earnings-related   114, 137, 161–2,
    164
  employment-related   80,114, 120,
    161, 171, 198
  flat-rate   36, 116, 136, 161, 163–4,
    201–2, 207, 223
  income-related   33, 35, 73
  in kind   159
  means-tested   35, 163, 207, 224
  targeted   81, 201, 207
  universal   201, 223, 224
  see also child, family, invalidity,
    old age, sickness, social
    security, survivors',
    unemployment
benefit family   89–91
Berghman, Jos   11, 22, 202
Berthod-Wurmser, Marianne   73–4
Beveridge, William   33, 136–7
Beveridgian social security   35, 224
Bimbi, Franca   110, 120
birth-rate(s)   52, 97, 114, 129–32
Bourdelais, Patrice   130
breadwinner   88, 114, 119–20, 204
Britain   *see* United Kingdom
Buckley, Mary and Anderson,
    Malcolm   102
Bundesministerium für Familie und
    Senioren   96
burden of proof   13, 111

cancer   75
  Europe against Cancer   63
care   29, 96, 121, 127–8
  see also health care, medical care
care insurance   141

care services   140–1
career break(s)   108, 116
carers   119, 140, 199
caring   29, 96, 119, 124, 127, 130,
    134, 135, 140–1, 163, 198
caring professions   113
Catholic lobby   88
Cedefop   48, 208
census(es)   [5.1], 83
Céreq   54
Chassard, Yves   23
child benefit(s)   90, 93, 96–8, 201,
    222, 224–5
childcare   90, 96, 98, 107–8, 110,
    115, 117–8, 120, 141, 208
children
  care for   117
  needs of   91
  protection of   41, 80–1, 197,
    207–8
  rights of   4, 91
  at risk   95
Child Support Act   91
Church   29, 34
citizenship   9, 33, 36, **102–23**, 135–6,
    174, 181, 185–7, 207
  European   47
  rights   16, 79, 100, 119–20, 151,
    186–7, 194, 197–9, 204
  of the Union   171, 187, 198
civil servants   179, 220–1, 223
code(s) of good practice   129, 212
co-existence   27, 201
cohabitation   83, 87, 90–1, 94
coherence   24
cohesion   8, 44, 193
  economic   6, 8, 39
  economic and social   8, 11, 25–6,
    109, 128, 143, 147, 149, 153,
    191, 198, 214
  social   7, 23,–6, 151
collective bargaining   3, 61, 63,
    70–2, 142
Collins, Doreen   3, 21, 169, 172, 174
Comett   50
Commission   64, 202, 214–5
  President of   6, 23, 191
  as a social actor   206–11
Committee of the Regions   217

common market 6, 20, 39, 61, 125, 206
communication(s) 218
  on education and training [3.4], 40
  on the elderly [7.5], 128
  on family policy(ies) [5.3], 80
  on frontier workers [9.10], 171
  on public health [4.7], 67
  on subsidiarity [1.10], 12
  on supplementary social security [9.11], 177
community care 74, 140
Community Charter of the Fundamental Social Rights of Workers (Community Charter) [1.7]
  application of [1.9, 1.11, 1.14, 1.15], 11–12
  and education and training 40–2
  and equal opportunities 105, 197
  and freedom of movement 171, 197
  and harmonisation 24
  and living and working conditions 63–4, 197
  and older and disabled people 126–7, 197
  and reconciling occupational and family obligations 105
  and the social dimension 8–10
  and social exclusion 149–50
  preamble to 9, 197, 199
  points 1–3 171, 197
  point 2 40
  point 3 24, 40, 44, 64
  point 5 150, 197
  point 6 81
  points 7–9 197
  point 7 63–4
  point 8 24, 64, 71
  point 10 24, 150, 200
  points 11–14 197
  point 15 40–1, 44, 197
  point 16 41, 105, 197, 199
  points 17–18 197
  point 19 24, 41, 64, 197
  points 20–3 197

point 20 41, 53
point 22 64
point 23 41
points 24–5 197
point 24 126–7, 200
point 25 126–7, 200
point 26 41, 126, 197
point 27 200
point 28 11
point 30 216
Community Support Frameworks (CSF) 149
competence/ies
  Community 11, 16, 194
  Council 183
  member states 185
  Union 12–14, 191, 193, 207, 209, 211, 213
competition 2–3, 10–11, 14, 15, 22–3, 38–9, 59, 72, 74, 102, 143, 173, 192, 200
competitiveness 11, 22–3, 25, 42, 44, 113, 121, 125, 155, 172, 192, 195–6, 199, 212
constitution(s) 98
  French 2, 88, 102, 110, 203
  German 88, 98, 221–2
  Greek 88, 99, 111
  Irish 88, 99
  Italian 88, 99, 100, 110
  Luxembourg 88
  Portuguese 88, 99, 111, 225
  Spanish 88, 99, 111, 226
consultation (of workers) 4, 6, 11, 12, 15, 63–4, 66, 197
contraception 83
contributions
  employee('s) 31–2, 125, 206, 220–1, 222–6
  employer('s) 31–3, 35, 125, 201, 206, 220–6
  employment-related 93
Convention on Human Rights 4, 8
convergence [2.1]
  and education 42, 44, 52, 57
  and equal opportunities 103, 117
  and family policies 97, 100
  and living and working conditions 75–6

convergence (*cont.*)
  and policy for older and disabled
    people 134, 138–9, 142–3
  and social policy 7, 21, 23–8, 31,
    34–6, 194, 199–202
convergence thesis 27–8
  see also recommendation on
co-operation 3, 6, 25–6, 38, 39, 42,
  44, 47–8, 49, 50, 61, 63, 67, 73,
  76, 154, 183, 199, 200–1, 209
co-operation procedure 7, 213, 216
co-ordination 7–8, 11, 21, 25–6, 57,
  100, 155, 198
core and periphery 69, 146, 158
corporatism 34, 36, 79, 222
Council (of Ministers) 21, 214
  as a social actor 209
Council of Europe 80
  see also Social Charter
Crawley, Christine 102, 105
culture(s) 46, 51, 179–80, 191, 198,
  217
  national 23

decisions 218
  75/458/EEC [8.1], 151, 156
  77/779/EEC [8.1], 151
  89/457/EEC [8.2], 152
Declaration against racism and
  xenophobia [9.9], 182
Delors, Jacques 6–8, 15, 16, 23–4,
  40, 63, 191, 209
demographic ageing 124, 130–3,
  141
demographic change(s) 56, 127,
  138
demographic trends 80–3, 97, 113,
  128, 181
Denmark
  ageing, older and disabled
    people 132, 135, 139–40,
    142–3
  Community membership 1
  education and training
    arrangements 52–4, 205
  equality legislation and equal
    opportunities 110–11,
    113–18, 120–1, 204
  family policy 88–90, 92–3, 96–8

family structure 83–7
health and safety at work 69
migration 175, 179, 182–4, 187,
  205
public health 73, 75
social exclusion 159, 163–5
social protection system 29, 33,
  36, 223–4
social spending 31, 201, 207
voting rights 214
working conditions 71–2
dependants 21, 73, 91, 119, 132,
  134, 137, 146
dependency ratio 129, 144
De Swaan, Abram 22, 187
directives 218
  68/360/EEC [9.3], 170
  73/403/EEC [5.1], 83
  75/117/EEC [6.1], 111
  76/207/EEC [6.2], 106, 111, 219
  79/7/EEC [6.3], 23, 106, 111, 126
  86/378/EEC [6.5], 106
  86/613/EEC [6.6], 106
  89/391/EEC [4.1], 65, 210
  89/48/EEC [3.2], 46
  91/383/EEC [4.3], 66
  91/533/EEC [4.4], 66
  92/51/EEC [3.3], 46
  92/85/EEC [4.6], 67, 107, 116
  93/104/EC [4.8], 65–6
Directorate-General (DG) V 215
disability 73, 135, 146, 206, 213
disability allowances 134
disabled people 41, 74, 96, **124–44**,
  149, 150, 155, 161, 192, 197,
  198, 199, 208, 221
discrimination 26, 41, 105–6, 121,
  129, 169–70, 182, 187, 195, 212,
  213
  positive 104
distance working 66
distribution of resources 194
diversity
  cultural 43, 184, 198
  linguistic 43
  between national systems 10,
    22–4, 26–9, 38, 50, 56, 79,
    161, 200, 205
  social 191

division of (household) labour 107, 119
divorce 85, 90, 97, 135
    rates 85–6
doctors 74
Drake, Keith 54–5
drug abuse 75
drug dependence 67
drug traffic 184
dualisation 157, 201
Dublin Convention 184

earnings 158
economic activity 73, 97, 102
economic activity rates 112, 114, 118, 121, 140, 181
    see also labour force participation rates
Economic and Monetary Union (EMU) 23
Economic and Social Committee 14, 215, 217, 218
Ects 49
education **38–58**, 94, 96, 105, 107, 128, 130, 135, 156, 158, 161, 168, 172, 177–8, 191, 195, 205, 207–9, 217
EEC Treaty establishing the European Economic Community [1.2]
    and freedom of movement 169–71, 182
    and harmonisation 20–21
    and living and working conditions 60–1
    and the social dimension 2–4
    and vocational training 39
    Article 2 2, 26, 61, 152
    Article 3 2, 148
    Article 7 169
    Articles 48–51 3, 169
    Article 48 169, 179
    Article 49 170
    Article 50 49, 170
    Article 51 21, 125, 170
    Articles 52–8 3
    Article 57 39
    Article 91 9
    Article 100 7, 20, 105, 200

Article 101 3
Articles 117–28 2
Article 117 19, 20, 21, 60, 125, 199, 206
Article 118 3, 7, 21, 39, 61, 125, 200
Article 119 3, 23, 102, 104–6, 203
Article 120 61, 64
Article 121 3, 21, 125, 170
Article 122 21
Articles 123–8 3
Article 123 43, 61, 148
Article 126 43
Article 128 39, 43
Article 235 105, 151
Elaine 183
eligibility 88, 137, 139, 156, 187, 198
employer(s) 6, 24, 65, 71, 76, 94, 111, 134–5, 173, 178, 221, 223
Employment 155
employment 3, 6, 94, 128–9, 151, 168, 176, 183, 186, 194, 198
    access to 32, 41, 105, 108, 111, 178,
    right to 157
employment contract(s) 59, 66, 72
employment law 23
Employment Observatory 154
employment patterns 104, 112
employment policy(ies) 208
employment relationship 67
employment rights 100, 121
employment status 33, 79, 187
employment structures 140
enlargement 42
environment 59
    social 152
    working 4–5, 7, 62, 75, 125, 176
equalisation 9, 59, 60
equality between men and women 12, 41, 81, 104–5, 108, 110, 121
    see also gender equality
equal opportunities 4, 14, 29, 40, 50, 81, 94–5, 103–5, 107–8, 110–11, 134, 154, 192, 208–10
equal pay 3, 15, 80, 203, 207, 212
equal rights 2, 111, 120

equal treatment 23, 26, 41, 60, 80–1, 102–6, 111, 198, 207, 218
equal value 106, 110, 113, 119
Erasmus 48–9, 51
Ergo 154
espace social 6
Esping-Andersen, Gøsta 28–9, 33, 136
ethnic groups 157, 182
ethnic origin(s) 32, 42
Eures 178
European Agency for Health and Safety at Work 208
European Agricultural Guidance and Guarantee Fund (EAGGF) 8, 148
European Anti-Poverty Network 153
European Atomic Energy Community (EAEC) [1.3], 2, 60
Articles 30–9 60
European base line of living (EBL) 160
European Centre of Public Enterprises (CEEP) 7
European Childcare Network 107
European Coal and Steel Community (ECSC) [1.1], 60
Article 3(e) 60
European Convention for the Protection of Human Rights and Fundamental Freedoms 198
see also Convention on Human Rights
European Court of Justice (ECJ) 102, 106–7, 210, 215–16
European Council 214
European Economic Community (EEC) [1.2], 1, 191
see also EEC Treaty
European Foundation for the Improvement of Living and Working Conditions 62, 208
European Institute of Social Security 24, 25

European Observatory on Ageing and Older People 124, 128, 138, 142
European Observatory on National Family Policies 81, 91, 96
European Observatory on National Policies to Combat Social Exclusion 153, 157
European Parliament 7, 14, 80–1, 103, 127, 171, 182, 209, 216, 217
European Regional Development Fund (ERDF) 8, 148
European Social Fund (ESF) 3, 5, 7–8, 40, 43, 61, 103, 148, 154, 215, 217
European social snake 202
European System of Integrated Social Protection Statistics (ESSPROS) 31
European Trade Union Confederation (ETUC) 7–8
European Women's Lobby 103
Eurostat 83
Eurotecnet 50
Eurydice 48
exchange of young workers 39, 50, 170
Exchange of Young Workers' Programme 49
extramarital births 83, 85, 87–8, 90, 97

Fagnani, Jeanne 117
family allowances 32, 33, 89–90, 93, 96, 98, 201, 221–3
family benefits 107, 130, 209
family credit 163, 224
family obligations 168
family policy/ies **79–101**, 204, 208
family responsibilities 80, 107, 135, 206
family reunification 171, 182, 185
family reunion 183
family size 90, 98, 147
family structure(s) 82–8, 94, 96, 99, 102, 103, 140
Federal Republic of Germany education 53
EEC membership 1

equal opportunities 113, 119–20
family policy 95
frontier workers 175
population ageing 132
see also Germany
feminism 102
fertility rates 83–4, 88, 97, 114
Finland
family policy 92
voting rights 214
welfare models 205
flexibility 70, 105, 212
Flora, Peter and Alber, Jens 27
Flynn, Pádraig 17, 207
Force 50
foreign residents 174
foreign workers 182, 184
Fortress Europe 169, 182, 199
framework directive(s) [4.1], 65, 67,
68, 69, 76, 107, 210
France
ageing, older and disabled
people 132–4, 140–3
education and training
arrangements 52–4, 205
EEC membership 1
equality legislation and equal
opportunities 102, 110,
114–18, 120, 204
family policy 88–90, 92–3, 95,
97–8, 204, 207
family structure 84–8
health and safety at work 69
migration 172, 174–5, 179, 182,
184–7, 205
public health 74–5
social charges 2
social exclusion 148, 159, 161–2,
204
social protection system 29,
32–3, 35, 204, 221
social spending 31, 201
voting rights 214
working conditions 70–2
freedom of movement 24, 38, 41,
56, 64, 186–8, 192, 195, 201, 212
of labour 59, 125, 143, 146, 149,
169–72, 182, 188, 198–9
principle of 168

free movement
of labour 197, 203
of persons, services and capital 3,
168
of students 40
of workers 218
frontier workers 171, 175

gender 32, 42, 70
gender equality 98, 102
gender stereotyping 108
Germany
ageing, older and disabled
people 131–5, 139–41, 143
education and training
arrangements 52–4, 205
equality legislation and equal
opportunities 110, 115, 119,
204
family policy 88–90, 92–3,
96–8
family structure 84–8
health and safety at work 69
migration 174–5, 179, 182, 185,
187, 205
public health 74, 75
social exclusion 159, 161–2
social protection system 32, 35,
204, 206, 221
social spending 31
unification 21, 185
voting rights 214
working conditions 70–2
Gillion, Colin 139
Ginn, Jay and Arber, Sara 134–7
Glendinning, Caroline and
McLaughlin, Eithne 141
Gold, Michael and Mayes,
David 195–6, 207
Greece
ageing, older and disabled
people 132–3, 137–9, 143
Community membership 10
education and training
arrangements 52–3
equality legislation and equal
opportunities 111, 116–18
family policy 88–90, 93, 97–9
family structure 83–7

Greece (*cont.*)
  health and safety at work 69
  migration 169, 172, 174–5, 179,
      181, 185, 187
  public health 73–5
  social exclusion 148–9, 158,
      164–5
  social protection system 29,
      34–5, 204, 225
  social spending 31
  voting rights 214
  working conditions 70–2
Green Paper on Education [3.6], 44
Green Paper on European social
    policy [1.12], 14–15, 17, 203,
    218
Guillemard, Anne-Marie 133

Handynet 128
harmonisation
  of conditions of residence 171
  of education and training 44–8,
      57
  of equal opportunities 105
  of living and working
      conditions 59–62, 64, 67,
      70, 76
  of social policy **19–37**, 73, 133,
      191, 199–202, 206
health 2, 94, 131, 133, 176, 206, 221
  see also public health
health care 32–4, 36, 73–4, 96, 121,
    125, 129, 132, 140, 143, 156,
    157, 201, 224–6
health and safety 60, 62, 193, 197,
    210, 215, 217
  at work 4, 6–7, 12, 41, 59, 65,
      68–9, 75–6, 107
health services 161, 222
  national health service(s) 32–3,
      73–4, 203, 222, 225–6
Heclo, Hugh 28
Helios 128
higher education 39, 46, 52–3, 57,
    205
Higgins, Joan viii
homeless 152
Hoover 10
hospital beds 74

household(s) 82–3, 89, 95, 156, 159,
    165
  one/single-person 83–4, 88
household size 83, 159
housing 96–8, 126, 128, 131, 156,
    157, 158, 163, 170, 176, 181
human resources 41, 51, 70, 212

ill health 73, 146
immigration 96, 130, 139, 146, 169,
    175, 199, 205
  illegal 182, 185
  non-European 169, 175, 181–6,
      199, 205
immigration policy(ies) 96, 182
  regimes 182, 205
    continental/Schengen 182–3,
        205
    liberal 182–3, 205
    Scandinavian 182–3
    semi-peripheral/
        Mediterranean 183, 205
improvement in living and working
    conditions 4–5, **59–78**, 171–2
income 176
income distribution 94
income maintenance 33, 96, 127,
    134, 139, 160–1, 194, 203, 209,
    224
income security 134–5, 204
income support 163, 224
income tax 120
  see also tax
individualisation of rights 99, 105,
    127, 211
industrial accidents, injuries and
    diseases 32, 59, 61, 68–9, 107,
    220, 223, 224
industrial relations 215
inequality(ies) 32, 107, 126, 142, 159
insurance *see* social insurance
insurance contributions 73
  employment-related 32, 35, 79,
      161, 164, 201, 203–4, 222
  income-related 19
insurance principle 93, 139, 161,
    164, 204
  see also private insurance, social
      insurance

integration 22, 125, 183, 188,
    198–9
  economic 1, 3, 10, 25, 127, 148,
    196
  economic and social 47, 128, 150,
    152, 172, 183, 209, 212
  European 42
  social 124, 126, 129, 170, 197
internal market 6–11, 16, 20, 25,
    42, 44, 63, 109, 149–50, 152,
    166, 172–3, 176, 191–2, 194–6,
    199
  see also Single European Market
International Convention on
  Children's Rights 91
invalidity
  benefits 32, 107, 133
  pensions 134–5, 136, 177, 161,
    223
Ireland
  ageing, older and disabled
    people 132–3, 136–7,
    139–41, 143
  Community membership 1
  education and training
    arrangements 53, 54
  equality legislation and equal
    opportunities 110, 113–19,
    204
  family policy 88–90, 93, 97–9, 2
  family structure 83–6
  health and safety at work 69
  migration 175, 179, 183–7
  public health 73–5
  social exclusion 148–9, 158–60,
    163–4
  social protection system 29, 33,
    224
  social spending 31
  voting rights 214
  working conditions 70
Iris 50
Italy
  ageing, older and disabled
    people 132–3, 139–43
  compliance 210
  education and training
    arrangements 52–4
  EEC membership 1

equality legislation and equal
    opportunities 110, 114,
    116–18, 120, 204
family policy 88–90, 93, 97–100
family structure 83–7
health and safety at work 69
migration 174, 179, 183–7, 203
public health 72, 74, 203
social exclusion 148–9, 158, 160,
    162, 165
social protection system 29,
    32–3, 35, 206, 222
social spending 31, 201, 222
voting rights 214
working conditions 70–2

James, Edward 151
James, Phil 75
job aspirations 80
job creation 11, 110, 165, 199, 212
job evaluation 106
job-seekers 162, 166, 175, 178
job-seeker's allowance 163
job shortages 186
job vacancies 176, 178, 188, 208
Jones, Hywel 47, 56

Kamerman, Sheila and Kahn,
    Alfred 91–2, 96, 98
Kleinman, Mark and Piachaud,
    David 16, 38, 207

labour costs 9–10, 20, 22–3, 32, 73,
    125, 127, 173, 196, 200, 201, 203
  see also social costs
labour force 39, 66, 114–15, 124,
    143, 181
labour force participation rates 39,
    139
  see also economic activity rates
Labour Force Survey (LFS) 173
labour law 38, 61, 72
labour market(s)
  and education and training 39,
    43, 54–6
  and family policies 81, 95, 209
  and gender equality 103, 107,
    112–14, 119, 121, 208

labour market(s) (*cont.*)
  and mobility   169, 172, 176, 178,
    181
  and policy for older and disabled
    people   129, 135, 139
  and social exclusion   147, 149,
    150, 154–5, 163, 165, 166
  and social policy   11–12, 14, 16,
    36, 197–8, 204, 205, 212,
    215
  and working conditions   66, 72,
    75
labour market policy(ies)   154–5,
  209
labour permits   174
labour shortage   169, 172
Land, Hilary and Parker, Roy   94,
  99
language(s)   47, 49, 55, 170, 179–80,
  186
  Community   48
  teaching of   43–4
language barriers   51
leave
  maternity   108, 112, 115–18, 120
  paid   24, 64, 71–2
  parental   98, 107–8, 112, 115–18,
    120, 141
  paternity   115–18
  sick   187
Leda   154
Leibfried, Stephan   202, 206
  and Pierson, Paul   10
Leonardo   50
level playing field   10, 200
Lewis, Jane   119, 120
life expectancy   129–32, 146
Lindley, Robert   55, 173
Lingua   49, 179
living and working conditions   2, 22,
  129, 178, 195, 207
  see also improvement of, working
    conditions
living standards   129, 141–4, 150,
  151
  see also standards of living
Lødemel, Ivar   164
logic of industrialism thesis   29, 34
lone parent(s)   87, 96, 221

lone-parent families   87–8, 90, 99,
  148
  see also single-parent families
lone parenthood   83, 87, 90–1, 94,
  147
Luckhaus, Linda   106
Luxembourg
  ageing, older and disabled
    people   133–4, 139, 143
  compliance   210
  education and training
    arrangements   52–3
  EEC membership   1
  equality legislation and equal
    opportunities   110, 115–18,
    204
  family policy   88, 90, 93, 97–8,
    204
  family structure   84–6
  foreign students   49
  health and safety at work   69
  migration   179, 182, 185–7
  public health   73–5
  social exclusion   159, 161–2
  social protection system   32,
    222–3
  social spending   31
  voting rights   214
  working conditions   70–1

Maastricht Treaty   [1.6]
  and education and training   42–4,
    47
  and freedom of movement   171–2
  and harmonisation   25
  and living and working
    conditions   67–8
  and the social dimension   12–13,
    195
  and social exclusion   149–51
  and subsidiarity   200, 210
  Article A   210
  Article B   198
  Article F   198
  Article K.1   183, 199
  Article 2   12
  Article 3   67, 210
  Article 3b   200, 210
  Article 6   105, 199

Article 8 171
Article 100c 171, 183, 199
Articles 118–129 191
Article 118a 213
Article 126 43, 51
Article 127 43, 51
Article 128 198
Article 129 67, 75, 198
Article 198a 217
  see also Treaty on European
    Union
managers 173
marginalisation 156–8
marital status 80, 88, 90
marriage 82–3, 85, 88
marriage rates 85, 97
maternity 208, 222–3
  benefit(s) 32, 118, 187
medical care 223–5
  see also health care
medical practitioner 74
medicines 74
Meehan, Elizabeth 119
memorandum 218
  on higher education [3.5], 41–2
Merger Treaty [1.4], 192, 217
Meulders-Klein, Marie-Thérèse 89
migrant(s) 149, 152, 158
  non-European 173, 185
migrant workers 16, 20–1, 61, 74,
    125, 170, 177, 186, 199, 206, 209
migration
  intra-European 169, 176, 181
  see also immigration
minimum income 147, 160, 166, 187
Misep 154
Mishra, Ramesh 35, 194
Missoc 220
Mitterrand, François 6, 203
mobility 41, 63, **168–90**
  barriers to 19, 168
  of disabled people 126, 128
  intra-European 49, 168, 172–5,
    181, 186
  of labour 10, 42, 44, 168, 195
  obstacle(s) to 44, 49, 59, 168–9,
    176–81, 188, 200
  of students 43, 46, 47, 49
  of teachers 43, 179

of workers 3, 57, 125, 127
model(s) of welfare 27–30, 194
  Anglo-Saxon 33–4, 163–4, 203,
    223–5
  Bismarckian 32, 35, 79, 161
  continental 19, 29, 32, 34, 73,
    134, 146, 161–3, 197, 203–5,
    220–3
  industrial achievement/
    performance 28–9, 134
  institutional redistributive 28–9,
    136
  Nordic 33–4, 163–5, 205, 223–5
  residual 28, 136–7, 204
  rudimentary 164–5, 204
  southern European 34, 161
  universalistic 161
  see also welfare regimes
monetary union 23, 42
mortality rates 130
mothers 80, 198
  lone 161
  rights as 95, 112–18, 198, 204
  working 61, 112
mutual recognition 38
  of qualifications 3, 25, 39, 42–6,
    56, 176
  of systems 23–6, 143, 187

Naric 49
nationality 162, 163, 169–70, 174,
    181, 182, 184–7, 199, 205
naturalisation 186, 187
Nec 154
Netherlands
  ageing, older and disabled
    people 133, 136–7, 139, 141,
    143
  education and training
    arrangements 52–5, 205
  EEC membership 1
  equality legislation and equal
    opportunities 110, 113–19,
    204
  family policy 96–8
  family structure 84–7
  health and safety at work 69
  migration 175, 179, 182, 185, 205
  public health 74

Netherlands (*cont.*)
  social exclusion   159, 161–2, 165
  social protection system   29,
    32–3, 223
  social spending   31
  voting rights   214
  working conditions   70–2
night work   64, 66, 71
Nordic countries   19, 204
Nordic states   183, 203
Now   50, 109

Objective 1 regions   148
occupational accidents and
  disease   *see* industrial accidents
old age   74, 206, 223
  benefits   32, 35, 107, 132
  pensions   133, 134, 135, 137, 177,
    221
older people   35, 74, 79, 96, **124–45**,
  146–8, 150, 152, 158, 161, 198,
  203, 208, 213, 218, 221
opinions   218
Ostner, Ilona   120

paid holidays   61, 66, 71
  see also leave
participation   197
part-time work   107–8, 114, 119–20,
  181
part-time workers   66, 107, 115, 136
part-time working   64, 66, 71–2,
  114, 118, 134
paternity   88–9
pensionable age   107
pension(s)   33, 112, 121, 124, 129,
  131–3, 142–3, 177, 187, 198,
  201, 203, 226
  flat-rate   135, 136, 137
  income-related   187
pension schemes   125–6, 129, 134,
  135, 137–9, 142, 143
  earnings-related   138, 142–3, 146
pensioners   73, 173
performance indicators   54
Petersen, Hanne   121
Petra   50
Pickup, Laurie   173, 176
Pieters, Danny   22–3, 202, 206, 220

platform of basic rights   8
polarisation   146, 157, 201
policy-making process   93, 100, 203
policy-making style(s)   92–4, 104,
  193, 203
political union   16, 42, 146
Portugal
  ageing, older and disabled
    people   132–3, 137–9, 143
  Community membership   10
  compliance   210
  education and training
    arrangements   52–3
  equality legislation and equal
    opportunities   111, 113–14,
    116–18
  family policy   88, 90, 93, 97–9
  family structure   84–6
  health and safety at work   69
  migration   169, 172, 174, 179,
    181, 183, 185
  public health   73–5
  social exclusion   148–9, 152,
    158–60, 164–5
  social protection system   29,
    34–5, 204, 225–6
  social spending   31
  voting rights   214
  working conditions   70–2
positive action   105, 108
poverty   6, 96, 136, 143, 146–60,
  165–6, 206, 208
  new   147, 157
poverty line   158
poverty trap   163
pregnant women   [4.6], 67, 71, 107
private health care   36
private insurance   35, 73, 136, 223
private pensions   135, 223
private sector   113, 121, 129, 154
privatisation
  of pension funds   139
  of services   207
professional workers   173
pro-natalism   94
proportionality   13, 16, 68
public health   59, 60, 67, 73–6, 191,
  198, 209, 217
public holidays   71

public sector 32, 36, 113, 121, 129, 154, 179
public service(s) 111, 169, 176–7, 220

qualifications 25, 32, 53–7, 168, 171–2, 176
see also mutual recognition of
qualified majority voting 7–8, 12, 16, 62, 65, 68, 171, 183, 193, 209, 210, 214
quality of life 5, 26
Quintin, Odile 23, 102

race 195, 213
racism [9.9], 182
recession 113, 132, 139, 201
recommendation(s) 218
  on childcare [6.10], 107–8, 117
  on convergence [2.1], 26–7, 81, 82, 127, 200–1, 208
  on dignity at work [6.9], 108
  on retirement age [7.2], 126
  on sufficient resources [8.4], 150–1, 160, 165, 208
reconciling work and family life 79, 81, 105, 107–9, 112, 114–15, 118, 141, 199, 209
recruitment 177–8
redistribution 32, 95, 194, 196
redistributive justice 100
redistributive principle 92
redundancies 59
referenda 193
refugees 152, 158, 182, 184
regions 195–6
regional development 148, 208
regional inequalities 192
regulations 21, 25, 218
  Nos 3–4 [9.1], 170
  No. 1612/68 [9.2], 170
  (EEC) No. 1408/71 [9.4], 171
  (EEC) No. 574/72 [9.5], 171
  (EEC) No. 311/76 [9.6], 182
religion 182, 213
resettlement allowance 148
residence 42, 73, 162, 170, 186–7
  condition(s) of 24, 64, 171, 177, 183

residence permits 170, 187
resolution(s) 218
  on education [3.1], 39
  on equal opportunities action programmes [6.7, 108–10
  on family policy [5.2], 80
  on a flexible retirement age [7.8], 127
  on health policy choices [4.5], 67–8
  on migration [9.7, 9.8], 182
  on a social action programme [1.8], 5–6
  services for the elderly [7.3], 127
  the situation of older people [7.1, 7.4], 127
restructuring
  economic 154, 198
  industrial 146
  of working hours 75
  of working time 72
retirement 32, 106, 161, 197, 204
retirement age 112, 126, 129–31, 136, 138–9, 143, 146
retirement pension(s) 134, 142, 161, 177
revenu minimum d'insertion (RMI) 36, 159, 162–3, 221
Rex, John 184
Richard, Ivor 15–16
right(s)
  of citizens 15
  employment-related 67, 80, 108, 146
  of establishment 3, 217
  see also mothers', women's, workers'
Rimet 183
road accidents 131
Roll, Jo 87
Rome, Treaty of *see* EEC Treaty
Room, Graham viii, 156
Rowntree, B. Seebohm 158

safety and health *see* health and safety
safety net, means-tested 136
Schengen Agreement 183–4
school-leaving age 41, 53

Schultheis, Franz 92, 98
Séché, Jean-Claude 45, 177
Sedoc 178
segregation 113
selection in higher education 53
self-employed workers 106, 111,
    126, 146, 179, 220
service sector 221
sexual harassment 108
Shanks, Michael 1, 151, 191,
    206–7
sickness 208, 221, 212
  benefits 32, 73, 198
Siim, Birte 121
Single European Act (SEA) [1.5]
  and the co-operation
      procedure 216
  and education 44–5
  and freedom of
      movement 171–2
  and harmonisation 23–4
  and living and working
      conditions 62–3
  and social exclusion 149–51
  Article 100a 62, 68, 171, 200
  Article 118a 24, 62, 65, 67, 68, 76
  Article 118b 62
  Article 130a-e 8, 191
  Article 130a 8
  Article 130b 16, 149
Single European Market (SEM) 10,
    11, 23, 172–3, 194–5
  see also internal market
single-parent families 87, 152, 158
  see also lone-parent families
single-parent households 147
skill shortages 55, 173
skilled workers 179
smoking 63, 131
social action programme [1.8], 5–6,
    39–40, 79, 80, 108, 127–8, 151,
    208, 219
social actor(s) 14, 205–11
  see also Commission, Council of
      Ministers
social assistance 33–5, 73, 90, 137,
    143, 146, 147, 150, 159–65, 177,
    187, 201, 204, 208, 220–5
  means-tested 33, 35, 135, 138, 164

social chapter 12–13, 192–3, 200
  see also Agreement on Social
      Policy
social charges 2
Social Charter (Council of
    Europe) 4, 8, 9, 80
social citizenship 33, 104, 119–21
social costs 9, 33
  see also labour costs
social devaluations 23
social dialogue 6–8, 11, 24, 63, 203,
    209, 215
social dumping 9–10, 22, 127, 143,
    166, 195–6
social exclusion 14, 36, 127, **146–67**,
    195, 208, 211, 218
social fund(s) 1, 2, 196, 217
  see also European Social Fund
social insurance 29, 32, 34, 118,
    125, 158, 164, 201, 220–6
  see also insurance contributions,
      insurance principle
social partners 7, 14, 63, 72, 108,
    200, 203, 211
social plinth 8–9, 16
Social Policy Research Unit 96
social protection system(s) 19, 22,
    26, 31, 73, 125, 128, 150, 160,
    187, 192, 195, 197, 200, 208,
    211, 222
social security 3, 9, 59, 89–90, 92,
    96, 106, 111, 124, 126, 134,
    141–2, 158, 163, 164, 170, 179,
    209–10, 215, 220
  of migrant workers 3, 21, 170,
      209
social security benefits 89–90, 115,
    156, 171, 176
social security entitlements 3, 88,
    112, 114, 118, 172, 206
social security rights 121, 139, 170
social security schemes 11, 35, 106,
    127, 171, 221
social security systems 21–3, 33–4,
    38, 73, 79, 93, 100, 128, 137,
    164, 187, 205–6, 211, 222
social services 124, 130, 195, 222–3
  means-tested 135, 140
social space 6, 8, 40, 191, 210

social spending 10, 30–1, 100, 196, 220–6
social state 203, 206, 221
socle social 8
Socrates 49
Soisson, Jean-Pierre 8
solidarity 26, 29, 47, 73, 94, 100, 120, 151, 160, 165, 193, 195–6
between generations 128–9
southern European countries 19, 29, 34, 36, 90, 100, 140, 164, 181, 200, 203–4
sovereignty 10, 14, 52, 166, 184, 193
Spain
ageing, older and disabled people 132, 137–9, 142–3
Community membership 10
education and training arrangements 52–3
equality legislation and equal opportunities 111, 114–18
family policy 88–90, 93, 98–9
family structure 84–7
health and safety at work 69
migration 169, 172, 174–5, 181, 183, 185–7
public health 73–5
social exclusion 148–9, 152, 158–9, 164–5
social protection system 29, 34–5, 226
social spending 31, 100, 201, 226
voting rights 214
working conditions 70–2
Spec 154
Spicker, Paul 13
standard(s) of living 2–3, 19, 26, 61, 132, 146, 148, 157, 197, 202
see also living standards
Standing Committee on Women's Rights 103
Structural Funds 8, 16, 25, 35, 109, 147–9, 154–5, 165, 208
subsidiarity [1.10], 5, 11–14, 16, 25, 38, 49, 50, 56, 64, 68, 73, 155, 160, 166, 193, 200, 210
subsistence 177, 201–2, 210–11
survivors' benefits 32, 107, 139

Sweden
voting rights 214
welfare models 29, 205
Sysdem 154

take-up 159, 166
targeted action 153
targeted funding 148
targeting 95
see also benefits
tax 96, 201, 222
tax allowances 141
taxation 22, 33–4, 73, 89, 121, 135, 139, 168, 201, 203, 222–5
tax law 89–90
tax relief 88–9, 97–8
Taylor-Gooby, Peter 29, 99
teachers 40
see also mobility
Teague, Paul 7–8
Teague, Paul and McClelland, Donovan 75
technological change 70, 155
technologies (new) 50–1, 55, 212
temporary contracts 70, 113
temporary work 64, 181
Tempus 49
terrorism 184
third-country nationals 12, 171, 182–3, 186, 188, 199
Titmuss, Richard 28, 38, 134, 136, 194
Townsend, Peter 156–8
trade unions 6, 24, 224
training 3, 6, 14, 23, **38–58**, 64, 96, 155, 163, 165, 168, 172, 177–8, 195, 205, 207, 212
transferability of labour 178
transferability of rights 168, 170–2, 176–7, 187
Treaty on European Union [1.6], 12, 217
see also Maastricht Treaty
Treaty of Paris 2
Treaty of Rome *see* EEC Treaty

unanimous voting 8, 12, 16, 67–8, 151, 170, 193, 209

unemployment 17, 39–40, 70, 72,
120, 135, 139, 146–7, 152,
154–5, 165, 169, 196, 201, 206,
208, 221
unemployment assistance 164–6
unemployment benefits 32, 138,
161–5, 177, 201, 204, 222
unemployment insurance 160, 24
unemployment rates 160
Union of Industrial and Employers'
Confederations of Europe
(UNICE) 7
United Kingdom
ageing, older and disabled
people 132, 136–7, 139–40,
143
Community membership 1
compliance 210
education and training
arrangements 52–5, 205
equality legislation and equal
opportunities 110–11,
113–15, 117–19, 204
family policy 89–91, 93, 95–6,
98–100, 204
family structure 84–8
health and safety at work 69
migration 174–5, 179–80, 182–7
opt-out 9, 12, 67, 193, 203, 211
public health 73–4
social exclusion 148–9, 152,
158–9, 163–4
social protection system 29, 33,
36, 204, 207, 225–6
social spending 31, 201, 225–6
voting rights 214
working conditions 70–2
universality 19, 28, 36, 98, 222, 225
unskilled workers 184
urban initiative 212

Val Duchesse 7, 209
Venturini, Patrick 47
visas 182–3, 199
vocational (re)training 3, 38, 40–3,
50–1, 54–7, 105–6, 108–11, 129,
148, 178, 191, 197, 208, 217
voluntary organisations 141
voluntary sector 33, 129, 153

wage costs 23
see also labour costs
wages 197
Walker, Andrew 129–30, 134, 138,
142–3
welfare
means-tested 159
mixed economy of 35, 79, 121
welfare pluralism 35–6
welfare principle 139
welfare regimes 27, 119, 161
corporatist 29, 32, 79, 134, 161
liberal 28–9, 136
social democratic 29, 33, 136
see also models of welfare
welfare state(s) 22, 27, 29–34, 82,
124
welfare tourism 22, 127, 143, 166
White Paper on European social
policy [1.13]
and convergence 201
and education and training 44,
57, 209
and equal opportunities 104–5,
108
and family life 81–2, 209
and the future of European social
policy 192–3, 196, 208–9,
211–13
and harmonisation 27
and living and working
conditions 76
and migration 183, 188
and older and disabled
people 129
and the social dimension 14–15,
17, 192, 211
and social exclusion 149–50, 154,
166
and subsidiarity 200
women's rights 80, 95, 102, 105,
106–8, 112–18, 121, 217
workers' rights 6, 8, 15, 79, 107,
121, 124, 146, 194, 197–9
workforce 2, 42, 132, 146
working age 174, 198
working conditions 3, 12, 19, 41,
59–78, 105–6, 108, 111, 113,
197, 199, 207, 209, 215

working hours   59, 64, 66, 70–1, 121
working population   174
working time   63, 66, 72
work-time organisation   65, 69–73

xenophobia   [9.9], 182

young people   39, 47, 64, 79, 95,
   155, 173, 199
   with disabilities   128
young workers   61, 197
youth   43, 51, 191, 217
Youth for Europe   49
Youthstart   155